STUDENT VIEWER'S HANDBOOK

TO ACCOMPANY

LE CHEMIN DU RETOUR

H. Jay Siskin
Cabrillo College

Ann Williams-Gascon
Metropolitan State College, Denver

Thomas T. Field
University of Maryland, Baltimore County

Boston   Burr Ridge, IL   Dubuque, IA   Mad   New York   San Francisco   St. Louis
Bangkok   Bogotá   Caracas   Kuala Lum   on   London   Madrid   Mexico City
Milan   Montreal   New Delhi   Santiago   ur   Singapore   Sydney   Taipei   Toronto

McGraw-Hill Higher Education

A Division of The **McGraw-Hill** *Companies*

This is an EBI book.

Student Viewer's Handbook
to accompany
Le Chemin du retour

This book is printed on acid-free paper.

1 2 3 4 5 6 7 8 9 0   CUS CUS   0 9 8 7 6 5 4 3 2 1

ISBN 0-07-289760-0

Editor-in-chief: *Thalia Dorwick*
Publisher: *William R. Glass*
Senior sponsoring editor: *Leslie Oberhuber*
Development editor: *Michelle-Noelle Magallanez*
Senior marketing manager: *Nick Agnew*
Senior project manager: *David M. Staloch*
Senior production supervisor: *Richard DeVitto*
Freelance design coordinator: *Michelle D. Whitaker*

Freelance interior and cover designer:
   Maureen McCutcheon/McCutcheon Design
Art editor: *Nora Agbayani*
Senior supplements producer: *Louis Swaim*
Photo research: *Judy Mason*
Compositor: *TechBooks*
Typeface: *10/12 Legacy Serif Book*
Printer and binder: *Von Hoffmann Graphics*

Grateful acknowledgment is given for use of the following:

Page 9 (top left) Beryl Goldberg, *(top right)* Franz-Mare Freil/Corbis, *(bottom right)* © Ann Williams-Gascon; *14* Becky Luigart-Stayner/Corbis; *15* © 2001, Les Éditions Albert René/Goscinny-Uderzo; *16 (clockwise from top left)* © Ann Williams-Gascon, Toutain Dorbec Pierre/Corbis Sygma, Hekimian/Corbis Sygma, Ann Williams-Gascon; *24 (clockwise from top left)* Walter Rapho/The Liaison Agency, Michael A. Dwyer/Stock Boston, Nik Wheeler/Corbis, Catherine Ursillo/Photo Researchers Inc., Lee Snider/The Image Works, James Andanson/Corbis Sygma; *29* R. Lucas/ The Image Works; *30 (clockwise from top left)* © Corbis, Corbis, Ann Williams-Gascon, Bill Ross/Corbis; *34 (top and bottom)* Lee Snider/The Image Works; *38 (top)* Owen Franken/Stock Boston, *(bottom)* R. Lucas/The Image Works; *39 (top left)* © Ann Williams-Gascon, *(top right)* Yann Arthus-Bertrand/Corbis, *(bottom right)* © Ann Williams-Gascon; *43* Steve Raymer/Corbis; *53 (top)* Catherine Karnow/Corbis; *54 (top left)* © Corbis, *(middle right and bottom right)* Ann Williams-Gascon, *(left)* Stefano Bianchetti/Corbis, *59* Farrell Grehan/Corbis; *62* Dean Conger/ Corbis; *67* Chip Hires/The Liaison Agency; *70* © Corbis, *71* Robert Holmes/Corbis; *72 (top)* © Ann Williams-Gascon, *(bottom left)* Yann Arthus-Bertrand/Corbis, *(bottom right)* Art on File/Corbis; *85* Lee Snider/The Image Works; *86* © Ann Williams-Gascon; *87 (top left)* Michel Caby, Musée du Désert, *(bottom left)* Michael Busselle/Corbis, *(bottom right)* Bob Gibbons, Eye Ubiquitous/Corbis; *90 (top)* Jonathan Blair/Corbis, *(bottom)* Stephane Ruet/Corbis Sygma; *101* Macduff Everton/Corbis; *102 (top)* Mike Southern, Eye Ubiquitous/Corbis, *(bottom)* Pascal Parrot/ Corbis Sygma; *103 (clockwise from top right)* Jean Marc Charles/Corbis Sygma, © Ann Williams-Gascon, Chris Hellier/Corbis; *107* Roger Wood/ Corbis; *108 (top right)* The Purcell Team/Corbis, *(bottom left)* Wolfgang Kaehler, *(bottom right)* Robert Holmes/Corbis; *113 (top)* Melies/Kobal Collection, *(bottom)* Kobal Collection; *114 (left)* Prods. Artistes Associes/DA MA/Kobal Collection, *(right)* United Artists/Kobal Collection.

http://www.mhhe.com

Contents

Le Chemin du retour:
What is it?

Imagine a film created specifically for students of French language and culture, a film that takes the viewer on an exciting journey through contemporary France and other areas of the French-speaking world. Welcome to *Le Chemin du retour*, an unparalleled cinematic adventure designed with beginning students in mind but appropriate for students at all levels. Through mystery and intrigue, drama and humor, the compelling story of Camille Leclair and her pursuit of the truth about her grandfather's past sets the stage for this two-hour feature film. Viewers—both students and professors—will be drawn into *Le Chemin du retour* as they follow Camille on her personal journey.

Le Chemin du retour and this accompanying *Student Viewer's Handbook* serve as an ideal supplement to any French textbook, enhancing the learning experience. Through Camille's quest, students review and learn language and culture in the functional context provided by the story. In addition, for instructors who might want to build an entire first year French course around *Le Chemin du retour*, the film is supported by the textbook *Débuts* and a full package of print and multimedia components.

Understanding French

As students begin their study of French, it is important that they examine their beliefs about the nature of language and the language-learning process. They may believe that they have little difficulty understanding what they hear in their native language, yet if they reflect on their interactions with others, they will find that this is not always true. They will see, for example, that in one's native language it is not unusual to ask someone to repeat or to clarify what he or she said. People who speak rapidly or indistinctly are harder to understand than people who speak more slowly or clearly. Students should recognize that when speaking with someone who mumbles, they are probably often reluctant to ask that person to repeat over and over again. In such a circumstance, they probably rely instead on the subject or direction of the conversation to fill in the gaps in their comprehension. Although they don't understand every word, they continue to listen to get the gist of the message.

When listening in a foreign language, however, students often set the bar higher. They are eager to understand every word, and when they don't, they become frustrated or they even give up. As they begin learning French, they should remember the following hints:

- Keep your expectations realistic.
- When you don't understand, keep listening!
- Try to fill in the gaps using context to help.
- See if you can get the gist of the message.

These strategies will be particularly important as students listen to the actors in the film. From the outset, they will be hearing authentic French spoken at a natural rate of speed. It has not been artificially slowed or simplified, because this will not be their experience when they travel in the French-speaking world or listen to French radio or television. But they should not worry. They will find that although they do not understand every word of the dialogue, they will still understand the story of *Le Chemin du retour*.

Cultural Competence

Cultural content was a central concern in the development of the plot of *Le Chemin du retour*. Through the film, students have the opportunity for intensive exposure not only to the language and communicative habits of French speakers, but also to the visual culture of objects and nonverbal communication and to the auditory culture of music and the sounds of everyday life.

The approach to culture in the *Student Viewer's Handbook* is content-based. Themes treated in the sections specifically devoted to culture derive from the film but consistently move students toward broader cultural issues; stimulating them to consider matters that are of concern to all people, whether or not they ever travel to the French-speaking world. The authors have made culture a "hook" in this program, to generate interest in longer-term language study and to place the study of language and culture within the larger context of a humanistic education. The cultural content aims to be thought-provoking and to expand students' horizons beyond simple "travelogue" facts toward understanding the roots of cultural differences.

The Structure of *Le Chemin du retour*

The film *Le Chemin du retour* is available in two versions: 1) a complete version that is the uninterrupted, full-length feature film, and 2) an instructional version of the film that divides the story into a preliminary episode, twenty-two story episodes, and an epilogue. Except for the **Épisode préliminaire**, which introduces students to the concept of learning French through film, each episode of *Le Chemin du retour* in the instructional version follows the same three-step format.

1. Students watch and participate in on-screen previewing activities.

   - **Vous avez vu...** Scenes from previous episodes are used to remind students about main events in the story that will help them understand the new episode.
   - **Vous allez voir...** Scenes previewing the upcoming episode set up the context for what students will see and hear in the episode.
   - **Paroles et images** This section, which occurs through Episode 11, introduces and practices a particular viewing strategy that students can apply to help them understand the language and events of the film.

2. Students view the complete episode.

3. Students watch and participate in on-screen postviewing activities.

   - **Vous avez compris?** Scenes from the episode are used in a variety of multiple-choice and true-false activities to help students verify their comprehension of the main ideas and the plot of the episode they've just viewed. Students who didn't understand an important point as they viewed the episode will find they understand more after doing these activities.
   - **Langue en contexte** This section identifies language functions and structures that are covered in *Débuts*, the textbook that accompanies *Le Chemin du retour*. Appropriate scenes from the film are subtitled in French and the targeted grammar and vocabulary are highlighted in yellow. Although keyed to *Débuts*, the *Langue en contexte* section does provide a review of general structures and vocabulary found in most beginning French textbooks. Some instructors may choose to skip this segment of the episode, depending on the correspondence between the textbook in use and the focus of the episode.

How to use *Le Chemin du retour*

With *Le Chemin du retour*, students will learn the basics of French within the functional context provided by this two-hour feature length film. As noted previously, the film is available in two distinct formats—the uncut two-hour film version and the eight-hour instructional version that divides the film into 24 individual episodes. Both formats are available on either VHS or DVD.

The choice of viewing format offers instructors the flexibility to decide how best to integrate the film into their language courses. With two formats of the film available, instructors may design a viewing program that suits their students' interests and linguistic needs.

The two-hour film version can be used as a supplement in a variety of French language courses from beginning French through advanced conversation and composition. The DVD allows inclusion of French or English subtitles, providing instructors the ability to monitor the level of language learning so that students are at once encouraged and challenged by their film viewing.

The eight-hour instructional version is comprised of 24 episodes, each of which includes on-screen pre- and postviewing activities. This version of the film can be viewed over the course of a semester or academic year, depending on the length and goals of the course. It is recommended that the episodes be available in the Language Laboratory or Media Center so that students who miss a class can view the episode they missed. If the eight-hour instructional version is made available to students in the Language Laboratory or Media Center, *Le Chemin du retour* can be used as a supplement out of class: Students can work on the materials on their own as a homework assignment. If time and class goals permit, the materials can be used in class as a supplement for linguistic and cultural discussions.

How to use the Student Viewer's Handbook

The *Student Viewer's Handbook* is designed to facilitate and assess students' comprehension of the film and to provide additional readings in French. When used in conjunction with other print and multimedia materials, *Le Chemin du retour* and the *Student Viewer's Handbook* play an important part in students' ability to develop proficiency in French language and cultures.

Each chapter of the *Student Viewer's Handbook* corresponds to an individual episode of the film.

The structure of each chapter is consistent across the *Handbook*, thus facilitating lesson planning and integration of the materials into the curriculum. Each chapter is organized as follows:

Visionnement 1: These activities support a first viewing of the episode.

- *Avant de visionner:* These are previewing activities that facilitate students' comprehension.
- *Vocabulaire relatif à l'épisode:* A brief list of useful vocabulary items culled from the episode.
- *Observez!:* These questions focus students' attention on what to watch and listen for in the story.
- *Après le visionnement:* These activities verify students' comprehension of the episode.

Regards sur la culture: A cultural note and its accompanying critical thinking question deepen students' awareness and understanding of cultural issues explored in the film's episode.

Visionnement 2: An optional second viewing section encourages students to watch the episode again, this time to concentrate on cultural information in the episode.

- *Avant de visionner:* These activities ask students to consider cultural issues raised in each episode.

- *Écrivez et explorez!:* These writing activities, introduced in the *Student Viewer's Handbook* and developed on the *Le Chemin du retour* website, direct students to write brief compositions related to the themes explored in each episode of the film.

Additional features:

- *Notez bien!:* These features present additional vocabulary that aids students' comprehension of the film.
- *Pour en savior plus:* This occasional feature provides further information concerning the cultural topics addressed in the film.

Following are suggestions for how you can make use of the chapter materials in class.

- Have students complete the *Avant de visionner* exercises in the *Visionnement 1* section before coming to class. You may then wish to go over the *Vocabulaire relatif a l'épisode* and the *Observez!* questions in class prior to viewing the episode.
- Watch the episode in class with your students and discuss answers to the *Observez!* questions.
- Have students work in pairs to complete the *Après le visionnement* activities.
- Assign the *Regards sur la culture* reading as a homework assignment to be reviewed in class.

The *Visionnement 2* section guides students in an exploration of the cultural content presented in the film.

- Have students complete the *Avant de visionner* activities in the *Visionnement 2* section before coming to class.
- Watch the episode for a second time in class, encouraging students to note cultural practices and social mores.
- Assign the *Écrivez et explorez!* writing activity found on the Web as homework.

Cast of Characters

Camille Leclair
A young television journalist who searches for the truth about her grandfather's past.

Mado Leclair
Camille's mother, who fears the truth and wants to keep her father's history hidden forever.

Bruno Gall
Camille's cohost on the morning television show "Bonjour!"

Rachid Bouhazid
A new reporter at "Bonjour!" who, with his family, must adjust to a new life in Paris.

Louise Leclair
Camille's grandmother, who encourages her granddaughter to pursue her quest for the truth.

Martine Valloton
Producer of "Bonjour!" who has to risk her job to support Camille's determination to find out about her grandfather.

Hélène Thibaut
A journalist from Quebec, and friend of Bruno and Camille.

David Girard
Historian, friend of Bruno, who researches information about Camille's grandfather.

Alex Béraud
A musician who plays in the Mouffetard Market. Friend of Louise, Mado, and Camille.

Sonia Bouhazid
Wife of Rachid and mother of their daughter, Yasmine.

Jeanne Leblanc
A woman who knew Camille's grandfather during the time of the German occupation of France.

Roland Fergus
A man who worked with Camille's grandfather during the German occupation and who holds the key to the truth.

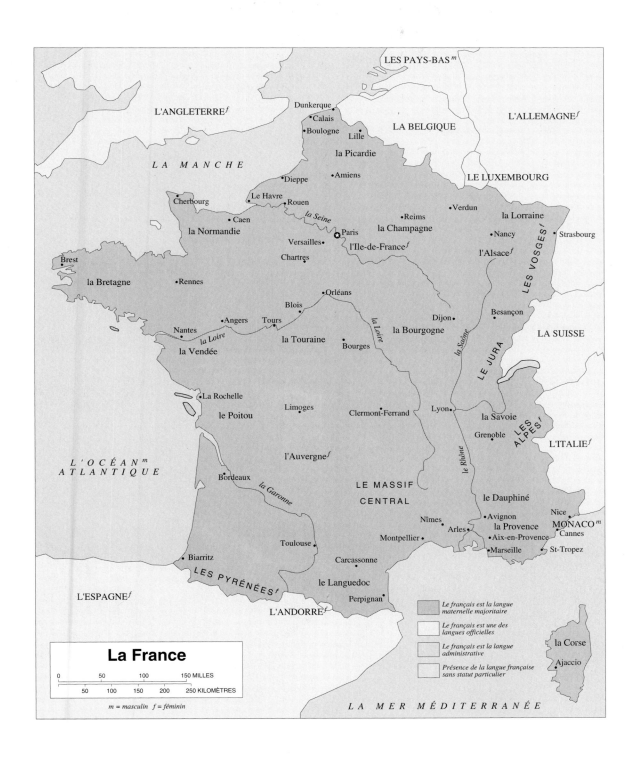

La France

LES PAYS-BAS *m*

L'ANGLETERRE *f*

L'ALLEMAGNE *f*

LA MANCHE

LA BELGIQUE

LE LUXEMBOURG

Dunkerque
•Calais
•Boulogne
•Lille
la Picardie

•Dieppe   •Amiens

•Cherbourg
Le Havre• •Rouen
la Seine
•Verdun
•Reims
la Champagne
la Lorraine
•Nancy
•Caen
la Normandie
Versailles• ✪Paris
l'Ile-de-France *f*
l'Alsace *f*
Strasbourg
LES VOSGES *f*

Chartres•

•Brest
la Bretagne

•Rennes

•Orléans

Blois•   Dijon•
la Bourgogne
Besançon•

•Angers Tours•
Nantes• *la Loire*
la Touraine *la Loire*
la Vendée   •Bourges
LE JURA
LA SUISSE
la Saône

•La Rochelle

le Poitou
•Limoges
Clermont-Ferrand•
Lyon•
la Savoie
LES ALPES *f*
Grenoble•
L'ITALIE *f*

L'OCÉAN *m*
ATLANTIQUE

l'Auvergne *f*

le Rhône

le Dauphiné

Bordeaux•
la Garonne
LE MASSIF
CENTRAL

Nice•
Nîmes• •Avignon MONACO *m*
•Arles la Provence •Cannes
Montpellier• •Aix-en-Provence
•Marseille •St-Tropez

•Toulouse

Carcassonne•

•Biarritz
LES PYRÉNÉES *f*

le Languedoc

Perpignan•

L'ESPAGNE *f*

L'ANDORRE *f*

Le français est la langue
maternelle majoritaire

Le français est une des
langues officielles

Le français est la langue
administrative

Présence de la langue française
sans statut particulier

la Corse

•Ajaccio

La France

0   50   100   150 MILLES
50 100 150 200 250 KILOMÈTRES

m = masculin f = féminin

LA MER MÉDITERRANÉE

L'Europe ^f

0   50 100   200   300   400   500 MILLES

0   100 200 300 400 500 600 700 800 KILOMÈTRES

m = masculin f = féminin

Le français est la langue
maternelle majoritaire

Le français est une des
langues officielles

Le français est la langue
administrative

Présence de la langue française
sans statut particulier

Reykjavik
L'ISLANDE *f*

LA SUÈDE

LA FINLANDE

LA NORVÈGE

Helsinki
St-Pétersbourg

Oslo
Tallinn
LA RUSSIE

Stockholm
L'ESTONIE
Moscou

LA MER BALTIQUE

Riga

L'ÉCOSSE *f*

LA MER
DU NORD

LA LETTONIE

L'IRLANDE DU NORD
LA GRANDE-
LE DANEMARK
LA LITUANIE

L'IRLANDE *f*   Dublin
BRETAGNE
Copenhague
Vilnius
Minsk

LE PAYS DE GALLES
L'ANGLETERRE *f*
Tver

Amsterdam
Berlin
LA BIÉLORUSSIE

Londres
LES PAYS-BAS *m*
Varsovie

LA BELGIQUE
L'ALLEMAGNE *f*

Jersey
Bruxelles Bonn
LA POLOGNE
Kyev

Luxembourg
Prague
L'UKRAINE *f*

LE LUXEMBOURG
LA RÉPUBLIQUE
TCHÈQUE
LA SLOVAQUIE

Paris
LA MOLDAVIE

L'OCÉAN
ATLANTIQUE *m*
Vienne
Bratislava
Chisinau

Budapest

LA FRANCE
Berne
L'AUTRICHE *f*
LA HONGRIE

Lausanne
LA SUISSE
Ljubljana
LA ROUMANIE

Genève
Zagreb
Bucarest

le Val d'Aoste
LA SLOVÉNIE
LA CROATIE
LA MER
NOIRE

L'ITALIE *f*
Belgrade

LA BOSNIE
LA MER
ADRIATIQUE
LA BULGARIE

LE PORTUGAL
L'ANDORRE *f*
HERZÉGOVINE
Sarajevo
LA SERBIE

LE MONTÉNÉGRO
Sofia
Istanbul

Lisbonne
Madrid
La Corse
Titograd
Skopje

L'ESPAGNE *f*
Ajaccio
Rome
Tirana
LA MACÉDOINE
LA TURQUIE

L'ALBANIE *f*

LA GRÈCE
LA MER ÉGÉE

LA MER MÉDITERRANÉE

Athènes

L'AFRIQUE *f*
LA CRÈTE

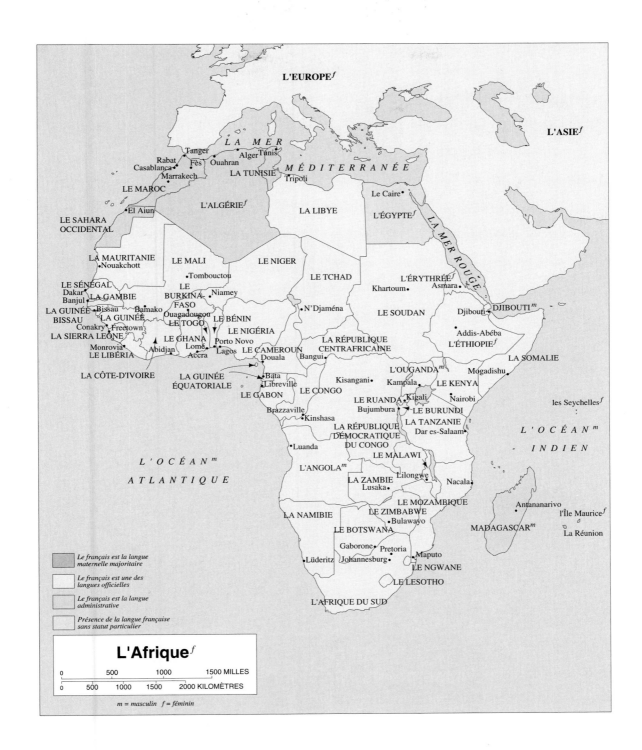

L'EUROPE *f*

L'ASIE *f*

LA MER MÉDITERRANÉE

Tanger
Rabat • Ouahran
Casablanca • Fès
Marrakech
LE MAROC
Alger Tunis
LA TUNISIE
Tripoli

Le Caire •

El Aiun

LE SAHARA
OCCIDENTAL

L'ALGÉRIE *f*

LA LIBYE

L'ÉGYPTE *f*

LA MER ROUGE

LA MAURITANIE
• Nouakchott

LE MALI

LE NIGER

LE TCHAD

• Tombouctou

LE SÉNÉGAL
Dakar •
Banjul •
LA GAMBIE
LA GUINÉE
BISSAU
Bissau •
LA GUINÉE
Conakry •
LA SIERRA LEONE
Monrovia •
LE LIBÉRIA

LE
BURKINA
FASO
• Niamey
Bamako •
Ouagadougou
LE TOGO
LE BÉNIN
LE NIGÉRIA
Freetown •
LE GHANA
Abidjan
Lomé
Accra
Porto Novo
Lagos
LE CAMEROUN
Douala

N'Djaména •

L'ÉRYTHRÉE *f*
Khartoum • Asmara •

LE SOUDAN
Djibouti • DJIBOUTI *m*

Addis-Abéba •
L'ÉTHIOPIE *f*

LA SOMALIE

LA CÔTE-D'IVOIRE

LA GUINÉE
ÉQUATORIALE
LE GABON

Bata
Libreville •
LE CONGO

Brazzaville
• Kinshasa

LA RÉPUBLIQUE
CENTRAFRICAINE

Bangui •

Kisangani •

L'OUGANDA *m*
Kampala •
LE RUANDA Kigali •
Bujumbura • LE BURUNDI

LA RÉPUBLIQUE
DÉMOCRATIQUE
DU CONGO

• Luanda

L'ANGOLA *m*

Mogadishu •

LE KENYA

• Nairobi

les Seychelles *f*

LA TANZANIE
Dar es-Salaam •

LE MALAWI
Lilongwe •

*L'OCÉAN *m*
ATLANTIQUE*

LA ZAMBIE
Lusaka •

Nacala •

*L'OCÉAN *m*
INDIEN*

LE MOZAMBIQUE

LA NAMIBIE
LE ZIMBABWE
• Bulawayo

Antananarivo •
l'Île Maurice *f*
MADAGASCAR *m*
La Réunion

LE BOTSWANA
Gaborone •
Pretoria •
Lüderitz • Johannesburg •
Maputo •
LE NGWANE

LE LESOTHO

L'AFRIQUE DU SUD

Le français est la langue
maternelle majoritaire

Le français est une des
langues officielles

Le français est la langue
administrative

Présence de la langue française
sans statut particulier

L'Afrique *f*

| 0 | 500 | 1000 | 1500 MILLES |

| 0 | 500 | 1000 | 1500 | 2000 KILOMÈTRES |

m = masculin   f = féminin

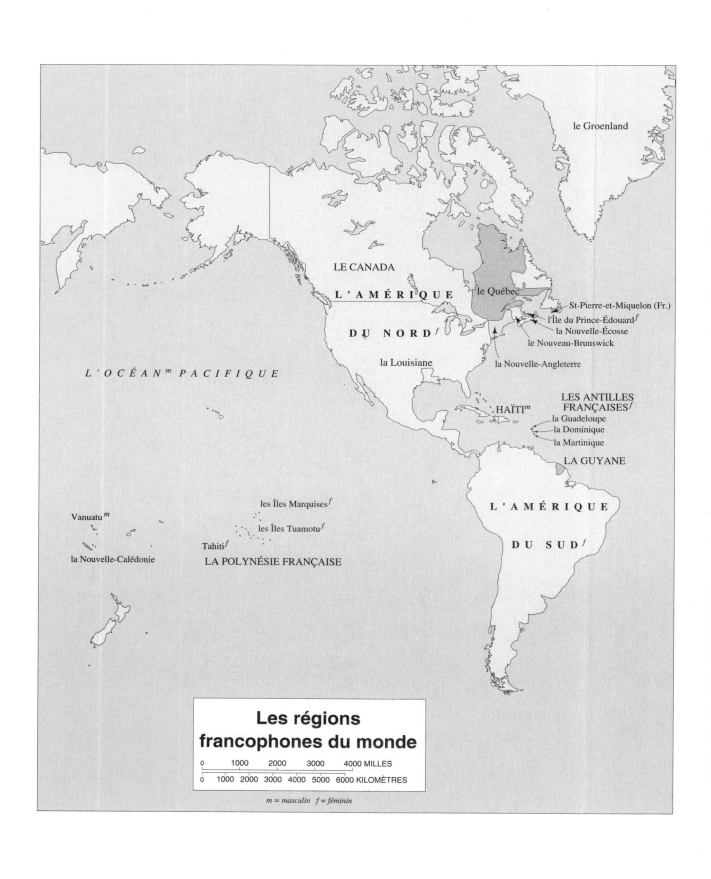

le Groenland

LE CANADA

L'AMÉRIQUE

le Québec

St-Pierre-et-Miquelon (Fr.)

l'Île du Prince-Édouard*f*

la Nouvelle-Écosse

DU NORD*f*

le Nouveau-Brunswick

la Louisiane

la Nouvelle-Angleterre

L'OCÉAN*m* PACIFIQUE

LES ANTILLES

FRANÇAISES*f*

HAÏTI*m*

la Guadeloupe

la Dominique

la Martinique

LA GUYANE

les Îles Marquises*f*

L'AMÉRIQUE

Vanuatu*m*

les Îles Tuamotu*f*

DU SUD*f*

Tahiti*f*

la Nouvelle-Calédonie

LA POLYNÉSIE FRANÇAISE

Les régions francophones du monde

| 0 | 1000 | 2000 | 3000 | 4000 MILLES |

| 0 | 1000 | 2000 | 3000 | 4000 | 5000 | 6000 KILOMÈTRES |

m = masculin   f = féminin

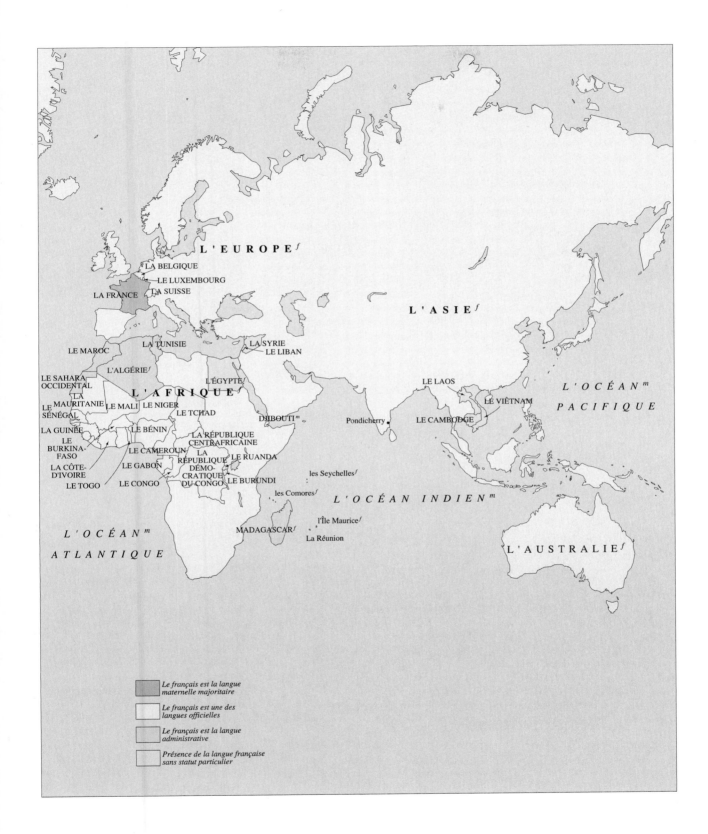

L'EUROPE ^{f}

LA BELGIQUE
LE LUXEMBOURG
LA SUISSE
LA FRANCE

L'ASIE ^{f}

LE MAROC
LA TUNISIE
LA SYRIE
LE LIBAN
L'ALGÉRIE ^{f}
L'ÉGYPTE ^{f}
LE SAHARA
OCCIDENTAL
LA
MAURITANIE
L'AFRIQUE ^{f}
LE
SÉNÉGAL
LE MALI
LE NIGER
LE TCHAD
DJIBOUTI ^{m}
LE LAOS
LE VIÊTNAM

L'OCÉAN ^{m}
PACIFIQUE

Pondicherry
LE CAMBODGE
LA GUINÉE
LE BÉNIN
LE
BURKINA-
FASO
LA RÉPUBLIQUE
CENTRAFRICAINE
LE CAMEROUN
LA
RÉPUBLIQUE
DÉMO-
CRATIQUE
DU CONGO
LE RUANDA
LA CÔTE-
D'IVOIRE
LE GABON
LE TOGO
LE CONGO
LE BURUNDI

les Seychelles ^{f}

L'OCÉAN INDIEN ^{m}

les Comores

l'Île Maurice ^{f}

L'OCÉAN ^{m}
ATLANTIQUE

MADAGASCAR ^{f}
La Réunion

L'AUSTRALIE ^{f}

Le français est la langue
maternelle majoritaire

Le français est une des
langues officielles

Le français est la langue
administrative

Présence de la langue française
sans statut particulier

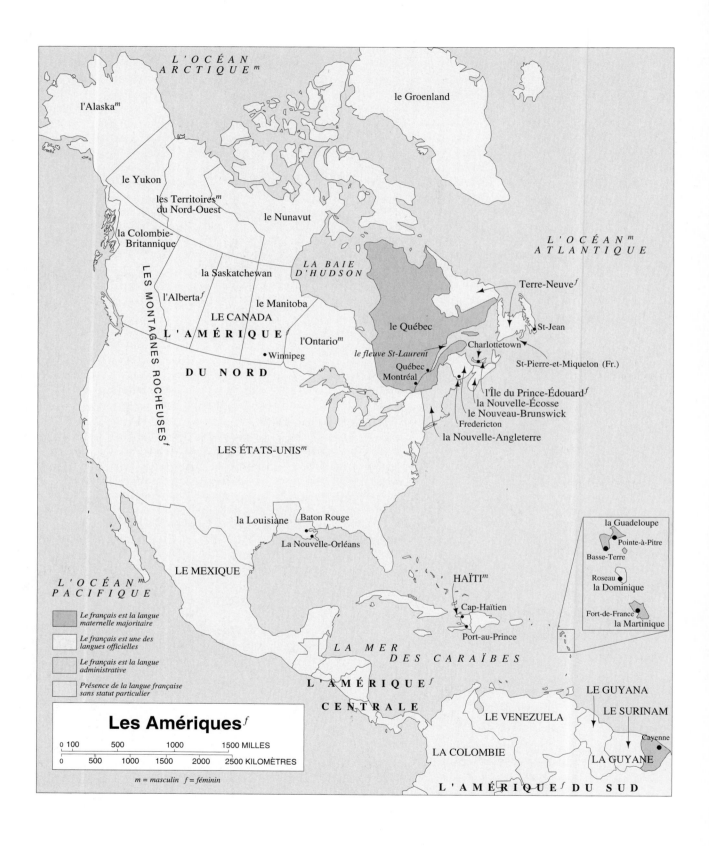

L'OCÉAN
ARCTIQUE^m

le Groenland

l'Alaska^m

le Yukon

les Territoires^m
du Nord-Ouest

le Nunavut

la Colombie-
Britannique

L'OCÉAN^m
ATLANTIQUE

la Saskatchewan

LA BAIE
D'HUDSON

Terre-Neuve^f

l'Alberta^f

le Manitoba

LE CANADA

St-Jean

L'AMÉRIQUE

le Québec

Charlottetown

l'Ontario^m

le fleuve St-Laurent

St-Pierre-et-Miquelon (Fr.)

DU NORD

• Winnipeg

Québec •
Montréal •

l'Île du Prince-Édouard^f
la Nouvelle-Écosse
le Nouveau-Brunswick

Fredericton

LES MONTAGNES ROCHEUSES^f

LES ÉTATS-UNIS^m

la Nouvelle-Angleterre

la Louisiane

Baton Rouge
•

la Guadeloupe

La Nouvelle-Orléans

Pointe-à-Pitre
•

Basse-Terre •

LE MEXIQUE

Roseau •
la Dominique

L'OCÉAN^m
PACIFIQUE

HAÏTI^m

Fort-de-France •
la Martinique

Le français est la langue
maternelle majoritaire

Cap-Haïtien
•

Le français est une des
langues officielles

Le français est la langue
administrative

Port-au-Prince
•

LA MER
DES CARAÏBES

Présence de la langue française
sans statut particulier

L'AMÉRIQUE^f

LE GUYANA

CENTRALE

LE VENEZUELA

LE SURINAM

Les Amériques^f

0 100   500   1000   1500 MILLES

Cayenne
•

LA COLOMBIE

0   500   1000   1500   2000   2500 KILOMÈTRES

LA GUYANE

m = masculin   f = féminin

L'AMÉRIQUE^f DU SUD

Ça tourne!°

Ça… *Action!*

Visionnement

*A*vant de visionner

Le film

Le Chemin du retour tells the story of Camille Leclair, a young TV journalist in Paris who risks her career to search for the truth about her grandfather. By following Camille's attempts to unravel the mystery surrounding her grandfather, you will learn about the culture of contemporary France and other French-speaking areas of the world, as well as historical information about France during the Second World War. *Le Chemin du retour* provides a natural, authentic context for learning to understand, speak, read, and write French.

Dans le studio avec Camille et Bruno

Pour utiliser le film°

Pour... *Using the film*

To use the film to its full advantage as a learning tool, you'll want to remember a few important pieces of advice.

Dans le studio, Martine présente de nouveaux collègues à Rachid. (new)

- Always participate fully in the activities that precede and follow your viewing of the film. These activities are specially designed to help you understand what you see and hear on-screen.

- As a beginning student of French, don't worry about understanding every word as you watch the film. Instead, just try to understand the gist (the main idea) of what is happening. You'll discover that you can figure out quite a lot by watching the action. Watch for body language and other visual clues that may clarify what is happening. Keep an ear tuned not only for vocabulary that you already know, but also for the tone people use as they speak. If you relax and don't worry about understanding every word, you'll find that you can still understand the story. As the course progresses, you will gradually understand more and more of what you hear.

- Watch, too, for similarities and differences between French culture and that of your own country. You may be surprised at some of the ways in which people interact, and you may see objects that you do not recognize. Think of the film as an immersion experience, like actually going to France, and pay attention to the place and to details of behavior just as carefully as you do to the plot. Many of the cultural features that you notice will be discussed in this book, but you may want to ask your instructor about others.

Camille et Mado

Camille au marché

Pour parler du film°

Pour... *Talking about the film*

To help you talk about the film, you will learn a few items of vocabulary in each chapter of the *Student Viewer's Handbook*. For a more complete list of vocabulary that relates to the film, please refer to the *Lexiques* found at the the end of the book. The following activity will teach you a few terms that you may need in class discussions and in your writing. See if you can match the English meanings with the French words. Note: The words **un** and **une** mean *a*.

1. film	**a.** un acteur
2. studio	**b.** une actrice
3. scene	**c.** un cinéma
4. actress	**d.** une femme
5. actor	**e.** un film
6. story	**f.** une histoire
7. person	**g.** un homme
8. character	**h.** un personnage
9. movie theater	**i.** une personne
10. man	**j.** une scène
11. woman	**k.** un studio

How many of these words are similar in both English and French?

$\mathcal{V}$isionnez!°

Watch!

Every chapter in the *Student Viewer's Handbook* contains previewing activities that you will do before watching the new episode of the story. In fact, you just did a previewing activity in the **Pour parler du film** section. In addition to these activities, however, there are on-screen previewing and postviewing activities to help you understand what you see and hear in the story. Go ahead and do the on-screen lesson for this chapter now. It will introduce you to the story of *Le Chemin du retour* and show you how the on-screen activities in the episodes work.

$\mathcal{R}$egards sur la culture

Le français dans le monde¹

Félicitations! You are among the 100 to 110 million people outside of the Francophone world who are studying French. Not only is French one of the five official languages of the United Nations, but it is important in many ways in places all around the world. French ranks tenth worldwide in terms of the number of native speakers—70 million—and, impressively, it ranks sixth in the world in the number of people for whom it is an official language—220 million. In fact, French ranks *second* in the world, after English and before Spanish, in the number of countries where it is an official language—28 countries, located on five continents. Take a look at the maps in the front of your textbook to see its distribution throughout the world.

¹Le... *French in the world*

FRANCE

CANADA

MAROC

ALGÉRIE

SÉNÉGAL

The ten countries with the largest numbers of French speakers are France, Algeria, Canada, Morocco, Belgium, Côte-d'Ivoire, Tunisia, Cameroon, the Democratic Republic of the Congo, and Switzerland. However, the official status of French varies from country to country. French is one of two or more official languages in Canada, Belgium, Cameroon, and Switzerland, and although it is spoken by many in Algeria, Morocco, and Tunisia it is not an official language at all in those countries. In Côte-d'Ivoire, however, French is the only official language and is used in some aspects of day-to-day life because there is no common African language that is used by all the people of the nation. In fact, Côte-d'Ivoire is one place in Africa where local innovations in French are giving birth to a new dialect of the language. In other countries, such as Senegal, French is again the only official language, but it is used almost exclusively in an administrative or educational context. As you can imagine, these two contexts mean a significant use of the French language there.

Numbers of speakers and status as an official language only tell part of the story of the importance of French in the world, however. Other factors must also be considered in order to appreciate fully the role of French in the community of nations. French is one of the world's major languages, not only because of the geographic spread of its speakers, but more importantly, because of the many contributions of French-speaking nations to the advancement of knowledge and artistic creation throughout the international community. France and the French language have had a profound influence on international culture in such areas as science, sociology, political theory, literature, the arts, fashion, and gastronomy. Furthermore, in the realm of international relations, France has had long historical ties with both the United States and Canada. You will explore some of these many influences in more detail throughout the *Student Viewer's Handbook* to accompany *Le Chemin du retour.*

Écrivez et explorez!

Visit the *Student Viewer's Handbook* link on the website for *Le Chemin du retour* at **www.mhhe.com/debuts** for the composition subject and activities related to this episode.

Un grand jour°

Un... A big day

Visionnement **1**

Before you watch each new episode of *Le Chemin du retour*, you will do several activities that prepare you to understand what you will see and hear.

*A*vant de visionner

A. La tour Eiffel a quatre pieds. (*The Eiffel Tower has four feet.*)   The film opens with children singing a **comptine**, a song somewhat like a nursery rhyme. A **comptine** often has an instructional purpose, for example, to help children learn months of the year, holidays, or telling time. **Comptines** are also used in school to help pupils improve their pronunciation. Read the following **comptine**. Later, as you hear it in the film, you can follow along.

La tour Eiffel a quatre pieds; Il en faut deux pour y monter (bis)
Et pour s'aider, on peut chanter (bis)
A...B...C...D...E...F...G...H...I...J...K...L...M...N... (bis)

The Eiffel Tower has four feet; You need two feet to climb it (repeat)
And to help, you can sing (repeat)
A...B...C...D...E...F...G...H...I...J...K...L...M...N... (repeat)

B. Moments importants. Here is a look at two important moments in Episode 1. Read the exchanges and answer the questions.

1. In this scene, a little girl named Yasmine and her father, Rachid, are arriving at school. How do you think she feels about being there?

    YASMINE: C'est ma nouvelle[a] école?
    PAPA: Mmm-hmm. La maîtresse est là.[b] Elle est très sympa. Regarde![c]
    YASMINE: Non, papa, je ne veux pas.[d] On repart à la maison![e]

    [a]ma... *my new*   [b]*over there*   [c]*Look!*   [d]je... *I don't want to (look at her)*   [e]On... *Let's go home!*

    a. Yasmine est contente.
    b. Yasmine est nerveuse.

2. What is the relationship between the people in this dialogue?

    ISABELLE: Vous êtes Monsieur Bouhazid?
    RACHID: Oui. Bonjour, madame.
    ISABELLE: Monsieur. Et toi, tu es Yasmine. Je m'appelle Isabelle.

    a. Isabelle et Rachid sont amis.
    b. Isabelle ne connaît pas (*doesn't know*) Rachid et Yasmine.

Vocabulaire relatif à l'épisode*

Here are a few more expressions from the film. Don't worry if you miss them as you are watching. You don't need to hear every word to understand the main idea of what is happening.

Qu'est-ce qu'il y a, ma puce?	What's wrong, sweetheart?
Pourquoi... ?	Why . . . ?
Où est... ?	Where is . . . ?
fatiguée	tired
le déménagement	move (to a new residence)
bonne chance	good luck

*O*bservez!

Now watch Episode 1. You already know that Yasmine is going to school. As you watch the film, see if you can answer these questions.

- What is Yasmine worried about?
- Why does she wish her father luck?

Remember—Don't expect to understand every word in the episode; you need to understand only the basic plot structure and characters. If you can answer the questions that follow the episode, you have understood enough. Your instructor may ask you to watch the episode again later. By then, you'll have additional tools and will be able to understand more of the details. The activities in **Visionnement 2** will help, too.

*A*près le visionnement

In this section of each chapter, you will review important information from the episode you have just watched.

A. Identifiez. Who makes the following statements to whom in Episode 1? Choose among Rachid, Yasmine, and the teacher (**l'institutrice**).

---

*For a more complete list of vocabulary items that relate to the film, please refer to the *Lexique* at the end of the book.

MODÈLE: La maîtresse est là. Elle est très sympa. →
Rachid parle à (*is speaking to*) Yasmine.

1. C'est ma nouvelle école?

2. Mais (*But*) où est-elle? Où est maman?

3. Au Jardin des Plantes (*To the Botanical Garden*), pour une leçon de sciences naturelles.

4. Au revoir, madame. Salut, ma chérie (*honey*)!

5. Pour toi aussi, c'est un grand jour, non?

B. Réfléchissez. (*Think.*)   Read the following dialogue exchanges and answer the questions.

1. In this episode, Yasmine asks where her mother is, but Rachid seems uncomfortable discussing her.

YASMINE: Pourquoi maman n'est pas là[a]?

RACHID: C'est, euh, Maman est fatiguée à cause du déménagement. Alors, elle se repose.[b]

YASMINE: Mais où est-elle? Où est maman?

RACHID: Allez viens,[c] ma chérie. Regarde les enfants.

[a]n'est... *isn't here*   [b]elle... *she's resting*   [c]Allez... *Come on*

Why might Rachid feel so uncomfortable? What does this scene tell you about his relationship with his wife?

2. As Yasmine begins her first day at her new school, she wishes her father luck.

YASMINE: Bonne chance, papa! Pour toi aussi, c'est un grand jour, non?

RACHID: Oui. Salut, ma chérie.

Why might Rachid have a big day ahead of him, too?

Regards sur la culture

*L'*enseignement° en France
Education

Les enfants à l'école

Here are some basic facts about the public school program in France.

- Discipline, memorization, and the imitation of good models are the fundamental principles of early education in French schools. Students do a lot of very careful copying of language (the teacher's notes on the board) and of images (the teacher's model of the umbrella indicating the day's weather, for example*). They also spend quite a bit of time memorizing and reciting poetry and **comptines**.

*Every morning in the early primary grades, many teachers draw a symbol on the board to indicate the day's weather—a sun for sunny weather, an umbrella for rain, a snowflake for snow, etc.

- The French educational system is very centralized. School programs and the requirements for diplomas are usually determined by the Ministry of Education so that all citizens, no matter where they live or what their social status, have the same educational opportunities.

- Nearly all French children enter elementary school having already been in public preschools for several years. Thirty-six percent of French children are in **l'école maternelle** (preschool) at age 2, and by age 3, 99.8% of all children attend. **L'école maternelle** is free and available to all.

- When they enter elementary school (**l'école primaire**), French children usually know how to copy cursive handwriting, but not how to read. "Printing" is never learned. The first year of elementary school in France is called **le cours préparatoire**. Children enter this class around age 6. In **le cours préparatoire**, they begin to learn to read.

Âge	Écoles	Classes
17		Terminale
16	Lycée	1
15		2
14		3
13	Collège	4
12		5
11		6
10		Cours moyen
9		
8	École primaire	Cours élémentaire
7		
6		Cours préparatoire
5		
4	École maternelle	
3		
2		

Considérez

Education in the United States is controlled locally and may vary greatly from county to county and from state to state. In Canada, education is the responsibility of each province and territory. What advantages and disadvantages do you see in local control of education? Are there advantages to a centralized system like the one in France? What about a compromise like the Canadian system?

Visionnement 2

Avant de visionner

A. Quelle classe? (*Which class?*)   The public school system in France is described in **Regards sur la culture**. Considering Yasmine's age, the type of field trip the class is about to take, and the song the class is singing as they line up, what grade do you think Yasmine is entering? Choose the best answer.

   a. Elle est à l'école maternelle.

   b. Elle est au cours préparatoire.

   c. Elle est au cours élémentaire.

Les environs de l'appartement des Bouhazid

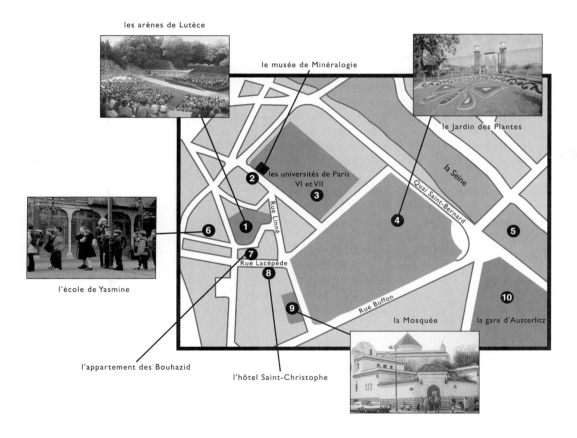

les arènes de Lutèce

le musée de Minéralogie

le Jardin des Plantes

la Seine

les universités de Paris VI et VII

Quai Saint-Bernard

Rue Linné

l'école de Yasmine

Rue Lacépède

Rue Buffon

la Mosquée

la gare d'Austerlitz

l'appartement des Bouhazid

l'hôtel Saint-Christophe

B. Points de repère. (*Landmarks.*) Look at this map showing the part of Paris where the action in this episode takes place. It is part of the **Quartier latin** (*Latin quarter*), so named because hundreds of years ago, Latin was the language of instruction at the university there. Rachid and Yasmine also live near the **Jardin des Plantes**, a botanical garden. The area around the **Jardin des Plantes** has always been a place where groups mixed: university students, wine merchants, and, since the 18th century, the scientists who have directed the **Jardin des Plantes**. Look carefully at the map and indicate the number and the name that correspond to the following landmarks in the neighborhood near Yasmine's school.

   a. un édifice (*building*) religieux **b.** une résidence **c.** des ruines romaines

   d. un fleuve (*large river*) **e.** une école

*O*bservez!

Rachid and the teacher greet each other in a typical French manner for people who don't know each other. Watch and listen to answer the following questions.

- Would you use a similar gesture when meeting a teacher for the first time?
- What level of language (formal, informal) does Rachid use when he speaks with the teacher? when he speaks with Yasmine? How do you know?

*É*crivez et explorez!

Visit the *Student Viewer's Handbook* link on the website for *Le Chemin du retour* at **www.mhhe.com/debuts** for the composition subject and activities related to this episode.

Bonjour!

 Visionnement 1

*A*vant de visionner

Un grand jour. At the end of Episode 1, Yasmine wished her father luck because he was going to have a big day too. To find out why, read the following exchange from Episode 2 and choose the response that best sums up the dialogue.

MARTINE: Alors, le déménagement[a]?

RACHID: Difficile... Tu vas bien?[b]

MARTINE: Mmm. C'est Roger, le réalisateur[c]... Et Nicole, la scripte.[d]

[a]*move (to a new residence)* [b]*Tu... Are you well?* [c]*director* [d]*script coordinator*

ROGER ET NICOLE:	Bonjour.
RACHID:	Bonjour.
MARTINE:	C'est Rachid, Rachid Bouhazid. ... (*à Rachid*) Et là, sur[e] l'écran, ...

[e]*Et... And there, on*

a. Rachid is saying goodbye before moving away.

b. He is starting classes at the university.

c. He is starting a new job.

*O*bservez!

Now watch Episode 2. See if you are right about Rachid's important day by looking for the following clues.

• Where does Rachid go after dropping Yasmine off at school?
• What does he do there?

Remember—Don't expect to understand every word in the episode; you need to understand only the basic plot structure and characters. If you can answer the questions that follow the episode, you have understood enough. Your instructor may ask you to watch the episode again later in the chapter. By then, you'll have additional tools and will be able to understand more of the details. The activities in **Visionnement 2** will help, too.

*A*près le visionnement

A. Quel travail? (*Which job?*) Now that you have watched Episode 2, match each job to the person you saw in the video.

1. Camille

2. Bruno

3. Martine

4. Hélène

5. Rachid

a. la productrice
b. un reporter canadien
c. un nouveau (*new*) reporter
d. un journaliste français
e. une journaliste française

B. Qu'est-ce qui se passe? (*What's happening?*) Tell what happens in Episode 2 by choosing words from the following list to fill in the blanks in the summary of the story.

Vocabulaire utile: béret, Camille, Canal 7, content, émission, médaillon, Montréal, pain, présente, prêt, test

Rachid arrive à _____[1]. Martine, la productrice, _____[2] ses nouveaux[a] collègues.

Rachid va travailler[b] avec _____[3] et Bruno.

Aujourd'hui,[c] pendant[d] l'émission «Bonjour!», Camille et Bruno inter-

viewent un boulanger parisien. Il y a un _____[4] sur le pain: pain artisanal ou

pain industriel? Bruno est _____[5] pour le test. Il identifie le _____[6] artisanal, et

il gagne[e] le _____[7] de la semaine[f]... mais il n'est pas _____[8].

Hélène, une amie de Bruno, arrive de _____[9]. Bruno est très content de la

revoir.[g] Plus tard,[h] Camille cherche son[i] _____[10]. Où[j] est-il?

[a]ses... his new [b]va... will be working [c]Today [d]during [e]wins [f]week [g]de... to see her again [h]Plus... Later
[i]her [j]Where

C. Réfléchissez. (*Think.*) Answer the following questions based on what you saw and heard in Episode 2.

1. Bruno and Camille work together as hosts of "Bonjour!" From what you have seen, would you guess that they are friends or simply coworkers? Or is it too early to tell?

2. Camille seems to have lost something. What do you think she has lost? What could its significance be?

Regards sur la culture

Perceptions et réalités

Stereotypes usually tell us as much about the values and customs of the people who use them as about those whom they are supposed to describe. There are a few North American stereotypes about the French that are shared by the French themselves, but many others are not.

- French people often think of themselves as particularly interested in food and gifted at appreciating it. They are especially concerned about bread, which is truly the staple food of French cuisine. Bread is eaten along with nearly every dish at every meal, and it is the main food eaten at breakfast and for most children's snacks. Bread made in the traditional craft sense (**le pain artisanal**) has to be bought daily because it contains no preservatives and dries out quickly. Mass-produced bread (**le pain industriel**) is also available in stores. Most French people are ready at any moment to engage in animated debates about the quality of bread today.

À la boulangerie

- The French do not think of themselves as eating rich food, however, but only *good* food. When asked what the typical French meal is, most people in France would probably answer **le steak-frites** (*steak with fries*). This may not correspond to North American ideas of what French people like to eat, but it is the kind of meal that a French traveler might think of first when he or she needs a quick dinner.

- The Eiffel Tower really is a landmark that the French think of as representing them in some sense. A hilarious 1999 film, *Le Voyage à Paris,* recounts the adventures of a rural highway toll collector with hundreds of models of the Eiffel Tower in his room at home. His dream is to visit Paris and see the real thing.

- The French like to think of themselves as the little guys who always win out because they are clever and quick. The popular comic character Astérix is a symbol of this sense of identity. He is a Gaul* who, in ancient times, lives in the one village that has not been conquered by the Roman legions. Astérix is always able to outwit the power of Caesar and his troops.

---

*In ancient times, France was part of an area known as Gaul. In 390 B.C., its inhabitants, called Gauls, attacked Rome and eventually swept farther east. Around 50 B.C., Julius Caesar and his Roman army had succeeded in turning the tide and had conquered all of Gaul, an area that comprised what is now France, Belgium, Luxembourg, and the parts of the Netherlands and Germany that are south and west of the Rhine River.

© 2001—Les Éditions Albert René/Goscinny-Uderzo

- Foreigners often think of the beret as typically French. To the French, however, it looks old-fashioned and reminds them of elderly people, farming life, and backwardness. Berets are not a common sight in Paris.

- The French are often surprised to find out that other people think of them as obsessed with love. As far as the French are concerned, the real lovers are the Italians.

- French people are also astonished to discover that people from some other cultures consider them rude. Later in this course, you'll learn reasons for this gap in perceptions, and you will also look at other aspects of French culture that may clash with North American stereotypes.

Considérez

To vouch for the kindness of someone, a French person might say: **Il est bon comme le pain.** Does this expression make any sense when translated literally into English? What would be the nearest English equivalent of this expression? What conclusions can you draw from this difference about the importance accorded to bread in France and in North American cultures?

Visionnement 2

*A*vant de visionner

A. **Points de repère. (***Landmarks.***)**   The following map shows the southeastern edge of Paris and the adjacent suburbs, where the Canal 7 studios are located. This whole area, on both banks of the Seine, became rather run-down after World War II, but recently, it has been attracting new development and prestige projects like the national library (**la Bibliothèque nationale de France**).

Look carefully at the map and indicate the number and name of the landmark that one would seek out in order to find the following:

Les environs de Canal 7

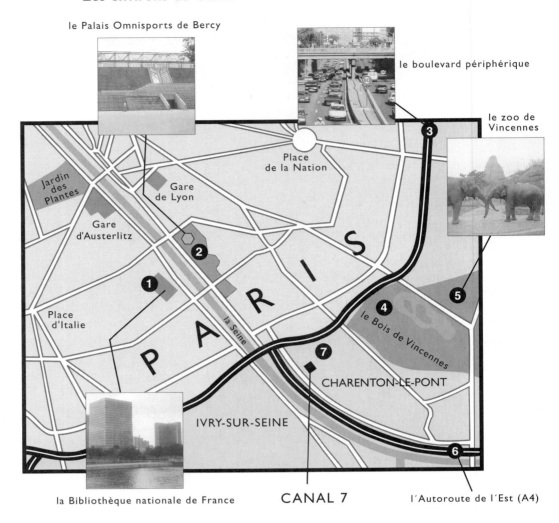

le Palais Omnisports de Bercy

le boulevard périphérique

le zoo de Vincennes

Place de la Nation

Jardin des Plantes

Gare de Lyon

Gare d'Austerlitz

la Seine

Place d'Italie

PARIS

le Bois de Vincennes

CHARENTON-LE-PONT

IVRY-SUR-SEINE

la Bibliothèque nationale de France

CANAL 7

l'Autoroute de l'Est (A4)

a. un manuscrit de la Renaissance

b. un tigre

c. un match de football (*soccer*)

d. des arbres et des fleurs (*trees and flowers*) magnifiques

e. une route autour de (*around*) Paris

f. Camille Leclair et Bruno Gall

B. Les pains en France. Match the description of the bread with the correct picture.

a.    b.

_____ **1.** Une baguette est longue et mince (*thin*).
_____ **2.** Un pain de campagne (*country*) est court et épais (*short and thick*).

Observez!

Consider the cultural information explained in **Regards sur la culture**. Then watch Episode 2 again, and answer the following questions.

• Why is Bruno embarrassed at the end of the show?
• What is the connection between the beret and the topic of the show?

$É$crivez et explorez!

Visit the *Student Viewer's Handbook* link on the website for *Le Chemin du retour* at **www.mhhe.com/debuts** for the composition subject and activities related to this episode.

Épisode *3*

Le Médaillon

Visionnement 1

Avant de visionner

Précisez. (*Specify.*) Which sentence best describes the dialogue? Choose from among the choices that follow the dialogue.

PRODUCTRICE:	Attends,[a] Camille. Je te présente Rachid Bouhazid. C'est notre nouveau[b] reporter.
RACHID:	Très heureux.
CAMILLE:	Enchantée.
RACHID:	«Bonjour!» est une émission très sympa. Vous êtes forts,[c] Bruno et vous!
CAMILLE:	Merci.

[a]*Wait* [b]*notre... our new* [c]*strong (a good team)*

a. Rachid critique l'émission.

b. Rachid admire l'émission.

c. Rachid préfère Bruno à Camille.

Observez!

Martine, the producer, makes an important discovery in Episode 3: she finds the locket Camille has lost. As you watch, try to answer the following questions.

- How does Camille react when Martine asks **Qui est-ce?**
- What is missing from the locket?

Vocabulaire relatif à l'épisode

C'est à toi?	*Is this yours?*
Tu viens de	*You come from*
Tu as faim?	*Are you hungry?*

Après le visionnement

A. Qu'est-ce qui se passe? (*What's happening?*) Tell what happens in Episode 3 by choosing words from the list to fill in the blanks in the summary of the story.

Vocabulaire utile: le bureau, chez, l'émission, invite, jolie, pense, une photo, présente, propose, «Qui est-ce?», trouve

Martine, la productrice, _____[1] le médaillon de Camille, et il y a _____[2] dedans.[a] Martine demande _____[3], mais Camille ne répond pas.[b] Ensuite,[c] Martine _____[4] Rachid à Camille. Il aime _____[5] «Bonjour!» et _____[6] que Camille et Bruno sont forts. Bruno _____[7] à Hélène de se marier avec lui,[d] mais c'est une plaisanterie.[e] Finalement, Bruno entre dans _____[8] et rencontre[f] Rachid. Il regarde une photo de la femme[g] de Rachid et pense qu'elle est _____[9], mais Rachid ne répond pas. Pour être sociable, Bruno _____[10] Rachid à déjeuner.[h]

[a]*in it* [b]*ne... doesn't answer* [c]*Then* [d]*de... to marry him* [e]*joke* [f]*meets* [g]*wife* [h]*have lunch*

B. Les personnalités. In this episode, several characters revealed a little more of their personalities. Read these exchanges and choose which sentence best describes each person's character.

1. Quel est le caractère de Bruno?

BRUNO: Hélène?... On se marie, toi et moi?

HÉLÈNE: Eh! Quelle bonne idée! D'abord, je divorce avec Tom Cruise, OK?

a. Il aime flirter. **c.** C'est un intellectuel.

b. C'est un menteur (*liar*).

2. Quel est le caractère de Camille?

MARTINE: C'est à toi... ? Le médaillon est ravissant. Qui est-ce?

CAMILLE: ... Merci, Martine. (Elle referme[a] le médaillon et part.[b])

[a]*closes* [b]*walks away*

a. Camille est heureuse.

b. Camille est discrète (*reserved*).

c. Camille est bavarde (*talkative*).

3. Quel est le caractère de Rachid?

BRUNO: Euh, excuse-moi, c'est mon^c bureau, ici. Ton^d bureau, il est là.

RACHID: Ah! Bon ben, pas de problème!

^cmy   ^dYour

a. Rachid est ridicule.

b. Rachid n'est pas gentil.

c. Rachid est sympathique.

Regards sur la culture

La communication non-verbale

Notice how close Martine, Rachid, and Camille stand when they are speaking. This illustrates one aspect of nonverbal communication that poses problems for many Americans and Canadians. Because we are not usually aware of our own gestures and needs for communication space, nonverbal communication can be one of the most difficult areas of adjustment when we visit another culture. Here are two examples.

Rachid fait la connaissance de Camille.

- The handshake, often consisting of a single quick up-and-down movement, is an obligatory greeting in France for all colleagues and friends the first time they meet each day. It can be replaced with a quick kiss on the cheeks (two or three or four times depending on the region) between two women or between men and women, when the people involved know each other well.

- Cultures differ in how they set interpersonal distances. In English-speaking North America, the distance people maintain in day-to-day business conversations with strangers and acquaintances (sometimes called "social" distance) starts at around 4 feet. In France, social distance tends to be smaller, starting at around 0.6 meters (2 feet). When English-speaking North Americans encounter French social distances, they may back up in an attempt to reset the situation with American spacing. The French person will normally move closer so as to reestablish the space with which he or she is comfortable. More than one American or Canadian has backed all the way across a room before the end of a French conversation.

Considérez

Many people have commented that it is extremely easy to spot North Americans in France just by the way they walk and stand. If you were studying abroad, would you want to try to adjust to the nonverbal habits of the culture in which you were living, or would that be unnecessary? How hard would it be?

Visionnement 2

*A*vant de visionner

Tu **ou** *vous***?** Read the following dialogues and choose the correct explanation(s) for why the highlighted pronoun **tu** or **vous** is used in that context.

1. RACHID: «Bonjour!» est une émission très sympa. **Vous** êtes forts, Bruno et vous.

   CAMILLE: Merci.

   a. C'est normal d'employer **vous** pour parler de deux personnes.
   b. Rachid vient de faire la connaissance de (*just met*) Camille.
   c. Rachid est un bon ami de Camille et de Bruno.

2. BRUNO: **Tu** es Rachid Bouhazid et **tu** viens de Marseille, c'est ça?

   RACHID: C'est ça, Bruno.

   a. Bruno vient de faire la connaissance de Rachid.
   b. Bruno accueille (*welcomes*) Rachid avec amitié (*friendship*).
   c. Bruno est beaucoup plus âgé que (*much older than*) Rachid.

*O*bservez!

Consider the cultural information explained in **Regards sur la culture**. Then watch Episode 3 again, and answer the following questions.

• What gesture do Rachid and Bruno use when they first greet each other?
• What behaviors do you notice when people greet each other that are different from the way people act in similar situations in your country?

*É*crivez et explorez!

Visit the *Student Viewer's Handbook* link on the website for *Le Chemin du retour* at **www.mhhe.com/debuts** for the composition subject and activities related to this episode.

Une nouvelle vie à Paris

*V*isionnement 1

*A*vant de visionner

Qu'est-ce que cela veut dire? (*What does it mean?*) In Episode 4, Rachid has the following conversation with Martine. Read the dialogue and then choose the most probable meaning of each of the sentences containing the word **appeler**, which means *to call*.

MARTINE: Ta femme vient d'appeler.

RACHID: Ma femme?

MARTINE: Oui... Il y a un problème?

RACHID: Sonia n'aime pas Paris. ...

MARTINE: (*donne son téléphone portable à Rachid*) Appelle ta femme.

1. Ta femme vient d'appeler.

    a. Your wife is going to call.   **c.** Your wife is coming to the studio.
    b. Your wife just called.

2. Appelle ta femme.

    a. Are you going to call your wife?   **c.** Call your wife.
    b. Your wife is calling.

Observez!

Now watch Episode 4. As you watch, try to fill in more details about Rachid.

- Where do Rachid's parents come from?
- What is Rachid's father's religion? What might Rachid's mother's religion be?

Vocabulaire relatif à l'épisode	
le jarret de porc aux lentilles	*ham hocks with lentils*
l'alcool	*alcohol*
le cochon	*pig; pork*
le jambon	*ham*
des nouvelles	*news*
tu l'attends	*you'll wait for her*

Après le visionnement

A. Un résumé. Fill in the blanks to finish the summary of events in Episode 4.

Vocabulaire utile: arrive, la cafétéria, l'école, la femme, un hamburger, lui, le mari, n'aime pas, séparés

Rachid et Bruno sont à _____[1]. Le chef de cuisine recommande le jarret de porc, mais Rachid commande[a] _____[2]. Martine _____[3] et annonce que _____[4] de Rachid vient d'appeler. Rachid explique que[b] Sonia _____[5] Paris. Rachid et Sonia sont _____[6]. À la fin de la journée,[c] Rachid va chercher Yasmine à _____[7]. Camille va avec _____[8].

[a]orders   [b]explique... *explains that*   [c]À... *At the end of the day*

B. Réfléchissez. (*Think.*) What type of relationship exists between Martine and Rachid? Is it professional (**un rapport professionnel**) or personal (**un rapport personnel**)? Explain your answer in French, using examples from the episode. Combine appropriate sentence fragments to form your examples.

MODÈLE: Martine et Rachid ont un rapport...
                 Par exemple, Martine...

	donne un conseil (*gives advice*) à	
	est la productrice de l'émission	
	montre (*shows*) son intérêt pour	«Bonjour!»
Martine	parle de sa (*his*) famille avec	Camille
Rachid	parle de soucis (*worries*) personnels à	Martine
	pose (*asks*) des questions à	Rachid
	présente le nouveau reporter, Rachid, à	
	travaille pour	

Regards sur la culture

La diversité de la France

Foreigners often have a view of France and French culture that doesn't actually match the truth; for them, Paris tends to represent the whole of France. In fact, the great diversity of the country makes it rather difficult to generalize about any aspect of culture.

- Geographically, France is one of the most diverse countries in Europe. It has warm Mediterranean coasts, the highest mountains on the continent, a range of extinct volcanoes, vast plains, deep canyons, and even landscapes that look like Arizona. Paris has a damp climate that is influenced by the Atlantic Ocean, whereas Marseille, located on the Mediterranean, in some ways is more like southern California than it is like Paris.

Cirque de Gavarnie, Pyrénées

Pointe du Raz, Bretagne

Èze-sur-Mer, Côte d'Azur

- This geographical diversity helps to explain the cultural diversity of France. Agriculture, architecture, and local traditions vary along with the landscapes. It is often clear when one has traveled from one province to the next, because the structure of the farm buildings, the layout of the villages, and the shapes of the fields have changed.

La Beauce

Le Périgord

L'Alsace

- The cuisine of the different regions of France varies, too. In the Southwest of France, food is traditionally cooked with goose fat, whereas in Normandy, butter is the essential cooking ingredient, and in Provence, it is olive oil.
- Recent immigration to France has added another level of diversity. The largest groups to arrive in France over the past fifty years have been the Spanish, the Portuguese, and, most recently, people from the Maghreb, which are the former French colonies of Morocco, Algeria, and Tunisia. Although these North Africans are Muslims, many of them have begun to assimilate into French society just as earlier groups did.

Considérez

Try to explain why the three farms pictured in this section would probably not be located in the regions that are represented in the photographs of the Pyrenees, Brittany, and the Riviera. Think about building materials, the layout of the farms, and the kind of agriculture that is possible in these places.

Visionnement 2

Avant de visionner

A. **J'ai faim!**   Bruno and Rachid decide to have lunch in the cafeteria. Here is their conversation with the chef. Stage instructions are included to portray the chef's reactions. Read the dialogue and then answer the question.

CUISINIER: Alors, pour aujourd'hui, en plat principal,[a] du jarret de porc aux lentilles! Vachement[b] bon, hein!

BRUNO: Ah bien, bien. Ça marche![c]

RACHID: Un hamburger, c'est possible?

CUISINIER (*se rembrunit*[d]):   Oh. D'accord! (*Il grommelle en s'éloignant.*[e])

[a]en... *as a main course*   [b]*Very*   [c]Ça... *That works (for me)*   [d]se... *frowning*   [e]Il... *He grumbles as he walks off.*

Pourquoi le cuisinier se rembrunit-il et grommelle-t-il? Il y a 2 ou 3 raisons.

   a. Préparer un hamburger, c'est beaucoup (*a lot*) de travail.
   b. Il pense que Rachid n'apprécie pas ses efforts culinaires.
   c. Il est toujours de mauvaise humeur (*in a bad mood*).
   d. Il pense que Rachid préfère un plat américain à un plat français.
   e. Certains Français sont parfois impatients avec les gens (*people*) d'origine étrangère.

B. La culture musulmane?   After ordering, Rachid and Bruno discuss their food preferences. Read their exchange and reflect on the cultural information it contains. Then answer the questions.

RACHID: Bonjour. Un verre d'eau,[a] s'il vous plaît. Merci.

BRUNO: Tu es musulman, je suppose? Pas d'alcool, pas de cochon...

RACHID: Mon père est algérien et musulman. Et ma mère est bretonne[b] et elle adore le jambon[c]!...

[a]Un... A glass of water   [b]Breton, from Brittany (a region in the northwestern part of France)   [c]ham

1. Pourquoi Bruno pense-t-il que Rachid est musulman?
2. Quelles viandes et boissons (*Which meats and drinks*) ne sont probablement pas permises (*permitted*) pour une personne musulmane?

Observez!

Consider the cultural information explained in **Regards sur la culture**. Then watch Episode 4 again, and answer the following questions.

- Why does Sonia not like Paris? What difference(s) between Marseille and Paris are implied by this explanation?
- Listen for the name and location of Yasmine's school. Locate the neighborhood on a map of Paris or on the map in **Visionnement 2** in Épisode 1. Which monuments and institutions are found near the school?

$É$crivez et explorez!

Visit the *Student Viewer's Handbook* link on the website for *Le Chemin du retour* at **www.mhhe.com/debuts** for the composition subject and activities related to this episode.

Secrets

Visionnement 1

*A*vant de visionner

Qu'est-ce que cela veut dire? (*What does that mean?*) In this episode, Rachid admires something in Camille's apartment. Read the following exchange and then answer the questions.

RACHID: Écoute, ce livre est vraiment,[a] euh... Il est vraiment magnifique!

CAMILLE: C'est un cadeau[b] de ma grand-mère... Tu aimes les Cévennes?

RACHID: Ah oui, beaucoup[c]... beaucoup.

[a]*truly* [b]*gift* [c]*a lot*

1. Qu'est-ce que Rachid admire? **2.** Qui a donné (*gave*) cette chose (*this thing*) à Camille? **3.** Est-ce que Rachid aime les Cévennes?

Vocabulaire relatif à l'épisode

Je ne me rappelle jamais.	I never remember (it).
J'apporte tout ce qu'il faut	I'll bring everything that's needed
Je peux t'emprunter le livre?	May I borrow the book from you?
De quoi se mêle-t-il?	What business is it of his?

Pour en savoir plus...

The **Cévennes,** a mountainous area in the southeast of France, is known for its magnificent scenery and its biodiversity. The region is quite isolated and relatively empty of young people, because many have moved away to find work. Lately, however, a diversified economic base, an influx of population, and the establishment of a national park in 1970 have brought more prosperity to the area.

Observez!

In Episode 5, Rachid goes to Yasmine's school and finds his wife there. Later on he meets Camille's mother. As you watch, answer the following questions.

- What does Rachid say to Yasmine's mother? What is her reaction?
- How does the attitude of Camille's mother, Mado, change during the episode?

Après le visionnement

A. Moments clés. (Key moments.) Here are some key moments from Episode 5. Fill in the blanks with the name of the appropriate person or thing.

1. Rachid rencontre (*meets*) _____ dans la cour (*courtyard*) de son école.
2. _____ demande pardon à Sonia. **3.** _____ invite Rachid et Camille à dîner.
4. Rachid admire _____ sur les Cévennes. **5.** Il examine _____ de la grand-mère de Camille. **6.** Mado ne veut pas parler de _____. **7.** _____ se méfie de (*distrusts*) Rachid.

B. Réfléchissez. (Think.) Answer the following questions about Camille's mother, Mado, according to your impressions from the episode.

1. Comment l'attitude de Mado change-t-elle envers (*toward*) Rachid dans cet épisode?
   Vocabulaire utile: aimable, content(e), cynique, horrifié(e), hostile, méfiant(e) (*suspicious*)

   - Au début (*At the beginning*)...
   - Pendant (*During*) la visite de Rachid...
   - À la fin (*At the end*)...

2. Pourquoi son attitude change-t-elle, à votre avis (*in your opinion*)? Choisissez (*Choose*) **a**, **b** ou **c**.

   a. Rachid n'accepte pas son invitation à dîner et part vite (*leaves quickly*).
   b. Mado a un secret de famille et Rachid pose trop de (*too many*) questions.
   c. Rachid est impoli avec Camille et Mado n'aime pas cela.

Regards sur la culture

La famille

As you noticed in this segment, Mado tries to discourage Camille from talking about family matters with Rachid. Although there is a very particular reason for this in the film (one that has not yet been made clear), it is also true that the family and its affairs are generally felt to be very private matters for French people.

- Unless the friendship is strong and well established, it is rather unusual for a visitor to France to be invited as a guest to the home of a French family. The home is a private domain, and even when one does enter a home in France, the visit is normally limited to the living room and dining room. One would almost never visit the entire house the way people do in North America. In addition, a French home is generally closed to the outside by a fence or wall and by shutters on the windows.

- French people often feel that they need to know something about a person's family in order to evaluate him/her. They sometimes judge an individual in part on the basis of the family's reputation or social standing within the community. Of course, because reputations are based partly on hearsay, the French know that such evaluations are only approximate.

- Meals are extremely important family affairs in France. It would be very unusual for a French person to schedule an event that would interfere with the family mealtime.

Un grand repas familial

- Competition between siblings is very strongly discouraged in France. North Americans tend to be surprised at how well French siblings appear to get along.

- To a greater extent than in North America, French children are discouraged from engaging in activities that would take them away from their families. Except in large urban areas, it is often expected that they will eventually find a job that will allow them to settle down relatively close to their parents.

- In France, it is traditionally considered shameful to the family if an elderly person ends his/her life in a retirement home or a hospital, rather than at home with the family.

Considérez

Why might a newcomer to a small town initially have a more difficult time assimilating in France than in Canada or the United States? Can you explain the origins of this difference?

Visionnement 2

Avant de visionner

Les environs de l'appartement de Camille

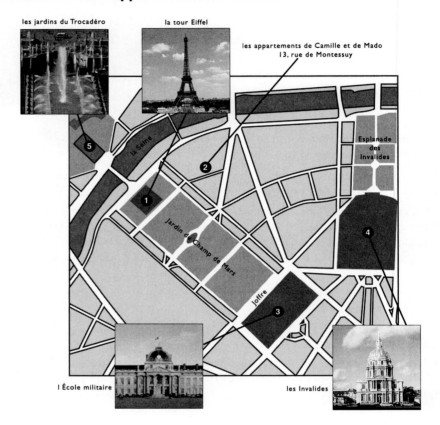

les jardins du Trocadéro

la tour Eiffel

les appartements de Camille et de Mado
13, rue de Montessuy

Esplanade des Invalides

la Seine

Jardin du Champ de Mars

Joffre

l École militaire

les Invalides

A. Visites dans le quartier. This map shows the elegant area of Paris in which Mado and Camille live. It wasn't until the time of Louis XIV, the Sun King, in the late 1600s, that this part of Paris began to be built. Louis XIV constructed **les Invalides**, an enormous complex of buildings, as a hospital and retirement home for the veterans of his many wars. Napoleon studied at the **École militaire**, and in 1840, nearly twenty years after his death, his remains were buried in the **Église du Dôme** at **les Invalides**. The **Champ de Mars** was the site of important ceremonies during the Revolutionary period in the late eighteenth century. But most of the buildings in this area date from the late nineteenth century, when the **tour Eiffel** was built. The **jardins du Trocadéro** are a reminder of the 1937 World's Fair.

Mado likes taking historical walks in her neighborhood. Indicate the number and name of the landmark that corresponds to each description.

    a. un ensemble architectural de 1676

    b. un bâtiment de 1773

    c. un tombeau (*tomb*) de 1840

    d. une construction de 1889

    e. des fontaines de 1937

B. Les relations familiales. What do you remember about Episode 5?

    1. Comment est la relation entre Camille et sa mère, Mado?

        a. Mado traite (*treats*) sa fille comme une enfant.

        b. Camille s'occupe de (*takes care of*) sa mère.

        c. Mado et Camille ont une vie (*life*) indépendante l'une de l'autre (*the other*).

    2. Selon les observations de **Regards sur la culture** dans ce chapitre, est-ce qu'il est normal que Mado invite Rachid à dîner? Expliquez.

*O*bservez!

Consider the cultural information explained in **Regards sur la culture**. Then watch Episode 5 again, and answer the following questions.

- What does Mado do to make Rachid feel welcome?
- What behaviors exhibited by Rachid might not conform to Mado's cultural expectations of a guest?

*É*crivez et explorez!

Visit the *Student Viewer's Handbook* link on the website for *Le Chemin du retour* at **www.mhhe.com/debuts** for the composition subject and activities related to this episode.

Épisode 6

Bonjour, grand-père!

Visionnement 1

*A*vant de visionner

Qu'est-ce que cela veut dire? (*What does that mean?*) In this episode, Rachid tries to learn more about Camille's family. After two or three questions, Camille responds with the following remark.

> Rachid, tu es gentil, tu me poses des questions, tu t'intéresses à ma famille... Mais, tu as peut-être autre chose à faire? Ton reportage, par exemple?

Match each of Camille's phrases to the most appropriate interpretation.

1. ...tu me poses des questions...
2. ...tu t'intéresses à ma famille...
3. ...tu as peut-être autre chose à faire...

a. ...tu dois (*must*) faire ton travail...
b. ...tu trouves ma grand-mère et mon grand-père intéressants...
c. ...tu es indiscret...

*O*bservez!

Two photographs are important to the story in Episode 6. As you watch, see if you can answer the following questions.

- Where does Rachid find a picture of Camille's grandmother?
- What is unusual about the picture?
- What other photograph is important?

Vocabulaire relatif à l'épisode

Du calme.	*Stay calm.*
coupée	*cut*
de l'autre côté	*on the other side*
le marié	*bridegroom*
vivante	*alive, living*

*A*près le visionnement

A. Vous avez compris? (*Did you understand?*) Summarize the episode by completing the paragraph with the correct word from the parentheses.

Au début de l'épisode, Camille est au _____¹ (plateau, maquillage) et Bruno devient _____² (ridicule, impatient). Aujourd'hui, le sujet de l'émission «Bonjour!» est _____³ (la mode, la cuisine). Rachid trouve _____⁴ (une photo, une carte) dans le livre sur les Cévennes. Selon[a] Camille, c'est une photo de Louise, le jour de _____⁵ (ses fiançailles,[b] son mariage). La photo n'est pas entière. Elle est _____⁶ (coupée, floue[c]). À la fin de l'épisode, Camille utilise _____⁷ (un ordinateur, un rétroprojecteur) pour agrandir[d] une autre photo de sa grand-mère. Elle trouve son _____⁸ (père, grand-père) sur cette photo.

[a]*According to* [b]*engagement* [c]*blurry* [d]*to enlarge*

B. Réfléchissez. (*Think*.) Choose what you think might be the most likely answer to each question. Explain your choice (in French).

1. Pourquoi Rachid pose-t-il beaucoup de (*many*) questions?
   - **a.** Il aime bavarder (*to gossip*).
   - **b.** Il s'intéresse à la famille de Camille et désire aider Camille.
   - **c.** Il aime les mystères comme la photo coupée.

2. Qu'est-ce qui explique (*What explains*) la réponse de Camille quand Rachid pose des questions sur la photo?
   - **a.** Camille désire parler de sa famille, mais l'histoire est trop (*too*) longue.
   - **b.** Rachid pose des questions troublantes pour Camille.
   - **c.** Camille s'impatiente parce que Rachid néglige (*is neglecting*) son travail.

C. Imaginez. In your opinion, what link might there be between the book on the Cévennes and the picture that Rachid finds in it? Use the expressions in two or three columns to form possible answers.

Pour en savoir plus...

Learn to recognize the following adverbs. They occur frequently in *Le Chemin du retour* and in your *Handbook*.

TIME: aujourd'hui, demain (*tomorrow*), plus tard (*later*)

FREQUENCY: encore (*again; still*), parfois, rarement, souvent, toujours

MANNER: bien, franchement (*frankly*), peut-être (*perhaps*), très, vachement (*very*), vite (*quickly, fast*)

PLACE: ici, là

MODÈLE: Louise s'est mariée dans les Cévennes, peut-être.

Camille	aime voyager	dans les Cévennes
le grand-père de Camille	est mort(e) (*died*)	de noces (*wedding*)
le livre	est né(e) (*was born*)	des Cévennes
Louise	est un cadeau (*gift*)	du mari de Louise
Mado	est un ensemble de photos	
	habite	
	s'est mariée (*got married*)	
	vient	

Regards sur la culture

Les habits et la mode°

Les… *Clothing and fashion*

In this episode, Bruno and Camille present a segment of "Bonjour!" devoted to fashion. The significance of clothing in French culture is very great and has been so for centuries. Clothing expresses a person's wealth and status, of course, and it may also serve as an indication of age group and ethnic origin. In addition, however, clothing expresses attitudes, including, in France, a concern for elegance and "good taste."

La mode "américaine" chez les enfants

- As a general rule, appearance is more overtly valued in France than in North America. In fact, most French children are taught that how they appear to other people (in clothing, in actions, in language) is extremely important.

- French people tend to comment explicitly on the way others dress. It would not be shocking or unusual for someone in France to say that so-and-so is attractive but badly dressed (**mal habillé**).

- French people pay a lot of attention to how they dress, but may not actually own very large wardrobes. The care with which items of clothing are combined is more important than the variety of items worn.

- French children spend much of their time dressed in what North Americans might think is rather fancy clothing. They are expected not to get dirty when they are playing.

- In North America, French clothing is usually associated with elegance and high style: classic fashion like Chanel or modern styles like those of Jean-Paul Gaultier, for example. In France, however,

La mode au masculin

young people love North American clothing for casual wear. In fact, there are several "imitation" American clothing companies in France. Chevignon, for example, was founded in 1979 and has created a very successful "American" style based on U.S. clothing of the 1950s.

Considérez

Someone who is passionately interested in clothing might be considered superficial by certain people in North America. This would not be the case in France. Do Americans or Canadians feel the same way about someone who has a passion for good food or for fancy cars? If not, what do you think is the difference?

Visionnement 2

Avant de visionner

La culture de la mode. In his introduction to the fashion segment, Bruno says:

...Mais, pour beaucoup d'entre nous, la mode reste un rêve. Eh oui, c'est cher, très cher! Alors, aujourd'hui, la question que l'on se pose, c'est: peut-on encore être à la mode? Est-ce que c'est possible? Combien ça coûte? Et surtout, où peut-on acheter au meilleur marché?

Reflect on what you have read in **Regards sur la culture**. What cultural assumptions about the importance of appearance does Bruno express?

Observez!

Consider the cultural information explained in **Regards sur la culture**. Then watch Episode 6 again, and answer the following questions.

- What compliment does Bruno give to Camille?
- What is her response? How might an American respond to this compliment?

Écrivez et explorez!

Visit the *Student Viewer's Handbook* link on the website for *Le Chemin du retour* at **www.mhhe.com/debuts** for the composition subject and activities related to this episode.

Préparatifs°

Preparations

Visionnement 1

*A*vant de visionner

La réponse logique. Choisissez la phrase qui suit (*follows*) logiquement l'expression donnée.

1. LOUISE: Alex. Tu m'achètes du champagne? Une bonne bouteille,[a] s'il te plaît!

   ALEX: _____

   a. Oui, d'accord, mais chez moi!

   b. Tu fais la fête[b] ce soir?

   c. Vous en prenez[c] un kilo?

   [a]*bottle* [b]*party* [c]*take*

2. MARCHANDE DE LÉGUMES: Qu'est-ce que je vous sers, mademoiselle?

CAMILLE: _____

a. Euh, des carottes, s'il vous plaît.

b. Non, juste deux ou trois...

c. Est-ce que vous pouvez me le couper en petits morceaux?[d]

[d]Est-ce... *Can you cut it into little pieces for me?*

Observez!

Dans l'Épisode 7, Camille va dîner avec quelqu'un (*someone*). Regardez l'épisode et essayez de trouver les réponses aux questions suivantes (*following*).

• Où va Camille et qu'est-ce qu'elle achète?

• Quel est l'état physique de la femme à qui Camille rend visite (*whom Camille visits*)?

Après le visionnement

A. Identifiez.   Qui dit (*says*) les phrases suivantes? Est-ce Camille, Louise (la grand-mère), Alex, le boucher ou la marchande de légumes?

MODÈLE: On dîne ensemble ce soir?   →
C'est Camille.

1. Oui, d'accord, mais chez moi!

2. Je fais la cuisine!

3. Tu m'achètes du champagne? Une bonne bouteille, s'il te plaît!

4. D'accord, mais vous signez un autographe!

5. Qu'est-ce que je vous sers, mademoiselle?

6. Tu vas bien? Tu as l'air en forme!

Maintenant, pensez à ces identifications pour raconter (*tell the story of*) l'Épisode 7. Commencez avec les phrases suivantes.

Camille invite sa grand-mère à dîner. La grand-mère invite Camille chez elle, et Camille propose de faire la cuisine...

B. Réfléchissez. (*Think.*)   Répondez.

1. Faites une liste des produits que Camille achète. Qu'est-ce qu'elle prépare, probablement—une quiche lorraine? un poulet rôti (*roasted*)? un bœuf bourguignon? des crêpes?

2. Pourquoi est-ce que Camille invite Louise à dîner? Est-ce qu'il y a une raison particulière, à votre avis? Expliquez.

Vocabulaire relatif à l'épisode

ensemble	*together*
vous en prenez un kilo?	*will you take a kilo (of them)?*
je vais prendre...	*I'll take ...*
du premier choix	*top quality*
tu as l'air en forme	*you seem to be doing well*
tu refermes... ?	*will you close ... ?*

Notez bien!

To talk about doing something with someone else, you can often use the word **ensemble** (*together*). Camille uses it to invite her grandmother to have dinner with her.

On dîne **ensemble** ce soir? *Shall we have dinner together tonight?*

Regards sur la culture

Le marché et la cuisine°

Le... The market and cooking

In this episode, you have seen Camille pick up a few items at an outdoor market as she prepares to make dinner for her grandmother. Food has a very high priority in French culture, and many social relations are maintained around home-cooked meals.

- One advantage of the traditional market is its appeal to the various senses. The displays are set up to highlight color and aesthetic appeal, and the mix of sounds (vendors calling, boxes being stacked) and smells (flowers, fruit, meat, cheese, fish) contributes to the experience. But for many people, the most important part of shopping at the market is the socializing that goes on.

Un marché en plein air

- Another advantage to the traditional market is that the vendor typically prepares the products to order for the customer, cutting the meat into particular sized pieces, for example, or slicing off just the right amount of cheese.

- In markets and in neighborhood grocery stores, customers do not pick out individual pieces of fruit or vegetables. They tell the vendor what they want, and the vendor picks out the produce. More than one North American has been thought to be shoplifting when picking out an apple from a market display.

Un supermarché

- Most French shoppers are very concerned about the quality of the food they buy, and they are often careful to buy pesticide-free products. They may want to know where the vegetables and beef come from or what kind of feed the chicken ate.

- Meals at home play a crucial role in family relationships. In addition, it is almost obligatory to treat guests to a meal consisting of three or more courses. Thus, having a large dining room is relatively important for French families, and one of the first pieces of furniture that many young couples purchase is a large dining table so that they can entertain family and friends appropriately.

- A French meal without some kind of first course is unusual. Even the simplest meal usually begins with the **entrée**—a few slices of salami, a bowl of soup, or a serving of marinated mushrooms—before the main dish (**le plat principal**) arrives. The distinction between **une entrée** and **un hors-d'œuvre** is based mostly on how many courses are served with the meal and whether the dish is served as part of the meal or before it begins.

Considérez

In France, **bien manger** means to eat delicious, refined food. What does *to eat well* mean in North America? Why the difference?

Le Quartier latin. (*The Latin Quarter.*) The area represented on the map is the southern part of the **Quartier latin**, which was first built up in the 12th and 13th centuries as the home of the great Parisian schools, renowned across all of Europe. **La Sorbonne**, originally a center of theological studies, today is just one part of the University of Paris. Many of the students who attend the numerous schools and universities of the Latin Quarter spend evenings in the restaurants and bars of the **rue Mouffetard**. **Le jardin du Luxembourg** is a large public park. The building that houses the French Senate, **le palais du Luxembourg**, is located within it. **Le Panthéon**, completed in 1789, honors great men and women of France. Among those buried there are Voltaire, Rousseau, Victor Hugo, Marie Curie, Louis Braille, and Jean Moulin, one of the most famous heroes of the Resistance. **L'Institut national des Jeunes Sourds**, founded in 1760, was a pioneering institution in the education of the deaf and is closely connected with the origins of American Sign Language.

Les environs de l'appartement de Louise

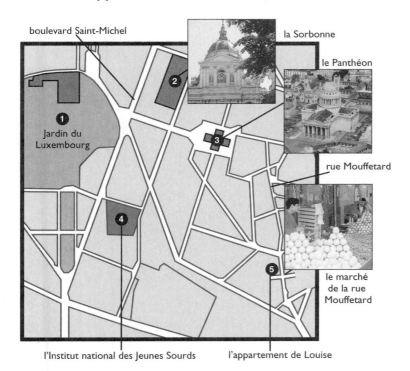

Un étudiant parle de sa journée. Complétez chaque phrase avec le nom de l'endroit qui convient.

1. Ce matin j'ai un cours (*class*) d'anthropologie à...
2. Après, j'ai un cours de la langue des signes française à...
3. À midi, je vais manger un sandwich en plein air (*outdoors*) dans...
4. Avec mon cousin, qui s'intéresse à l'histoire, je vais visiter...
5. Le soir, nous allons chercher un bon petit restaurant dans la rue...

Observez!

Considérez les aspects culturels expliqués dans **Regards sur la culture**. Ensuite (*Then*), regardez l'Épisode 7 encore une fois, et répondez aux questions suivantes.

- Quelles expressions Camille et les marchands emploient-ils pour montrer leur souci (*concern*) pour la qualité des produits?
- Que fait et que dit Camille au marché Mouffetard? Comparez ce marché avec un marché près de chez vous.

Écrivez et explorez!

À explorer: **www.mhhe.com/debuts** pour trouver le sujet de composition et plus d'informations sur les thèmes de cet épisode.

C'est loin, tout ça.°

C'est… *All that was long ago.*

Visionnement 1

Avant de visionner

In this episode, you will hear examples of two new verb tenses: The **passé composé** (in **boldface** type) is used to talk about past events; the *imparfait* (in **bold italic** type) is used to talk about past conditions or states of mind, and ongoing action in the past.

Vous comprenez? Essayez de comprendre les deux extraits (*extracts*) du film.

Camille pose une question à sa grand-mère, Louise.

CAMILLE: C'*était*ᵃ quand, la dernièreᵇ fois qu'il t'**a contactée**ᶜ?

LOUISE: En 1943. Il *était* dans les Cévennes. Il m'**a envoyé** une lettre… pour l'anniversaire de ta maman. Elle *avait* quatre ans.

ᵃ*It was* ᵇ*last* ᶜ*il… he contacted you*

Plus tard,[d] Mado parle à Camille.

MADO: D'où sort-elle[e] cette photo?! Pourquoi tu **as montré** ça à ta grand-mère?

[d]Plus... *Later*   [e]D'où... *Where does it come from*

Maintenant, indiquez si les phrases suivantes sont vraies ou fausses. Corrigez les phrases qui sont fausses.

1. Quelqu'un (*Someone*) contacte Louise pour la dernière fois en 1940.
2. Il est à Paris.
3. Il envoie une lettre pour l'anniversaire de Mado.
4. Mado a quarante ans à cette époque (*at that time*).
5. Mado demande pourquoi Camille montre une photo à sa grand-mère.

Observez!

Dans cet épisode, Camille cherche des informations sur le rôle de son grand-père pendant (*during*) la Deuxième Guerre mondiale (*Second World War*).

• Comment Louise réagit-elle (*does Louise react*) à la demande de Camille?
• Comment réagit Mado? Pourquoi?

Après le visionnement

A. **Vrai ou faux?**   Indiquez si les phrases suivantes sont vraies ou fausses. Corrigez les phrases fausses.

1. Camille montre une lettre d'Antoine à Louise.
2. Louise aime parler de son mari.
3. Louise raconte la visite de son mari dans les Cévennes.
4. Mado est furieuse parce que Camille a montré la photo à Louise.
5. Mado pense qu'on ne doit pas (*should not*) parler de son père.

B. **Réfléchissez. (*Think*.)**   Répondez aux questions.

1. Quels mots et expressions montrent que Louise et Mado considèrent encore Camille comme une enfant?
2. Comment Camille essaie-t-elle de montrer son indépendance?

Regards sur la culture

Principes de conversation

When people are angry with each other, they tend to use confrontational language, as Camille and Mado do in this episode. In this case, Mado is extremely angry, but in France, argument and debate can also be a normal part of any conversation. In fact, there are several aspects of French conversational practices that North Americans in France generally have to adjust to.

Une conversation animée

- A conversation between two French people may sometimes sound aggressive to North Americans. This impression is partly due to the lively tone of French dialogue, and it is partly because conversation in France is an art that requires some degree of expertise in argument and disagreement. This approach to conversation may surprise English-speaking North Americans who expect exchanges to sound calm even when disagreement is involved. Some North American conversations may feel spiritless and uninteresting to French people, who are accustomed to defending their own point of view in a lively way.
- In a French conversation, it may be more important for a participant to state his/her point of view and to defend it well than it is to come to an agreement or compromise on the subject being discussed.
- It is also typical in French conversation to be critical. Criticism of food and of people's physical appearance in France may seem especially striking to North Americans, who sometimes find such comments impolite. The French, on the other hand, think of criticism as something constructive and tend to find the North American hesitation to be frank about these things insincere or even hypocritical.
- Being a conversational partner is serious business in France! A French child learns early to speak in a lively and interesting manner.
- In the English-speaking parts of North America, conversational etiquette requires a slight pause between speakers' turns. In France, such pauses would be unusual: One begins talking just as the preceding speaker is finishing his/her turn. The result is that some North Americans find it quite challenging to get a word in when they are communicating with a group of French people: They are waiting for a tiny pause so that they can politely begin to speak, and often, the pause never arrives!
- In public places, French people tend to talk more quietly than North Americans. In France, the ideal is to speak in such a way that conversations cannot be overheard by others. North American groups often stand out in France because they tend to talk more loudly than the French in restaurants and shops.
- Conversations between strangers are rather unusual in France. It would be quite normal to spend several hours on a train face to face with three or four French people and never exchange a word with them.*

---

*Some European trains are different from North American trains in that travelers may be seated in compartments rather than rows. Each compartment is like a small room with two seats facing each other. Several people can fit on each seat and they face the people across from them for the duration of their trip.

Considérez

How would you react if you arrived in France for the first time and soon faced contradiction and opposition to your point of view from conversational partners? What do you think you could learn in order to cope with these new patterns of dialogue? Do you think you could learn to enjoy or appreciate these practices? How would these new practices help you improve the way you express your ideas?

Visionnement 2

Observez!

Considérez les aspects culturels expliqués dans **Regards sur la culture**. Ensuite, regardez l'Épisode 8 encore une fois et répondez aux questions suivantes.

- Est-ce que la conversation entre Mado et Camille est un échange vif (*intense*) mais normal, ou est-ce que les deux femmes sont fâchées?
- Quelles expressions Mado emploie-t-elle pour indiquer son attitude?
- Est-ce que Camille répond à sa mère calmement ou avec colère (*with anger*)?

Écrivez et explorez!

À explorer: **www.mhhe.com/debuts** pour trouver le sujet de composition et plus d'informations sur les thèmes de cet épisode.

Inquiétudes°

Worries

 Visionnement 1

Avant de visionner

Qu'est-ce qui se passe? Voici des extraits du dialogue du film. Choisissez la réponse qui explique le dialogue.

1. LOUISE: Oh, chérie!

   CAMILLE: Grand-mère, à quoi tu joues...ª? Tu veux me faire peur?

   LOUISE: Je suis en pleine forme!

   ªà... *are you playing games?*

   a. Camille est inquiète pour la santé de sa grand-mère.

   b. Camille est fascinée par le jeu (*game*) de sa grand-mère.

   c. Camille est contente de voir sa grand-mère.

2. HÉLÈNE: Bon ben, voilà, c'était[a] Hélène Thibaut, sur les bords[b] de la Seine, avec Camille Leclair à mes côtés. Avec un temps radieux,[c] mais un «Bientôt à Montréal» à tous.[d] Ciao!

[a]*I'm (lit., this was)* [b]*sur... on the banks* [c]*Avec... With great weather* [d]*everyone*

   a. Hélène va quitter Paris pour rentrer (*return*) à Montréal.
   b. Hélène aime Paris et ne rentre pas à Montréal.
   c. Hélène fait un reportage sur les monuments du Québec.

3. CAMILLE: On va au restau? J'ai faim!

BRUNO: Tu as faim? Je ne le crois pas... !?[a] Eh! Eh oh! Appelez les photographes! Là, vite,[b] j'ai un scoop! Camille arrête son régime,[c] elle va faire un vrai repas! Ce n'est pas un scoop, ça?!

[a]*Je... I don't believe it . . . !?* [b]*quickly* [c]*arrête... is going off her diet*

   a. Bruno ne veut pas aller au restaurant avec Camille.
   b. Bruno taquine (*teases*) Camille, parce que d'habitude (*usually*) elle mange très peu.
   c. Bruno est surpris parce que Camille préfère en général manger chez elle.

Vocabulaire relatif à l'épisode	
un malaise	*weakness, fainting spell*
Vous devez	*You must*
Tu connais... ?	*Do you know ...?*
inutile	*useless*
au plus mal	*very ill*
Tout va bien.	*Everything's fine.*
Ne t'inquiète pas.	*Don't worry.*

*O*bservez!

La grand-mère Louise figure dans l'Épisode 9. Regardez l'épisode et répondez à ces questions.

• À quel sujet Mado ment-elle à Camille? Qu'est-ce qu'elle dit (*say*)?
• Qu'est-ce que Louise suggère à Camille de faire avec elle?

*A*près le visionnement

A. Vous rappelez-vous? (*Do you remember?*) Complétez le paragraphe pour résumer l'Épisode 9. Choisissez une expression de la liste pour remplir chaque blanc (*to fill each blank*).

Vocabulaire utile:

à l'hôpital	en France	sa mère est au plus mal
à Montréal	ment	elle est en pleine forme
au lit	va bien	près de la cathédrale
au restaurant	va mieux	Notre-Dame
dans la chambre	ce n'est pas vrai	
dans la rue Mouffetard		
dans les Cévennes		

L'épisode commence _____[1] de Louise. Elle est _____[2], et le médecin l'examine.[a]

Il encourage Louise à aller _____[3]. Elle refuse et dit[b] à Camille qu' _____[4].

Camille voit[c] que _____[5]. Louise demande à Camille si Alex est là _____[6].

[a]*is examining her* [b]*says* [c]*sees*

Camille dit oui et elle va dans la rue pour lui parler. Pourquoi? Le médecin dit
à Mado que _____⁷. Mais Mado _____⁸ à Camille et dit que tout^d _____⁹.

Hélène interviewe Camille au bord de la Seine _____¹⁰. C'est pour une
émission _____¹¹. Camille dit qu'elle vit^e bien _____¹², et que la famille est très
importante pour elle.

Quand Louise _____¹³, elle invite Camille à faire un voyage _____¹⁴. Camille
est très heureuse et elle invite Bruno à venir avec elle _____¹⁵.

^deverything   ^elives

B. Réfléchissez.   Répondez aux questions suivantes. Choisissez parmi les idées
suggérées, ou formulez (*make up*) votre propre (*own*) hypothèse.

1. Pourquoi est-ce que Louise envoie Camille parler à Alex (l'homme avec
l'accordéon)?

   a. Louise cherche un prétexte pour terminer sa conversation avec Camille.
   b. Louise veut entendre une chanson familière pour la réconforter (*comfort*).
   c. Camille et Alex sont comme frère et sœur.

2. Pourquoi Mado ment-elle quand Camille demande l'opinion du médecin?

   a. Mado et Camille n'ont pas une relation très ouverte.
   b. Mado ne veut pas faire peur à Camille.
   c. Mado a du mal à parler de la maladie et de la mort.

3. Pourquoi Louise veut-elle faire un voyage aux Cévennes?

   a. Elle cède (*gives in*) toujours aux demandes de Camille.
   b. Elle veut montrer la région à Camille, qui ne la connaît pas.
   c. Elle veut apprendre plus de détails sur l'histoire de son mari.

Regards sur la culture

La santé en France

The United Nations has consistently placed France at or near the top of its world
ratings based on access to health care. We tend to think of health as a rather
objective matter, but cultural attitudes and traditions always play a large role in
people's sense of what is healthful and what is not and in the development of
policies for health care delivery.

- In part, culture determines what we think makes us healthy or sick. North
Americans think of apples as especially healthful. In France, apples are
considered hard to digest. On the other hand, many French people consider
nearly any moving air a draft (**un courant d'air**) and a threat to one's health.

- Many common digestive complaints are referred to in France as **une crise de foie** (literally, *a liver attack*). Doctors even use this term in their diagnoses. The **crise de foie**, from which so many French people suffer, does not correspond to any single Anglo-American illness.

- French doctors make house calls, even in the middle of the night when necessary. They tend to prescribe larger numbers of different medicines than do their counterparts in North America. In fact, the French consume more medicine than any other nationality in

Le médecin examine Louise chez elle.

  Europe, though the government is now urging doctors to prescribe less. French doctors are also relatively generous in prescribing long hospital stays and time off from work.

- The French system of **Sécurité sociale**, established in 1945, reimburses about 72 percent of health care expenses, and about 70 percent of prescription medicine costs, although the average patient is expected to pay the doctor or pharmacist at time of service. However, many people in France take out additional insurance policies so that nearly all of their expenses are covered. Prenatal care, as prescribed by French Social Security, is virtually free and is considered a world-class model by most professionals.

- French pharmacists have a good deal of medical training and are often consulted for common health problems. They are also expected to be able to examine mushrooms collected in the woods to indicate if they are edible or not. The Health Code limits the number of pharmacies that may be opened, through a licensing process. In a city of over 30,000 people, for example, there may be only one pharmacy for every 3000 inhabitants. One of the functions of such limits is to protect the integrity and prestige of the profession.

Considérez

The French Social Security system was founded on the explicit need for maintaining "national solidarity." This is related to the notion of **fraternité** that was one of the founding principles of the French Revolution. In what ways do the health care systems in North America relate to general cultural and political principles?

*O*bservez!

Considérez les aspects culturels expliqués dans **Regards sur la culture**. Ensuite, regardez l'Épisode 9 encore une fois, et répondez aux questions suivantes.

- Quelle pratique particulière aux médecins français voit-on dans cet épisode?
- Parlant de la France avec Hélène, Camille dit: «C'est un pays que j'aime. On y vit bien.» Dans cet épisode, et dans le film en général, qu'est-ce qui montre qu'on vit bien en France?

*É*crivez et explorez!

À explorer: **www.mhhe.com/debuts** pour trouver le sujet de composition et plus d'informations sur les thèmes de cet épisode.

Rendez-vous au restaurant

Visionnement 1

*A*vant de visionner

Histoire de couples. Dans cet épisode, vous allez voir Camille et Bruno et le patron et la patronne du restaurant, un couple marié. Lisez (*Read*) le dialogue entre ces deux derniers (*latter two*), et choisissez la phrase qui résume la scène.

1. PATRONNE: Tu as vu ça?^a C'est étonnant^b!

   PATRON: Quoi?

   PATRONNE: Ils sont à nouveau ensemble^c, ces deux-là?

   PATRON: Ben, apparemment, oui. Il faut croire.^d

^aTu… *Did you see that?* ^b*amazing* ^cà… *together again* ^dIl… *It looks like it.*

a. Le patron et la patronne connaissent déjà (*already know*) Bruno et Camille.

b. Le patron et la patronne n'aiment pas bien Bruno et Camille.

c. C'est la première fois que Camille et Bruno viennent dans ce restaurant.

2. PATRONNE: Tu regardes trop de sitcoms à la télévision!

PATRON: Mais, je ne regarde que toi, mon amour!

PATRONNE: Regarde plutôt^a ta sauce! Elle brûle^b!

PATRON: Oh, nom d'un chien!^c

^aRegarde... *Better look at*   ^b*is burning*   ^c*nom... damn!*

a. La patronne critique son mari.

b. Le patron et la patronne se taquinent (*are teasing each other*).

c. Le patron et la patronne ne s'aiment plus.

Observez!

Dans cet épisode, vous allez apprendre quelques détails supplémentaires sur la relation de Camille et Bruno. Ces deux personnages vont aussi révéler des détails sur leur famille.

• Est-ce que Bruno se considère comme un bon fils? Pourquoi ou pourquoi pas?

• Est-ce que Camille se considère comme une bonne fille? Pourquoi ou pourquoi pas?

• Quelle sorte de rapport Camille et Bruno avaient-ils (*did they have*) avant? Quelle sorte de rapport semblent-ils avoir (*do they seem to have*) maintenant?

Après le visionnement

A. Avez vous compris? (*Did you understand?*) Faites un résumé de l'épisode en complétant chacune (*each one*) des phrases suivantes avec une des options de la colonne de droite (*on the right*).

1. Le patron est étonné de voir Camille et Bruno...

2. Bruno n'est pas marié...

3. Camille n'est pas une bonne fille...

4. Comme plat principal, Bruno commande...

5. Comme vin, Bruno choisit...

6. Selon la patronne, son mari regarde trop de...

7. Mais il ne regarde pas...

a. parce qu'elle est nerveuse et impatiente.

b. des œufs en meurette.

c. sa sauce. Elle brûle.

d. parce qu'il ne les a pas vus (*hasn't seen them*) depuis quelque temps.

e. sitcoms à la télé.

f. parce qu'un bon fils ne devient pas toujours un bon mari.

g. du vin rouge.

B. Hypothèses. Réfléchissez aux questions suivantes.

1. Selon vous, est-ce que le patron et la patronne sont mariés depuis longtemps? Comment peut-on décrire leur relation?

2. Est-ce qu'on découvre un nouveau côté de Bruno dans cet épisode? Expliquez.

Notez bien!

The phrase **ne... que** means *only*. The **ne** precedes the verb and **que** precedes the person or thing that is restricted or limited.

Je **ne regarde que** toi. *I look only at you.*

Camille **ne parle de son père qu**'à Bruno. *Camille speaks only to Bruno about her father.*

Vocabulaire relatif à l'épisode

dragueur	*pick-up artist*
tellement	*quite, somewhat*
depuis quelque temps	*for some time*
comme d'habitude	*as usual*
à part la nôtre, évidemment	*except for ours, obviously*

Regards sur la culture

Les cafés et les restaurants

In this episode, Camille and Bruno have dinner in what is a rather typical French restaurant. As we have already seen, food is very important in France, and the experience of eating out is somewhat different there from what we know in North America. Cafés, for example, have a different function in France from restaurants, even though it is possible to get something simple to eat in many of them.

- The average French restaurant is family-owned and operated. There are very few large chain restaurants in France. This means that the owners or chefs are likely to know some of their customers quite well and may come out to speak with them.

- When French people go to a restaurant, they are looking forward to real culinary pleasure: something unusual to eat, or something that is difficult to make at home. The notion of going to a place that serves "homestyle cooking" would not be appealing to the French. They often say that there is no point in going to a restaurant if you could eat just as well at home.

Bruno et Camille dînent au restaurant.

- Because the focus on the quality of the food is so strong, a restaurant's décor is less important in France than it is in North America. Although successful restaurants tend to be very comfortable, French people delight in finding a place **qui ne paie pas de mine** (that is not much to look at), but that serves wonderful food.

- Waiting on tables in France is a professional (and usually male-dominated) activity. Service is expected to be efficient and unobtrusive. No French waiter will ever introduce himself. Professionalism and courtesy are more important to the French than the "friendliness" of the service.

- French people spend lots of time looking for good restaurants, and comparing notes on restaurants is a big part of everyday conversation. The average French person judges an establishment on the basis of the cost and apparent quality of the "menus" that it serves. A **menu** in France is a fixed-price meal with at least two courses. These menus are always posted outside the restaurant door.

- In contrast to restaurants, the focus in cafés is not so much on the food or drink as it is on the social scene. Every café has its own particular clientele. In university towns, for example, law students might have a café where they meet and where students of philosophy, for example, would never go. Their gathering place would be another café where law students would not go.

- Because one can order just a simple drink at a café and then stay seated for quite a long time, people use the café as a meeting place. They may read, write, or study at a café table. They may simply want to watch people going by (staring at others is not nearly as impolite in France as it is in North America). They may sit down and order a coffee in order to rest in the middle of a long walk.

Un café à Paris

- The social functions of the café have declined somewhat over the past 30 years, particularly in the evening. Many French people feel that having a drink at a café has become too expensive. Probably more important is the fact that people tend to stay home at night and watch television, rather than go out to socialize at the café.

Considérez

Why do you think there aren't many establishments in North America that serve the functions cafés do in France? Where in North America does café-style socializing exist?

Visionnement 2

Le Quartier des Halles.   Bruno and Camille have gone to dinner in another part of Paris, on the right bank of the Seine. This area housed the central market of Paris until 1969; it was both picturesque and run-down. The district was redeveloped in the 1970s and '80s. The **Centre Pompidou,*** completed in 1977, was built to house the National Museum of Modern Art and other cultural services. It has remained a controversial piece of architecture. **Le Forum des Halles** is a complex of shops, movie theaters, and restaurants, rising in tiers from a sunken patio. Much of the rest of the old market area is occupied by gardens. Nearby stands the **église Saint-Eustache**, where Richelieu[†] was baptized and where Molière's[‡] funeral was held. It is probably the best architectural example of a French Renaissance church in Paris. Near the Seine, the **Hôtel de Ville**, the city hall of Paris, is a replica of the 17th-century building that was burned down when the army put down a revolutionary government that had taken over Paris in 1871.

---

*Le Centre national d'art et de culture Georges Pompidou** porte le nom de Georges Pompidou (1911–1974), qui a été Premier ministre (1962–1968) sous le Président Charles de Gaulle et président de 1969 à 1974.
[†]Le cardinal Richelieu (1585–1642), grand homme d'État, ministre de Louis XIII. Il a fondé l'Académie française pour créer un dictionnaire de la langue française.
[‡]Molière (1622–1673), auteur célèbre de nombreuses pièces de théâtre comiques.

Les environs du restaurant préféré de Camille et Bruno

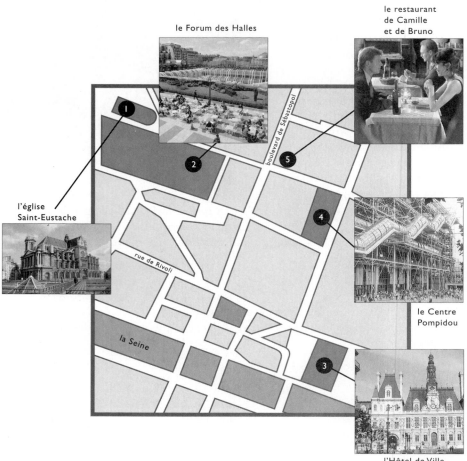

le Forum des Halles

le restaurant de Camille et de Bruno

l'église Saint-Eustache

le Centre Pompidou

l'Hôtel de Ville

Vous recherchez une atmosphère particulière. Indiquez où vous voulez aller. Plusieurs (*Several*) réponses sont possibles.

MODÈLE: la tranquillité et les plaisirs gastronomiques
Je veux aller au restaurant où vont Camille et Bruno.

a. des souvenirs historiques   **c.** une atmosphère mouvementée   **e.** la solitude
b. une ambiance esthétique   **d.** une ambiance de méditation

*O*bservez!

Considérez les aspects culturels dans **Regards sur la culture**. Ensuite, regardez l'Épisode 10 encore une fois, et répondez aux questions suivantes.

- Comment est le décor du restaurant? Selon vous, quelle sorte de clientèle fréquente ce restaurant?
- Comment peut-on qualifier le rapport entre Bruno, Camille et le serveur? Le serveur est-il froid? réservé? respectueux? familier? trop familier? Expliquez son comportement (*behavior*).

Écrivez et explorez!

À explorer: **www.mhhe.com/debuts** pour trouver le sujet de composition et plus d'informations sur les thèmes de cet épisode.

Épisode **11**

Bonjour!

Visionnement 1

*A*vant de visionner

A. Révision du passé composé. Dans cet épisode, il y a beaucoup d'exemples de verbes au passé composé. Lisez les phrases suivantes et donnez l'infinitif de chaque (*each*) verbe.

Verbes utiles: disparaître (*to disappear*), écrire (*to write*), faire, pouvoir, raconter (*to tell*), revoir, surprendre (*to surprise*), voir

1. Et il a disparu de tous (*all*) les albums-photos?
2. Et qu'est-ce qu'on t'a raconté sur lui?
3. Et pendant la guerre (*during the war*), qu'est-ce qu'il a fait?

4. Toute petite, à l'âge de sept ou huit ans, j'ai surpris une conversation entre ma grand-mère et ma mère.

5. Il a écrit une lettre pour le quatrième anniversaire de sa fille.

6. Il a disparu. Louise ne l'a jamais revu. (deux verbes)

7. Ça fait longtemps que je ne l'ai pas vu. (*I haven't seen him for a long time.*)

B. Les dates et les événements. Lisez les dialogues suivants et ensuite, donnez la date qui correspond aux événements mentionnés.

Bruno parle avec Camille de son grand-père.

BRUNO: Et maintenant, Camille, raconte-moi ton histoire. Ton grand-père est toujours vivant[a]?

CAMILLE: Non, il est mort[b]... pendant la guerre, en 1943.

[a]*alive* [b]*il... he died*

Plus tard...

BRUNO: Ta grand-mère a toujours habité le quartier Mouffetard?

CAMILLE: Oui, à partir de[c] 1938, avec son mari.

BRUNO: Antoine? Et quel âge a-t-il à cette époque-là[d]?

CAMILLE: 20 ans.

BRUNO: Il a déjà son atelier d'ébéniste[e]?

CAMILLE: Oui, il en a hérité[f] de son père. Les affaires marchent[g] bien. Il a trois employés avec lui.

BRUNO: Et ta mère? Elle est déjà née[h]?

CAMILLE: Pas encore. Elle est venue au monde[i] en septembre 1939.

BRUNO: Oh. 1939? La déclaration de guerre contre[j] les Allemands...

[c]*à... beginning in* [d]*à... at that time* [e]*atelier... cabinetmaker's workshop* [f]*il... he inherited it* [g]*are going* [h]*born*
[i]*est... came into the world* [j]*against*

1. Louise et Antoine s'installent dans la rue Mouffetard.

2. date de naissance de Mado

3. date de la déclaration de guerre aux Allemands

4. date de la mort d'Antoine

Observez!

Dans l'Épisode 11, Camille parle à Bruno des expériences de ses grands-parents pendant la guerre. Pendant votre visionnement du film, essayez de trouver les réponses aux questions suivantes.

• Qui est Samuel Lévy? Où va-t-il et pourquoi?

• Que fait Antoine?

• De quoi est-ce qu'Antoine est accusé?

• Comment Bruno offre-t-il d'aider Camille?

Après le visionnement

A. Un résumé. Faites un résumé de l'histoire d'Antoine pendant la guerre en complétant le paragraphe suivant.

Vocabulaire relatif à l'épisode	
presque	*almost, practically*
non plus	*neither*
juif	*Jewish*
personne n'envoie	*nobody sends*
Que Dieu te protège	*May God protect you*
Prenez soin de vous	*Take care of yourself*
ce qui est juste	*what is right*
plus rien	*nothing more*
est-ce qu'il vit toujours	*is he still living*

Vocabulaire utile: 1939, a trahi (*betrayed*), dans les Cévennes, la déclaration de guerre, ébéniste (*cabinetmaker*), en Amérique, un historien, juif, quatrième, dans la rue Mouffetard, trois, vingt

À partir de 1938, Antoine et Louise habitent _____[1]. À l'époque, Antoine a _____[2] ans. Il travaille comme _____[3] avec _____[4] employés. Sa fille, Mado, naît[a] en _____[5]. C'est une année importante, parce qu'elle marque _____[6] aux Allemands. Un des employés d'Antoine—Samuel Lévy—est _____[7]. Hitler veut exterminer les Juifs, alors, Samuel part _____[8] pour rejoindre[b] sa femme.

Antoine va _____[9]. Il écrit une carte pour le _____[10] anniversaire de sa fille. Ensuite, on perd sa trace. Le bruit court[c] qu'il _____[11] son pays. Bruno connaît _____[12] et espère qu'il peut aider Camille à découvrir la vérité.[d]

[a]*is born* [b]*to join* [c]*Le... Rumor has it* [d]*découvrir... to discover the truth*

B. Questions. Faites une liste de questions dont (*whose*) les réponses peuvent éclaircir (*shed light on*) ce mystère familial. Utilisez les mots **où**, **quand**, **pourquoi**, **comment**, **combien de**, **qu'est-ce que**, etc.

MODÈLE: Pourquoi Antoine va-t-il dans les Cévennes?

Ensuite, essayez de répondre aux questions de vos camarades de classe. À quelles questions est-ce qu'on ne peut pas encore répondre?

Regards sur la culture

Le couple

In this segment of the film, we see Louise and Antoine together as a young couple. The other important couple in the story, Camille and Bruno, is linked by a somewhat ambiguous relationship, although it is clear that the two Canal 7 reporters share very strong emotional ties. Their interactions illustrate some differences between France and North America in the relations between the sexes.

- French children are usually brought up to be very happy about their sex. Both males and females are taught that they have many advantages being the sex that they are.
- In adolescence, there is no such thing as "dating." Rather than engage in the kind of one-on-one formalized "trial" relationship that is common in North America, French young people usually go out in groups. If two people do become a couple, they still may prefer to go most places with friends, rather than by themselves.
- Adolescent boys in France sometimes utter exaggerated compliments or engage in mock boasting about their sex appeal in front of girls their own age. These

girls learn very young how to appreciate the attention but to deflate the pretensions of the male. Some of this male-female sparring continues later in life. Young North American women who encounter it are often at a loss about how to react. An uncomfortable smile is often the result, just the opposite of the culturally appropriate reaction.

- Anthropologist Raymonde Carroll has stated that French couples tend to manifest their relationship through the kinds of verbal interactions they have: They tease each other in front of friends and may argue, say, about politics or the choice of a restaurant. In fact, she claims that French people might be suspicious of a couple who is always in agreement, thinking that there is no "spark" in the relationship.

Yves Montand et Simone Signoret, un couple célèbre

- The partners in a French couple tend to maintain more independence than do those in North America. They continue to frequent their own friends individually.

- Even when there is no question of a romantic or sexual relationship, French people enjoy trying to be attractive to the opposite sex. They do not find this demeaning. One might even speak of "the game between the sexes" in France, in opposition to the North American "war between the sexes."

Considérez

What possible conflicts could emerge in an intercultural relationship between a mainstream North American and a French person?

Visionnement 2

Observez!

Regardez l'Épisode 11 encore une fois, et répondez aux questions suivantes.

- Pourquoi Samuel Lévy et sa femme ont-ils décidé de quitter la France?
- Est-ce que les Allemands sont les seuls à vouloir exterminer les Juifs?

Écrivez et explorez!

À explorer: **www.mhhe.com/debuts** pour trouver le sujet de composition et plus d'informations sur les thèmes de cet épisode.

Épisode 12

C'est à propos de Louise.

C'est... *It's about Louise.*

Visionnement 1

Avant de visionner

Pour parler du passé. Vous avez déjà appris le **passé composé**. Mais en français, on utilise aussi un autre temps—l'**imparfait**—pour parler du passé. Mais maintenant, pour comprendre l'Épisode 12, lisez (*read*) les phrases suivantes et faites attention au sens (*meaning*).

Elle **était**[a] très calme...
Ses yeux **brillaient**,[b] comme les yeux d'un enfant à Noël...
Je **voulais**[c] discuter avec elle.

[a]*was* [b]*were shining* [c]*wanted*

Regardez encore une fois les verbes en caractères **gras**. Quels verbes décrivent (*describe*) des émotions? Quels verbes décrivent une action qui continue dans le passé?

Observez!

Dans l'Épisode 12, Camille apprend un autre détail important sur son grand-père. Pendant votre visionnement, essayez de trouver la réponse aux questions suivantes.

- Pourquoi Mado s'impatiente-t-elle contre Camille?
- Quelle est l'importance du titre de la chanson (*song*) préférée de Louise, *Mon Amant de Saint-Jean*?

Vocabulaire relatif à l'épisode	
elle a souri	*she smiled*
un drôle de…	*a funny, strange …*
doucement	*gently*
qui a déchiré	*who tore up*
au moins	*at least*
une bourgade	*village*

Après le visionnement

A. Les détails. Qu'est-ce qu'on apprend dans cet épisode sur l'histoire de la famille Leclair? Répondez **vrai** si on trouve cette information dans l'épisode. Répondez **faux** si on ne la trouve pas.

Dans cet épisode, on apprend…

1. qui a déchiré les photos d'Antoine.
2. l'état d'esprit (*state of mind*) de Louise au moment de sa mort.
3. où Antoine est allé dans les Cévennes.
4. pourquoi on a déchiré les photos d'Antoine.
5. pourquoi *Mon Amant de Saint-Jean* était la chanson préférée de Louise.
6. où on a enterré (*buried*) Louise.

B. Réfléchissez. Selon vous, pourquoi Mado a-t-elle révélé le nom du village où Antoine est allé en 1943? Est-ce qu'elle se prépare à raconter l'histoire d'Antoine à Camille? Essaie-t-elle d'apaiser (*appease*) Camille? Ou y a-t-il une autre explication?

Regards sur la culture

Les étapes de la vie

Louise's death in this episode upsets Camille and seems to dash her hopes of finding out about what happened to her grandfather during World War II. It also modifies the relationship between Mado and Camille in subtle but important ways. In every culture, deaths, like births and marriages, are treated in special ways.

- French people don't give baby showers. A birth announcement is usually sent to family and friends, and many of these people visit the new baby, bringing gifts of the kind that North Americans give at a shower.
- Most French people see having a child as a major investment of time, energy, and affection. Children are looked after very closely all the way through childhood. As a result, many French families have only one child, and there is no particular sense that being an only child is a disadvantage. People who have many children are sometimes jokingly accused of being clumsy or of wanting to take advantage of the additional Social Security payments that they receive.

Un mariage civil à la mairie

- French marriages take place in two parts. The civil ceremony is obligatory and is usually carried out complete with flowers and bridal gown. A religious ceremony is optional and in itself is not sufficient to legalize a marriage. This dual ceremony is the result of the separation of church and state that was mandated in early 20th-century France. The wedding reception usually consists of a huge dinner: As many as twelve or thirteen courses are presented over 5 hours or so, with dish after dish being commented on and appreciated. The meal is punctuated by individual speeches, toasts, and songs, and often is followed by dancing.

- Career choice is often class-related. Since World War II, young people have often been discouraged by their families from entering agriculture, blue-collar jobs, and crafts. Another very important criterion in the choice is security. Finding a permanent, secure job (**une situation**) has traditionally been an obsession with French people. Most look for a job they can keep all their lives. This often means trying very hard to get a civil service job (anything from staff positions in government offices to teaching). Another criterion is location: Most people expect to find a job near home and family and to stay in it.

- **Ambition** is a word that has mainly negative connotations in France. It is impolite, at best, to be **ambitieux**. But for the French, ambition is not really necessary: French education and the system of competitive examinations are oriented toward finding people exactly the kind of job they should have.

- The average retirement age in France is 60. Most people receive 60 to 70% of their salary in retirement benefits. Many consider it selfish not to plan for an inheritance for one's children.

- Nearly every French person dreads the idea of dying in a hospital. People want to die at home, where friends and loved ones can watch over them and come to pay their last respects. Funerals and the clinical procedures surrounding death and burial are far simpler in France than they are in North America.

Considérez

Contrast French attitudes toward having children with those of your culture. What different values are involved? Why might this be? What might be the outward signs of these differences?

*O*bservez!

Considérez les aspects culturels expliqués dans **Regards sur la culture**. Ensuite, regardez l'Épisode 12 encore une fois, et répondez aux questions suivantes.

- Louise meurt dans son lit, chez elle. Est-ce que cette scène reflète une situation typique en France ou non?
- Camille a-t-elle tort de vouloir parler de son grand-père juste après l'enterrement de Louise?

*É*crivez et explorez!

À explorer: **www.mhhe.com/debuts** pour trouver le sujet de composition et plus d'informations sur les thèmes de cet épisode.

Épisode 13
Documents

*V*isionnement 1

*A*vant de visionner

Les actes de parole. Lisez les extraits suivants du scénario de l'Épisode 13. Ensuite, analysez les phrases en italique. Quelles sont leurs fonctions? Choisissez parmi les possibilités suivantes.

demander une opinion   exprimer la reconnaissance (*gratitude*)
demander une précision   exprimer les condoléances
exprimer l'accord   faire un compliment
exprimer l'incrédulité   faire une demande

1. RACHID: Et je fais quoi, là-bas?

   CAMILLE: Interroge les gens sur la vie du village, pendant la guerre. Surtout les années 1942–43.

   RACHID: *D'accord.*

2. PRODUCTRICE: *Je suis désolée pour ta grand-mère.*

3. CAMILLE: L'autre jour, tu m'as parlé d'un ami historien, non?

   BRUNO: Je ne sais pas où il est, Camille. J'ai téléphoné, mais il a déménagé (*moved*).

   CAMILLE: *Dépêche-toi de le retrouver, s'il te plaît.*

4. HÉLÈNE: (après la mort de Louise) *Camille! Camille, je suis de tout cœur avec toi.*

5. CAMILLE: Au revoir. Merci, Bruno. Et toi aussi, Hélène. *Je suis contente de vous avoir comme amis.*

6. BRUNO: Alors? *Qu'est-ce que tu penses de... de David?* Un peu bizarre, non?

   HÉLÈNE: Non. *Non, il est plutôt* (rather) *bel homme... Hmmm?*

   BRUNO: *Bel homme? David?*

*O*bservez!

Dans l'Épisode 13, Hélène et Bruno essaient de trouver l'historien qui peut aider Camille. Pendant le visionnement, essayez de trouver la réponse aux questions suivantes.

- Où est-ce que Camille demande à Rachid d'aller?
- Quelles méthodes de communication utilise-t-on pour trouver l'historien? Est-ce qu'on réussit?
- Qu'est-ce qui semble impliquer Antoine dans un acte de trahison (*treason*)?

*A*près le visionnement

A. Vrai ou faux? Vérifiez votre compréhension de l'épisode en indiquant si les phrases suivantes sont vraies ou fausses. Répondez **incertain** si l'épisode ne vous donne pas l'information nécessaire.

1. Rachid va à Alès pour parler aux gens du grand-père de Camille.
2. Bruno a du mal à trouver son ami historien.
3. Hélène trouve des renseignements sur Antoine Leclair aux Archives nationales.
4. Les Allemands et certains Français ont détruit beaucoup d'archives à la fin de la guerre.
5. Le laissez-passer (*pass*) que possédait (*possessed*) Antoine était contrefait (*counterfeit*).
6. Le laissez-passer a été signé par un officier allemand.
7. Il était normal de posséder un laissez-passer comme celui (*the one*) qu'avait Antoine.

Vocabulaire relatif à l'épisode	
type étrange	*strange guy*
vous avez découvert quelque chose	*you discovered something*
ont été détruites	*were destroyed*
partout	*throughout, everywhere*
aussi bien... que	*just as easily ... as*
la preuve	*proof*
indice sérieux	*serious indication, clue*

B. Réfléchissez.   Selon l'historien, le laissez-passer n'est pas preuve de la culpabilité d'Antoine, mais c'est un indice sérieux. À votre avis, y a-t-il d'autres scénarios qui pourraient (*that could*) expliquer le laissez-passer? Voici quelques possibilités. Quelle explication est la plus convaincante?

1. Antoine a contrefait (*counterfeited*) le laissez-passer pour obtenir des renseignements sur les activités des Allemands.

2. Les Allemands ont fabriqué ce laissez-passer pour faire croire aux Français (*to make the French believe*) qu'Antoine était un collaborateur.

3. Tous les résistants avaient un laissez-passer contrefait pour les protéger (*to protect them*) au cas où ils seraient arrêtés (*in case they were arrested*) par la gestapo.

Avez-vous une autre idée?

Regards sur la culture

L'enseignement supérieur°   L'enseignement... *Higher education*

In this episode, Bruno locates David, the college history professor. He is not teaching at the moment because he is writing his thesis. A North American would probably expect a college professor to have finished writing his thesis before getting a job in higher education. In fact, French higher education is different in many ways from the North American model.

• Almost everyone who receives a higher education in France attends public institutions, which are very inexpensive. The curricula are supervised by the Ministry of Education. Anyone who has earned the **baccalauréat*** may study at a public university.

---

*The **baccalauréat** is a comprehensive examination of general knowledge and studies done in high school. It is taken in two parts: the first at the end of the next-to-last year of high school, the second at the end of the final year. The **bac** is essential for many jobs in France. About 77% of high school students pass it.

- Students at the university are called **étudiant(e)s**. This is seen as a social, and almost a professional, category in France. College students have many advantages (reduced prices at the movies, for example) and generally enjoy a rich social life by taking advantage of the services of the city where their university is located.

- College courses revolve around the end-of-year examinations. Some (not all) students rarely go to class and work only in the late spring before exams.

- Relationships between students and professors at the university in France are usually impersonal and distant compared with those in North America.

- Some college professors or researchers work on **le doctorat d'État**, a degree that requires two theses. Many finish this at age 40 or even later. David, in the film, is working on a **doctorat d'État**.

- Some young people (around 10%) hope to enter one of France's **grandes écoles**, which is an entirely different educational track. Entry into one of these institutions requires two years of very stressful preparatory studies beyond the **baccalauréat**, followed by extremely difficult competitive examinations called **concours** that involve both written and oral tests. Only a small number of positions are available in the **grandes écoles**, and those with the best scores in the **concours** get them. Students on this track do very little but study. If they gain entry into a **grande école**, they are guaranteed a salary, great social prestige, and a very useful social network. Those who are not accepted start university studies from scratch.

Une cérémonie à l'École polytechnique

Considérez

Compare the system of higher education in France with that of your own country. What are some of the advantages of each? What do you think are some of each system's weaknesses?

Visionnement 2

*O*bservez!

Considérez les aspects culturels expliqués dans **Regards sur la culture**. Ensuite, regardez l'Épisode 13 encore une fois, et répondez aux questions suivantes.

- À votre avis, est-ce que David va finir sa thèse de doctorat bientôt? Pourquoi (pas)?
- Selon Hélène, pourquoi est-ce que Bruno est «un vrai Français»? Qu'est-ce qu'elle veut dire en ce qui concerne les Français et Internet?

*É*crivez et explorez!

À explorer: **www.mhhe.com/debuts** pour trouver le sujet de composition et plus d'informations sur les thèmes de cet épisode.

Une lettre

Visionnement 1

*A*vant de visionner

La répétition. Parfois, la même idée est répétée dans une phrase sous des formes différentes. Il s'agit de paraphrases ou d'explications du mot-clé. Analysez les phrases suivantes. Les mots en *italique* ont le même sens ou renforcent le sens des mots en caractères **gras**. Que signifient les mots en italique?

1. CAMILLE: Regarde. Louise a gardé[a] cette photo **intacte**. Elle *ne l'a pas déchirée*, comme les autres.
2. CAMILLE: Elle aimait son mari. Elle l'a **toujours** aimé, *jusqu'à la fin de sa vie*.
3. MADO: J'avais 10 ou 11 ans. Un jour, à l'école, mes camarades *m'ont surnommée* la **fille du traître**. D'autres **disaient** la «fille du pourri[b]», la «fille du collabo».

[a]*a… kept* [b]*rotten pig*

*O*bservez!

Dans cet épisode, Camille et Mado apprennent des détails importants sur la vie d'Antoine pendant la guerre. Pendant votre visionnement de l'Épisode 14, essayez de trouver les réponses aux questions suivantes.

- Qu'est-ce que Rachid a appris pendant son voyage?
- Qu'est-ce que Mado et Camille ont trouvé dans le coffret (*little box*) de Louise?
- À quel sujet Mado a-t-elle changé d'avis (*changed her mind*)?
- Qui a découpé les photos de Louise avec son mari? Pourquoi?

Vocabulaire relatif à l'épisode	
la serrure	*latch*
verrouillé(e)	*locked*
Il faut chercher la vérité.	*We must look for the truth.*
en courant	*running*
des ciseaux	*scissors*

*A*près le visionnement

A. Un résumé. Complétez le résumé de l'Épisode 14 en mettant dans chaque cas un des deux verbes proposés au passé composé ou à l'imparfait.

Rachid revient de son voyage dans les Cévennes. Il y _____[1] (rencontrer,[a] rentrer) des gens intéressants, mais il _____[2] (ne rien apprendre, ne rien comprendre) sur le grand-père de Camille.

Plus tard, chez Mado, Camille _____[3] (cacher,[b] trouver) un coffret qui _____[4] (rendre, appartenir) à sa grand-mère. Dans ce coffret, Mado a découvert[c] les bijoux[d] de sa mère. Le coffret _____[5] (contenir, vouloir) aussi une lettre d'Antoine. Il avait écrit[e] cette lettre en 1943, quand il _____[6] (travailler, habiter) dans les Cévennes, chez Pierre et Jeanne Leblanc.

Le coffret _____[7] (tenir, contenir) également une photo de Louise avec Antoine. Louise _____[8] (garder, mentir) cette photo intacte; elle _____[9] (ne pas la montrer, ne pas la déchirer[f]).

De toute façon,[g] ce n'était pas Louise qui avait découpé[h] les photos; c'était Mado. Pourquoi? Parce qu'à l'école, tout le monde l'_____[10] (acheter, appeler) la «fille du collabo». Elle _____[11] (avoir honte, avoir froid). Alors,[i] elle _____[12] (décider, savoir) de «tuer» son père en découpant les photos avec des ciseaux.

[a]*to meet, run into* [b]*to hide* [c]*a... discovered* [d]*jewelry* [e]*avait... had written* [f]*to rip up* [g]*De... In any case* [h]*avait... had cut up* [i]*So*

B. Réfléchissez. Répondez aux questions suivantes.

1. Au début, Mado n'a pas voulu entendre parler de son père. Maintenant, elle encourage Camille à trouver la vérité à son sujet. Selon vous, pourquoi Mado a-t-elle changé d'avis (*changed her mind*)? Est-ce à cause de la mort de sa mère? du contenu du coffret? de l'insistance de Camille?

2. Mado a voulu «tuer» son père en découpant ses photos. Est-ce que cette action l'a aidée à surmonter sa honte? Expliquez.

Regards sur la culture

Les transports et la société

When Rachid tells Camille how to get to Saint-Jean de Causse, he assumes that she will take the train, not drive there. Even in the area of transportation, French cultural attitudes differ greatly from those of North Americans.

Le Train à Grande Vitesse (TGV)

- In France, nearly everyone uses the train. Although the network of rail lines has diminished since World War II, with many smaller and out-of-the-way places now linked to the rest of France by bus, people can get to most places quickly and easily by rail. The **Société nationale des chemins de fer français** (SNCF) is a public service known for its efficiency.

- The **SNCF** is also known for its advanced technology. The **TGV** is a model of modern rail technology. In fact, Amtrak's high-speed train Acela, introduced in late 2000 on the East Coast, uses an electric propulsion system developed for the TGV. Designed by the French, the trains were built by a company in Quebec, Bombardier, which also invented the snowmobile.

- The **SNCF** is one of the leading employers in France. It also has one of the largest budgetary deficits of any French organization, but no government administration would dream of radically cutting rail services in order to balance the budget. Transportation is one of the services that the French expect from the government in return for their taxes.

- For many years, French experts downplayed the need for limited-access highways—**les autoroutes**. The Ministry of Transportation wanted to promote train travel and discourage long-distance car and truck use; this is one reason for the long delays in the development of the **autoroute** system in France as compared with Germany or Italy, for example. Although the attitude has changed in recent years, many large cities are still not linked to nearby urban areas by **autoroute**.

- The French sometimes find the North American atittude toward the automobile peculiar. They are surprised that people may prefer to live far from their place of work, take the car for the slightest errand, and often treat their cars with something akin to affection.

- In French cities, modes of transportation vary. There is a subway system—**le métro**—in cities such as Paris, Toulouse, Lyon, and Marseille. The Paris **métro**, opened in 1900, is famous for its completeness and ease of use. Its Art Nouveau entryways are considered artistic masterpieces.

- Most French cities did away with their tram lines in the 1950s, and bus transportation became the norm. Today, bus service is usually extensive and efficient in French cities. Like the trains, the buses often run at a deficit but are nonetheless considered an essential public service.

- In recent years, many French cities have reintroduced tram lines (**les tramways**), partly for ecological reasons, because trams do not pollute the way buses do. Lyon reintroduced the tram in 2000, and several other French cities, including Bordeaux, have plans to do the same thing by 2005.

Une entrée de métro à Paris

Considérez

In what ways do French cultural attitudes toward transportation differ from those in North America? Why did the automobile replace other forms of transportation in North America so much more than in Europe? How do you feel about government support for and control over transportation systems?

Visionnement 2

*A*vant de visionner

La gare de Lyon. In this episode, Rachid comes back to Paris with his report on Saint-Jean de Causse. Because he has been in the Cévennes, he comes into the **gare de Lyon**, where the trains from southeastern France arrive. The following map shows the area around this train station. Just across the Seine is the **gare d'Austerlitz**, named for a great victory in the Napoleonic wars. This is the station that serves southwestern France (Bordeaux, the Pyrenees, the Basque Country, etc.). You may recall from Episode 1 that the **gare d'Austerlitz** is close to the **Jardin des Plantes** and Yasmine's school. Just to the north of the **gare de Lyon** is the **place de la Bastille**, former site of the infamous prison. Visitors to the square today see a monument to the July Revolution of 1830 and the new buildings of the **Opéra Bastille**. The outline of the now demolished Bastille is inscribed in the pavement of the square. South of the **gare de Lyon** is the **Ministère de l'Économie**, **des Finances et de l'Industrie**, one of the last great public building projects of the 20th century in Paris. In Episode 2, you saw that Canal 7 is located not too far away, just down the right bank of the Seine, beyond the city limits.

Maintenant, regardez le plan ci-dessous et donnez le nom du bâtiment célèbre (*famous*) qui est en question dans les phrases suivantes.

1. Sylvie veut aller à Lourdes dans les Pyrénées. Vers quel bâtiment doit-elle aller?
2. Philippe veut voir *Carmen*. Vers quel bâtiment doit-il aller?
3. Bruno et Camille vont des Studios Canal 7 à la gare de Lyon. Quel bâtiment vont-ils voir en route?
4. Rachid va de la gare de Lyon à l'école de sa fille. Quel bâtiment va-t-il voir en route?
5. Hélène va de la gare de Lyon à la place de la Bastille. Quel bâtiment moderne va-t-elle voir en passant?

Les environs de la gare de Lyon

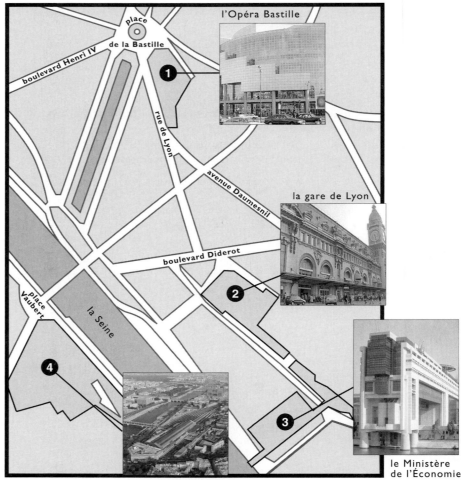

l'Opéra Bastille

la gare de Lyon

le Ministère de l'Économie

la gare d'Austerlitz

*O*bservez!

Considérez les aspects culturels expliqués dans **Regards sur la culture**. Ensuite, regardez l'Épisode 14 encore une fois, et répondez aux questions suivantes.

- Quand Camille voit Rachid à la gare après son retour à Paris, il semble reposé et de bonne humeur. Que peut-on en conclure sur la qualité du service des trains en France?
- Enfant, Mado a été tourmentée par ses camarades à cause de son père. Que peut-on en conclure sur l'attitude des Français vis-à-vis des collaborateurs après la guerre?

*É*crivez et explorez!

À explorer: **www.mhhe.com/debuts** pour trouver le sujet de composition et plus d'informations sur les thèmes de cet épisode.

Épisode 15
Une piste!°

Une... *A lead!*

Visionnement 1

Avant de visionner

Un dialogue incomplet. Voici l'extrait d'un dialogue entre Camille et Rachid, où on parle du voyage de Rachid dans les Cévennes. Complétez le passage en choisissant les mots logiques.

CAMILLE: _____¹ (Personne, Rien) ne t'a parlé de la guerre, apparemment?

RACHID: Les vieux sont discrets. Ils _____² (veulent, ne veulent pas) s'exprimerᵃ devant une caméra. Et les jeunes n'ont pas _____³ (connu, su) cette période.

CAMILLE: Comment faire pour _____⁴ (retrouver, retourner) la trace de mon grand-père?

ᵃ*to express themselves*

RACHID: 60 ans après la guerre, c'est _____[5] (utile, difficile).

CAMILLE: _____[6] (Pourquoi, Où) tu dis ça? On sait aujourd'hui comment vivait l'homme du Néandertal.[b] Et c'était _____[7] (quand, où)? Il y a 75.000 ans!

RACHID (*sourit*): Tu n'es jamais _____[8] (encouragée, découragée), hein?

[b]l'homme… *Neanderthal Man (ancient human ancestor)*

*O*bservez!

Dans l'Épisode 15, Camille pose des questions à Rachid sur son voyage dans les Cévennes. Pendant votre visionnement, essayez de trouver les réponses aux questions suivantes.

- À quels obstacles Rachid doit-il faire face dans ses recherches?
- De quelle piste est-ce que Camille parle?

Vocabulaire relatif à l'épisode	
y a séjourné	*stayed there*
une petite goutte	*a little drop*
as-tu rencontré	*did you meet*
C'est comme ça que ça s'écrit?	*Is that how it's spelled?*
c'est génial	*that's fantastic*
surtout pas	*definitely not*

*A*près le visionnement

A. Racontez l'épisode! Un étudiant donne une phrase qui commence le résumé. Un autre étudiant reprend le récit, jusqu'à ce que tout l'épisode soit (*is*) reconstitué.

B. Réfléchissez. Répondez aux questions suivantes.

1. Pourquoi les vieux de Saint-Jean de Causse sont-ils «discrets»? Pourquoi ne veulent-ils pas parler de la guerre? Est-ce qu'ils veulent oublier les événements tragiques? Est-ce qu'ils ont quelque chose à cacher (*hide*)? Se méfient-ils des inconnus (*Do they mistrust strangers*)?

2. Pourquoi Camille ne veut-elle pas appeler les Leblanc tout de suite? A-t-elle peur d'apprendre la vérité? Veut-elle réfléchir avant d'agir (*before acting*)?

*R*egards sur la culture

*T*ransformations de la culture en France

In this episode, Rachid and Sonia have prepared **couscous**, a traditional North African dish, for Camille. In fact, **couscous** is one of a number of cultural elements from the Maghreb that are becoming assimilated into French culture. Immigration often changes the host society.

- People of North African origin are now the largest immigrant cultural group in France. Originating in Morocco, Tunisia, and especially Algeria, many of these people originally arrived in hopes of finding temporary work.

- At the time of Algeria's independence in 1962, nearly 1.5 million French citizens who had lived their entire lives in North Africa arrived en masse in France. These people included the **pieds-noirs**, who were descendants of European settlers; Algerian Jews, whose ancestors had lived in North Africa for centuries; and North African Muslims.

- Among the customs brought by these people are a number of culinary specialities: **merguez** (a kind of spicy beef or lamb sausage), **méchoui** (a way of preparing a whole lamb on a spit over open coals), and **couscous**.

- Couscous is based on semolina wheat, which is steamed with the vapor from a stew of meat (usually lamb) and vegetables. At the table, one generally helps oneself to the couscous grain itself, the vegetables, the bouillon, and chickpeas out of separate serving dishes. One can then add **harissa**, a hot pepper sauce.

Les éléments du couscous

- Because of recent immigration patterns, Islam is now the second-largest religion in France after Roman Catholicism, with more adherents than Judaism or Protestantism. The children of North African immigrants, often called **beurs**, may or may not follow Islamic traditions.

- The wearing of the veil among certain Muslim groups has been a very touchy issue in France, because French public schools have traditionally forbidden the wearing of any outward religious symbol.

- The presence of **pieds-noirs** and, more recently, of **beurs** in French entertainment has brought a new accent to the culture. The most striking recent development has been the rising popularity among French young people of **raï**, the distinctive popular music of Algeria.

Considérez

What immigrant groups have succeeded in bringing changes to your own culture in recent times? What kinds of changes are these—food? games? music? something else?

Visionnement 2

La ville de Paris

As you followed the lives of the characters through the first fifteen episodes of *Le Chemin du retour*, you examined six areas of Paris in some detail. Each of these is indicated by an episode designation in a box on the following map. As you can see, most of the action of the film has taken place near the center of Paris. Because the scene is about to shift focus to other parts of France, this is a good time to consolidate your knowledge about Paris.

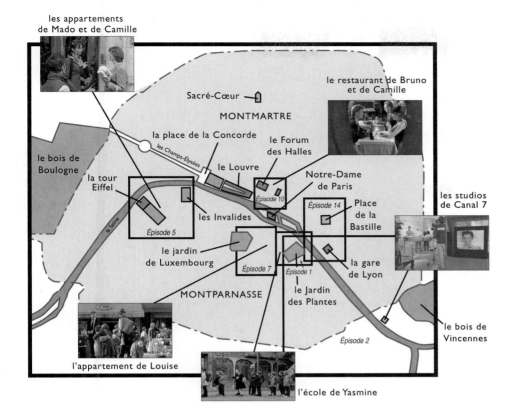

les appartements
de Mado et de Camille

le restaurant de Bruno
et de Camille

Sacré-Cœur

MONTMARTRE

la place de la Concorde

le Forum
des Halles

les Champs-Élysées

le Louvre

le bois de
Boulogne

la tour
Eiffel

Notre-Dame
de Paris

Épisode 10

les studios
de Canal 7

Épisode 14

Place
de la
Bastille

les Invalides

la Seine

Épisode 5

le jardin
de Luxembourg

Épisode 7

Épisode 1

la gare
de Lyon

MONTPARNASSE

le Jardin
des Plantes

Épisode 2

le bois de
Vincennes

l'appartement de Louise

l'école de Yasmine

Vous souvenez-vous? Composez des phrases pour situer les endroits de la liste A par rapport (*with respect to*) aux endroits de la liste B.

Vocabulaire utile: près de, loin de, au nord de, au sud de, à l'est de, à l'ouest de

MODÈLES: Le Jardin des Plantes est près de l'école de Yasmine.
La place de la Concorde est loin des studios de Canal 7.
Montmartre est au nord du restaurant de Bruno et de Camille.

A	B
la Seine	l'appartement de Louise
la tour Eiffel	l'appartement de Mado
le Louvre	l'école de Yasmine
Montmartre	les studios de Canal 7
Notre-Dame de Paris	le restaurant de Bruno et de Camille
les Champs-Élysées	
Montparnasse	
la place de la Concorde	
le Jardin des Plantes	
la gare de Lyon	

Observez!

Considérez les aspects culturels expliqués dans **Regards sur la culture**. Ensuite, regardez l'Épisode 15 encore une fois, et répondez aux questions suivantes.

- Comment le couscous est-il présenté? Qu'est-ce qu'il y a dans un grand bol et qu'est-ce qu'il y a dans plusieurs petits bols?
- Quelle sorte de musique Rachid met-il à la radio? Pourquoi, à votre avis?

$É$crivez et explorez!

À explorer: **www.mhhe.com/debuts** pour trouver le sujet de composition et plus d'informations sur les thèmes de cet épisode.

Le départ

Visionnement 1

*A*vant de visionner

Une discussion. Voici des phrases tirées de l'Épisode 16. C'est une conversation entre Camille et Martine, la productrice de «Bonjour!». Considérez l'histoire jusqu'ici et essayez de déterminer si c'est Camille ou la productrice qui parle.

1. Je pars en vacances aujourd'hui! **2.** Tu es folle? Tu penses à l'émission? **3.** Mais remplace-moi [...]! J'ai besoin de partir! **4.** Inutile (*It's pointless* [*to insist*]). J'ai pris ma décision... **5.** Tu es une professionnelle! Tu dois respecter ton contrat! **6.** Je suis mal en ce moment et j'ai besoin de repos (*rest*), tu peux comprendre ça? **7.** Incroyable (*Unbelievable*)! Cette fille a perdu la tête.

Vocabulaire relatif à l'épisode	
deux semaines de congé	two weeks of vacation
C'est si grave que ça?	Is it as serious as that?
le plus vite possible	as soon as possible
je tiens à toi	I care about you
elle a des soucis	she has worries
le moindre problème	the slightest problem

*O*bservez!

Camille et la productrice se disputent dans l'Épisode 16. Essayez de répondre aux questions suivantes pendant votre visionnement de l'épisode.

- Qu'est-ce que Camille veut faire absolument?
- Quelle solution trouvent-elles pour régler (*resolve*) leur problème?

*A*près le visionnement

A. Une vive discussion. (*An intense discussion.*) Martine n'est pas contente de la décision de Camille de partir en vacances. Voici quelques-unes de ses objections. Comment est-ce que Camille y répond? Choisissez parmi les possibilités données.

1. MARTINE: Tu ne peux pas partir! C'est impossible...
CAMILLE: Pourquoi?
MARTINE: Tu es la vedette° de l'émission!   °star
CAMILLE: a. Tu plaisantes!
     b. Elle a des soucis!
     c. Personne n'est irremplaçable.

2. MARTINE: Camille, tu as des responsabilités.
CAMILLE: a. C'est le plus mauvais jour de ma vie.
     b. Inutile. J'ai pris ma décision.
     c. Tu es le meilleur.

3. MARTINE: Tu as signé un contrat avec moi! Tu es une professionnelle! Tu dois respecter ton contrat!
CAMILLE: a. Pourquoi?
     b. Vraiment? C'est si grave que ça?
     c. Peut-être, mais il est essentiel de vivre, aussi!

B. Les subtilités de l'amour. Quelle sorte de relation existe entre Camille et Bruno, selon vous? Est-ce un rapport d'amitié, d'amour, ou est-ce un mélange des deux? Considérez les scènes suivantes avant de répondre.

Regards sur la culture

L'amitié°

°*Friendship*

In Episode 16, Bruno reminds Camille that she can always count on him, that he is ready to join her immediately in the Cévennes if she should encounter any problem at all. Camille recognizes that Bruno is her best friend.

Une amitié intime entre Bruno et Camille

- French people generally have only a few friends, because friendship to them is a deep relationship and one that makes serious demands on one's time and attention. They check up on a friend nearly every day, and they expect to go out of their way frequently to do good turns for a friend. In short, a friend in France would expect you to participate fairly intensely in his or her life.

- Friends are not expected to agree on everything. The pleasures of debate and argument are a normal part of friendship.

- Married people in France, both men and women, may maintain friendships that they do not share with their spouses.

- Neighbors in France, whether in single-family homes or in apartments, do not expect to be friends. Proximity does not inspire friendship; shared interests and personal trust do.

- In France, people do not usually invite acquaintances to their homes. They might go out to dinner with people they know casually, but only good friends are invited into the closed domain of the home. Many North Americans who live in France are frustrated at not being invited home by the people they know. In the South, however, people tend to meet with friends in less planned, more spontaneous ways than in the North.

- Even good friends would normally not consider that they have the right to go beyond a few areas of a friend's home. They would probably not go into the kitchen, for example, and might not ever see the bedrooms. French people are shocked at the freedom that visitors seem to have in North American homes. The idea of serving oneself something from the refrigerator is anathema to the French!

- Most French people who visit North America are thrilled to find that they make many friends so quickly. They comment favorably on the openness and kindness of Americans and Canadians. However, those who stay for more than a couple of weeks are often bitterly disappointed when they find out that what seemed like "friendships" to them in fact have none of the depth and intensity that they expect of such a relationship in France.

Considérez

What is your reaction to the French notion of friendship? Would you prefer to have just a few very intense friendships, or maintain a larger number of less committed relationships? Why? What are the advantages and disadvantages of each custom?

quatre-vingt-un   81

*O*bservez!

Considérez les aspects culturels expliqués dans **Regards sur la culture**. Ensuite, regardez l'Épisode 16 encore une fois, et répondez aux questions suivantes.

- Pourquoi Martine laisse-t-elle partir Camille? Est-ce une décision basée sur des critères professionnels ou sur une amitié personnelle?
- Comment Bruno montre-t-il son amitié pour Camille?

*É*crivez et explorez!

À explorer: **www.mhhe.com/debuts** pour trouver le sujet de composition et plus d'informations sur les thèmes de cet épisode.

Je cherche la trace d'un homme.

Visionnement 1

Avant de visionner

A. Le contexte. À la fin de l'Épisode 16, Camille est partie pour Saint-Jean de Causse. Martine n'était pas contente. Lisez cette conversation téléphonique qui introduit l'Épisode 17. Utilisez le contexte pour deviner (*guess*) la signification des mots en italique.

BRUNO: En fait,[a] tu sais, on a des problèmes ici, hein...

CAMILLE: Tu m'as choisi une remplaçante[b]? Comment est-elle?

BRUNO: Non, Camille. Je ne plaisante pas,[c] là! Je suis vraiment très *embêté...*

CAMILLE: Un problème d'argent. Combien te faut-il,[d] cette fois-ci?

[a]En... *In fact*   [b]*replacement*   [c]Je... *I'm not joking*   [d]te... *do you need*

BRUNO: Mais non, ce n'est pas ça! En fait, le problème, Camille, c'est toi, voilà! Ton absence est très mal acceptée par le président, et...

CAMILLE: Ah! Qu'est-ce qu'il a dit?

BRUNO: Ben,ᵉ officiellement, rien, mais, euh, il y a des rumeurs, hein! On parle d'un *licenciement* possible...

CAMILLE: Quoi, le président me met à la porte?!

BRUNO: *Méfie-toi*, il en est capable, tu sais!

CAMILLE: *Je m'en fiche!*

BRUNO: Quoi... ?

CAMILLE: Je m'en fiche, Bruno! Ce voyage est très important pour moi. Tu comprends, c'est pff!ᶠ

ᵉWell ᶠc'est... *the rest is nothing!*

B. Quel ton? Regardez encore une fois le dialogue dans l'Activité A. De quel ton Bruno et Camille doivent-ils dire chacune (*each one*) des phrases dans cette scène?

d'un ton compatissant (*caringly*)	d'un ton indifférent
d'un ton fâché	d'un ton inquiet
d'un ton grave	d'un ton sérieux
d'un ton impatient	en plaisantant (*jokingly*)
d'un ton incrédule (*incredulously*)	

MODÈLE: En fait, tu sais, on a des problèmes ici, hein... →
Bruno dit ça d'un ton inquiet. (Bruno dit ça d'un ton sérieux.)

Observez!

Dans l'Épisode 17, Camille arrive à Saint-Jean de Causse. Regardez l'épisode, et trouvez les réponses aux questions suivantes.

- Qui est Éric? Qu'apprenez-vous sur sa famille et sur l'endroit où il habite?
- Est-ce que les attitudes de Louise et de Jeanne Leblanc envers (*toward*) la guerre se ressemblent?

Vocabulaire relatif à l'épisode

à peine	*hardly*
j'ai hérité de la ferme	*I inherited the farm*
il a disparu	*he disappeared*
ne vous le dira pas	*won't tell you*
son mari était un résistant	*her husband was a resistance fighter*
l'ont tué	*killed him*

Notez bien!

To say that you miss someone or something, use the verb **manquer à**. In French, the person or thing missed is the subject of the sentence; an indirect object is used to identify the person who misses.

Tu **me manques**. *I miss you.*

Antoine **manque à** Louise. Il **lui manque**. *Louise misses Antoine. She misses him.*

Après le visionnement

A. Pourquoi? Expliquez pourquoi les personnages du film font les actions suivantes dans l'Épisode 17.

1. Pourquoi Bruno téléphone-t-il à Camille?
2. Pourquoi Camille semble-t-elle indifférente à l'idée d'un licenciement éventuel?
3. Pourquoi Camille ne veut-elle pas téléphoner au président?
4. Pourquoi Camille cherche-t-elle à parler avec Éric?
5. Pourquoi y a-t-il peu de jeunes dans le village?
6. Pourquoi est-ce qu'Éric tient particulièrement à (*is fond of*) sa grand-mère?
7. Pourquoi Camille veut-elle parler avec la grand-mère d'Éric?
8. Pourquoi, selon Éric, est-ce que sa grand-mère ne va pas parler avec Camille?

B. Réfléchissez. Répondez aux questions suivantes.

1. Comprenez-vous l'attitude du président envers Camille? Est-ce qu'il a tort?
2. Bruno suggère à Camille de parler avec le président. Elle refuse, disant qu'elle ne le connaît pas. Prend-elle la bonne décision, ou non?

Regards sur la culture

*L*e déclin de la campagne

Camille notices that there are not many people around in Saint-Jean de Causse. Éric tells her, however, that a new road has been built to the village and that this will certainly bring in many tourists during the summer months. The situation of Saint-Jean de Causse is similar to that of many other villages in France.

- Paris has long been the undisputed center of France. In French, one is by definition either **Parisien** or **provincial**. Even those who live in large cities such as Lyon or Marseille are "provincials."

- At the same time, the villages of rural France are the backbone of many French people's vision of their country. Many urban dwellers speak of a rural region as their family's place of origin, even if they have lived their whole lives in the city.

- At the time of the Second World War, a very high percentage of France's population did work in agriculture as compared with other developed countries such as Britain and Germany. But today, fewer than 30% of the farms of that period are still active. This relatively rapid depopulation of rural France has been called **l'exode rural**.

Ancien village de Conques, Aveyron

- The economic shift away from agricultural work since the Second World War has also been a cultural shift, as young people moved to the cities. Young women were in the forefront of this movement, and, for the past forty years, young men who wanted to maintain the family farm were sometimes unable to find wives.

- Along with the decline of traditional agriculture, France is experiencing the decline and loss of many regional traditions that had their roots in rural populations, including the daily use of languages such as Breton, Basque, and Occitan.

- Villages such as Saint-Jean de Causse in the Cévennes that today might have fifty or sixty inhabitants could have had as many as five hundred in 1880. Two institutions seem to symbolize to local people the survival of a living village community: the local grocery store and the elementary school. The closing of the school is always a particularly dramatic—and sad—event.

Dans les Pyrénées

- One result of the rural exodus is the existence of abandoned or nearly abandoned villages, particularly in areas that are difficult to reach. These places are often extraordinarily picturesque, and, in some cases, have been bought up by Europeans from other countries or by wealthy Parisians to serve as vacation sites.

- Despite this dramatic decline in rural populations and traditional farming, France is still a very important power in agriculture: It produces 21.4% of the agricultural output of the European Union, by far the largest percentage of any of the members (the next highest is Italy, with 16%).

Considérez

French attitudes toward farming as a career have been relatively negative for quite a long time. Today, a young person who decides to go into farming often feels a bit defensive. Why would this be? What perceptions and attitudes related to farming as an occupation are there in your culture?

Visionnement 2

Les Cévennes.   In order to get to Saint-Jean de Causse, Camille rode the train down the Rhône Valley and over to Nîmes. There, she changed to a local train that took her to Alès, a former center of silkworm breeding that lies in the plains near the edge of the Cévennes mountains. From Alès, Camille drove a rented car up to Saint-Jean de Causse. This is a region of rocky soils that has always been poor and isolated from the rest of France. It is one of the areas that has lost the largest percentage of its population over the past half century.

The Cévennes were a center of the Resistance in World War II, but the area's history of resistance goes much further back. In the early 1700s, it was a hotbed of Protestant revolt against royal authority. One tourist attraction in the Cévennes is the village of Le Mas Soubeyran (*The Upper Hamlet* or *Farm* in the Occitan language). It is the location of the house of the Protestant chief Roland and a museum dedicated to the Protestant resistance.

Imaginez que vous allez passer une journée dans les Cévennes. Complétez les phrases suivantes à l'aide de la carte à la page 87.

Demain, nous ferons une excursion dans le Massif central. Nous prendrons

le train de nuit. Il passera à Avignon, mais il ne s'y arrêtera pas.[a] Nous

[a]ne... *will not stop there*

descendrons à _____¹ pour prendre le train régional jusqu'à _____².
Là, nous louerons une voiture et nous monterons vers les _____³. Nous nous
arrêterons pendant une heure au _____⁴, parce que nous voulons comprendre
l'histoire du protestantisme en France. Ensuite, nous monterons voir le village
de _____⁵, pour visiter la ferme de Jeanne Leblanc. Plus tard, nous irons faire
du bateau dans les _____⁶. Et après, nous descendrons vers la Méditerranée
pour passer la soirée[b] dans la ville de _____⁷.

[b]*evening*

Les Cévennes

le Mas Soubeyran

Saint-Jean de Causse

les Causses des Cévennes

les gorges du Tarn

le Tarn · Millau LES CÉVENNES · Alès le Rhône · Avignon Nîmes · Montpellier · Aix-en-Provence · Marseille LA MER MÉDITERRANÉE

*O*bservez!

Considérez les aspects culturels expliqués dans **Regards sur la culture**. Ensuite,
regardez l'Épisode 17 encore une fois, et répondez aux questions suivantes.

- Est-ce qu'il y a beaucoup de jeunes dans le bar des Cévennes? Quel rôle le bar
  semble-t-il jouer dans ce petit village?
- Est-ce qu'il y a beaucoup de chômage dans cette région? Quel était le métier
  traditionnel dans cette région? Qu'est-ce qui va le remplacer?

*É*crivez et explorez!

À explorer: **www.mhhe.com/debuts** pour trouver le sujet de composition et plus
d'informations sur les thèmes de cet épisode.

Histoires privées

Visionnement 1

*A*vant de visionner

La narration de Jeanne Leblanc.   Dans cet épisode, Jeanne Leblanc raconte le séjour (*stay*) d'Antoine dans sa famille. Sa narration est au passé. Complétez le dialogue avec le passé composé ou l'imparfait. Justifiez votre choix en vous rappelant la fonction de chaque temps du verbe: le passé composé s'emploie pour raconter des événements achevés dans le passé; l'imparfait s'emploie pour des descriptions des circonstances et des situations, pour des actions habituelles et pour des actions en train de se dérouler (*unfolding*).

> JEANNE: [Antoine] _____¹ (vouloir) faire de la Résistance. Pierre l'_____² (accueillir) avec sympathie, et très vite ils _____³ (devenir) copains[a]...
>
> CAMILLE: Il _____⁴ (habiter) dans cette maison?

[a]*friends*

JEANNE: Oui... Pierre lui _____5 (faire) visiter la région. Puis il lui
_____6 (présenter) nos amis résistants. Antoine _____7
(être) serviable,[b] sympathique.

CAMILLE: Il vous _____8 (parler) souvent de sa femme?

JEANNE: Oui, et de sa fille aussi, qui _____9 (être) encore toute
petite. Antoine _____10 (s'inquiéter) beaucoup pour elles. Il
les _____11 (savoir) seules à Paris. Elles n'_____12 (avoir)
pas d'argent...

CAMILLE: Mais alors, il _____13 (lutter[c]) dans la Résistance avec votre
mari?

JEANNE (*acquiesce*): Oui. Il y _____14 (avoir) quatre copains avec eux. Ils
détruisaient des ponts et des voies de chemin de fer.[d] Il
_____15 (être) essentiel de retarder les troupes allemandes...
Mais Antoine _____16 (être) impatient. Il _____17 (dire) à
mon mari: «Il faut frapper plus fort![e]».

CAMILLE: Plus fort?

JEANNE: Oui. Il _____18 (vouloir) monter des opérations plus
importantes! Et je vous le dis, Camille, notre malheur
_____19 (venir) de là!

[b]*willing to help*   [c]*to fight*   [d]*détruisaient… destroyed bridges and railroads*   [e]*Il… We have to strike harder!*

Observez!

Dans l'Épisode 18, Camille essaie d'apprendre plus de détails sur Antoine.
Écoutez la conversation entre Camille et Jeanne, en réfléchissant aux questions
suivantes.

- Quel rapport s'établit (*is established*) entre Jeanne Leblanc et Camille?
- Pourquoi Antoine est-il allé dans les Cévennes? Comment a-t-il fait la
connaissance de Pierre et Jeanne Leblanc?

Après le visionnement

A. Le carnet de Camille. (*Camille's notebook*.)   Avant de rencontrer Jeanne,
Camille a préparé une liste de questions qu'elle voulait lui poser. Voici les
questions tirées de son carnet. Quelles réponses a-t-elle reçues?

1. Quand est-ce que mon grand-père Antoine est arrivé chez vous?   **2.** Est-ce
qu'il habitait dans votre maison?   **3.** Est-ce qu'il vous parlait souvent de sa
femme ou de sa fille?   **4.** Quel était son état d'esprit quand il parlait de sa
famille? Pourquoi?   **5.** Est-ce qu'il a vraiment lutté dans la Résistance avec
votre mari?   **6.** Les opérations se sont-elles bien passées?

B. Réfléchissez.   Répondez aux questions suivantes.

1. Quelle sorte de personne est Jeanne? Est-elle généreuse? contente? amère
(*bitter*)? Expliquez, en donnant des exemples de l'épisode.   **2.** Est-ce qu'elle
mène (*leads*) une vie moderne ou plutôt (*rather*) traditionnelle? Justifiez votre
réponse.   **3.** Selon vous, pourquoi Jeanne décide-t-elle de raconter l'histoire
d'Antoine à Camille?

Vocabulaire relatif à l'épisode	
Tenez!	*Take this!*
C'est une lettre qu'a écrite mon grand-père.	*It's a letter my grandfather wrote.*
la vérité	*truth*
cacher	*to hide*
Asseyez-vous	*Sit down*
l'aligot	*regional potato-and-cheese soup*
de la part d'un ami	*on the recommendation of a friend*
c'était de la folie	*it was madness*

Regards sur la culture

La vie en ville et à la campagne

As you saw in this episode, Camille eventually finds the house in Saint-Jean de Causse where her grandfather spent part of the war. Jeanne and her grandson seem to have a fairly comfortable life.

Le village de Sainte-Engrâce dans les Pyrénées

- A farmhouse in the Cévennes would usually have the stable and barn on the ground floor. The family would live on the second floor, which would have an exterior stone staircase leading up to it. The roof would be covered with rough stone tiles. Jeanne's house is more elaborate and southern-looking. It has certainly been modified as the family became more prosperous. However, like most village homes in France, it is filled with a curious mix of traditional and modern elements.

- French people, both urban and rural, are very much attached to certain local traditions. For example, in the Central **Pyrénées**, everyone wants to be able to enjoy **la garbure** (a thick stew of cabbage, pork, rye bread, and preserved goose meat). And on special occasions, for example at a wedding dinner, everyone will sing the song "Aqueras montanhas" (*Those Mountains*) in Occitan, the traditional language of southern France.

- Until the 1970s or 1980s, the borders separating city from country were very distinct in most areas of France. Except for the special cases of a few very large cities, urban sprawl was absent. The past few decades, however, have seen the development of huge supermarkets and malls around even small towns.

- At the same time, the desire for North American–style suburban living is growing, not among the wealthiest people, who prefer urban environments, but in the middle class. Hosts of large **lotissements** (*developments*) are appearing all over France. More and more people want to have their own **pavillon** (*small single-family home*), with garden and lawn.

- Today, the major cities of France are developing very specific looks and personalities. Lille, in the north, aims to promote a modern image, with its Euralille district and high-tech public transportation. Montpellier, on the Mediterranean coast, has renovated its 18th-century center and has linked it to what is probably the most ambitious postmodern architectural development in France. Though they differ considerably one from the other, cities in France are in general very livable and intensely lived in. The North American city that is in large part emptied of its inhabitants at night is a shock to the French.

Lyon la nuit

Considérez

The majority of French people would probably prefer to live in a city. Why do you think that this is true when so many North Americans would rather live in the suburbs or in the country?

*V*isionnement 2

*O*bservez!

Considérez les aspects culturels expliqués dans **Regards sur la culture**. Ensuite, regardez l'Épisode 18 encore une fois, et répondez aux questions suivantes.

- De quelle région de la France la famille de Jeanne vient-elle?
- Quelle est l'attitude de Jeanne envers son héritage régional? Que fait-elle dans cet épisode pour vous donner cette idée?

*É*crivez et explorez!

À explorer: **www.mhhe.com/debuts** pour trouver le sujet de composition et plus d'informations sur les thèmes de cet épisode.

Épisode 19

Un certain Fergus

Visionnement 1

*A*vant de visionner

Jeanne raconte son histoire. Dans le passage suivant, Jeanne raconte les événements de la nuit du 17 décembre 1943. À votre avis, qu'est-ce que les résistants allaient faire ce soir là. Qu'est-ce qui ne s'est pas passé comme prévu (*as planned*)?

Mon mari est arrivé le premier, avec les autres résistants. Antoine était en retard. Il devait le rejoindre[a] avec un camion, pour transporter les armes. Pierre était nerveux. Il savait qu'il risquait sa vie et celle[b] de ses camarades. Mais mon

[a]*meet* [b]*that*

mari avait confiance^c: Il croyait qu'Antoine était son ami. Et Antoine leur avait

assuré^d qu'il y aurait^e très peu de soldats ce soir-là.

^cavait... *trusted him* ^dleur... *had assured them* ^eil... *there would be*

*O*bservez!

Regardez l'épisode pour répondre aux questions suivantes.

- Qui était Fergus? Quelle «preuve» (*proof*) a-t-on de sa trahison?
- Qui a accusé Antoine de trahison? Pourquoi?

*A*près le visionnement

A. Ordre chronologique.   Classez les événements suivants par ordre chronologique de 1 à 10.

_____ **a.** Pierre est arrivé le premier au rendez-vous, avec les autres résistants.

_____ **b.** Antoine a voulu frapper plus fort.

_____ **c.** Éric donne une photo de Fergus à Camille.

_____ **d.** Pierre a été grièvement blessé.

_____ **e.** Fergus a demandé à Pierre de réunir (*gather together*) tous ses amis résistants.

_____ **f.** Pierre s'est traîné jusque chez lui.

_____ **g.** Fergus est arrivé de Paris.

_____ **h.** Jeanne a soigné (*took care of*) Pierre.

_____ **i.** Pierre a accusé Antoine de trahison.

_____ **j.** Pierre a pu s'échapper.

B. Réfléchissez.   Répondez aux questions suivantes.

1. À la fin de l'épisode, Jeanne demande à Camille de partir. Selon vous, regrette-t-elle sa décision d'accueillir Camille? Est-ce que le récit des événements de la nuit du 17 décembre 1943 a été trop pénible (*painful; difficult*) pour elle? Jeanne ressent-elle de la haine (*does she feel hatred*) envers Camille, la petite-fille d'Antoine?

2. Jeanne demande à Éric de donner la photo de Fergus à Camille. Est-ce que les remarques de Camille l'ont incitée à revoir sa façon de penser en ce qui concerne l'histoire d'Antoine? Veut-elle savoir elle-même la vérité?

Vocabulaire relatif à l'épisode	
il faut les empêcher de combattre	*we have to keep them from fighting*
un type	*guy*
nous saisirons ces armes	*we'll seize these arms*
tout s'est précipité	*everything began happening quickly*
se traîner	*to move slowly, with difficulty; to crawl*
il a disparu	*he disappeared*
le chagrin	*pain, sorrow*

*R*egards sur la culture

*L*a Résistance

During the years immediately following the Second World War, those who had served in the Resistance were seen as heros and saviors of France.

- In 1940, shortly after the French defeat, General Charles de Gaulle made a radio broadcast from London, encouraging the French nation not to cooperate

Antoine avec ses camarades de la Résistance

with the German victors or their French allies but rather to fight to free France. By this act, he became the leader of the Free French forces.

- The Resistance movement that emerged little by little in occupied France engaged in secret military action (sabotage, assassinations, etc.), intelligence missions, medical service, and political contact. It had its own underground newspapers and periodicals. With the Resistance fighting both the German occupiers and the French Vichy government, World War II became a French civil war.

- After Germany turned against Russia in 1941, many well-organized French Communist groups became active members of the Resistance. The participation of these people made the movement far more effective.

- Much of the Resistance operated out of remote areas in the French countryside. Many groups were centered in rural southern France, where they came to be known as **maquisards** after the region's scrubby vegetation, **le maquis**.

- By the time of the Allied landings in Normandy in 1944, many who had originally supported Vichy started considering themselves members of the Resistance. By the end of the war, the number of **résistants** had multiplied considerably.

- A number of well-known French writers joined the Resistance through the underground **Comité national des écrivains**. Among these were Camus, Aragon, Éluard, and Malraux. One of the most important outcomes of this period was the tendency for intellectuals to become **engagés**, in other words, to be political activists. Many joined the French Communist Party. For nearly 25 years after the war, famous literary figures, like Jean-Paul Sartre, were significant political opinion makers.

Considérez

In 1940, France was defeated and partly occupied, but there was a French government operating from Vichy, with a popular man (le Maréchal Pétain) at its head. Why might some people have joined the Resistance when it seemed like a doubtful cause and when it made them traitors to the existing government?

Visionnement 2

Observez!

Considérez les aspects culturels expliqués dans **Regards sur la culture**. Ensuite, regardez l'Épisode 19 encore une fois, et répondez aux questions suivantes.

- Comment la Résistance a-t-elle essayé d'infiltrer les Allemands?
- Dans quel quartier de Marseille Fergus habitait-il avant la guerre?

Écrivez et explorez!

À explorer: **www.mhhe.com/debuts** pour trouver le sujet de composition et plus d'informations sur les thèmes de cet épisode.

Risques

Visionnement 1

A vant de visionner

Confrontation professionnelle.   Dans l'Épisode 20, la productrice, Martine, doit parler avec le président de Canal 7. Il est furieux à cause de l'absence de Camille. Voilà quelques paroles du président. À votre avis, qu'est-ce que Martine pourrait répondre?

1. Martine, vous me connaissez depuis longtemps. Je n'accepte pas les caprices. L'attitude de Camille est intolérable!
2. Personne n'a le droit (*right*) de déserter son poste. Rien ne peut le justifier.
3. C'est nous qui l'avons découverte, formée et rendue célèbre. Elle nous doit quelque chose, n'est-ce pas?
4. Je lui accorde (*I'll give her*) deux jours. Pas un jour de plus!

Vocabulaire relatif à l'épisode	
elle était censée être...	she was supposed to be ...
elle a changé d'avis	she changed her mind
démissionner	to quit, resign
rédactrice	editor
faites-lui confiance	trust her
Vous êtes de passage...	Are you traveling through ...

Observez!

Dans cet épisode, Martine est convoquée (*summoned*) chez le président. Ils discutent les actions de Camille. Maintenant, regardez l'Épisode 20 et répondez aux questions suivantes.

- Quel effet a l'absence de Camille sur les indices d'audience (*ratings*) de Canal 7?
- À quelle solution de compromis est-ce que Martine et le président arrivent à la fin de leur discussion?
- Que fait Camille pour essayer de trouver Roland Fergus?

Après le visionnement

A. Reconstituez. Mettez les répliques du dialogue dans l'ordre logique.

DIALOGUE A: MARTINE ET BRUNO

_____ MARTINE: À Marseille. Qu'est-ce qu'elle va faire à Marseille?

_____ MARTINE: Elle a changé d'avis. Et pourquoi?

_____ MARTINE: Est-ce que quelqu'un a des nouvelles de Camille?

_____ BRUNO: Oui. Elle a appelé. Elle est à Marseille.

_____ BRUNO: Elle a peut-être changé d'avis!

DIALOGUE B: LE PATRON DU BAR ET CAMILLE

_____ PATRON: Alors, vous êtes de passage à Marseille?

_____ PATRON: Fergus... ? Fergus... ? Je connais tout le monde dans cette ville.

_____ PATRON: Oui. Je vous trouve son adresse pour demain matin.

_____ CAMILLE: C'est vrai?

_____ CAMILLE: Je cherche cet homme. Il s'appelle Roland Fergus... . Autrefois, son père avait un garage sur le Vieux-Port.

B. Réfléchissez. À votre avis, est-ce que le président est trop sévère envers Camille ou a-t-il raison? Justifiez votre réponse.

Regards sur la culture

Le monde du travail

You have probably noticed that the working relationships between Camille, Bruno, Rachid, and Martine are quite informal. In this segment, however, you see that the president of Canal 7 maintains a somewhat different connection with those who work there.

- Relationships in the workplace in France are changing, but in most cases they are more formal than in North America. The fact that Martine addresses her boss as **Monsieur le président**, even in an industry like broadcasting where informal relationships are more common, would not surprise French people. Coworkers rarely call each other by their first names, unless they have become friends outside of work. Familiarity in the world of work is not equated with friendship.

Martine parle avec le président de Canal 7

- Adhering to schedules is not as important in the French workplace as it is in North America, probably because people expect to be taking care of several things at once and know that new obligations may easily take precedence over old ones.* There is also a sense that relationships need to be maintained even at the expense of deadlines and promptness for appointments.

- It is usually considered rude in a meeting to "get down to business" right away. The French expect a certain amount of time to be spent on general conversation, making the personal relationships work, before real work can get done.

- The French are raised to be individualists. They do not join clubs and organizations nearly as much as North Americans do and sometimes consider that those who do are unacceptably conformist. As a result, French people in the workplace often resist teamwork, preferring to do their jobs separately.

- At the same time, however, the French have a long tradition of joining together for the defense of their professions and jobs. The power and appeal of labor unions in France is much greater than it is in North America, partly because social class is perceived to be a more important factor in one's identity in France.

- Just as authority is centralized in the French political system (although that is changing slowly), control tends to be vested in a few individuals in the workplace. Decisions made by the central power source seem more natural to French workers than attempts at creating consensus, which are often felt to be a waste of time.

- Mealtimes are usually considered more important than any normal work obligations. Traditionally, French businesses and offices were closed for two hours between 12:00 and 2:00 P.M., so that employees could go home for lunch and relaxation. This is still considered the norm, although the situation is slowly changing. The expression **la journée continue** describes business situations where this lunch break is not taken.

- July and August are vacation time in France, and, because everyone has at least five weeks of paid vacation, many businesses simply shut down for several weeks during this period.

Considérez

Few people in France would admit to being workaholics. What differences in priorities regarding work do you see when you compare the French situation with that in your culture?

---

*Edward Hall, an anthropologist particularly interested in nonverbal communication, has called this approach "polychronic." He contrasts French attitudes with respect to time to the "monochronic" approach of North Americans, for whom fixed deadlines are a fairly serious matter.

Visionnement 2

Observez!

Considérez les aspects culturels expliqués dans **Regards sur la culture**. Ensuite, regardez l'Épisode 20 encore une fois, et répondez aux questions suivantes.

- Écoutez le français du patron du bar. En quoi son accent est-il différent du français que vous avez entendu jusqu'ici?
- D'après ce que dit le patron du bar, qu'est-ce qui indiquerait que Marseille a certaines caractéristiques d'une petite ville?

Écrivez et explorez!

À explorer: **www.mhhe.com/debuts** pour trouver le sujet de composition et plus d'informations sur les thèmes de cet épisode.

D'où vient cette photo?

Visionnement 1

*A*vant de visionner

Vrai ou faux? Lisez le dialogue. Ensuite, lisez les phrases qui suivent et dites si elles sont vraies ou fausses. Si elles sont fausses, corrigez-les (*correct them*).

—Cet homme, Roland Fergus, qui est-il exactement? Vous savez quelque chose sur lui?

—Je sais qu'il est marseillais et qu'il a quitté la ville au début de la guerre pour se rendre dans les Cévennes.

—Ici, nous conservons les photos qui sont de provenance[a] incertaine ou douteuse.

[a]*origin*

—C'est-à-dire?[b]

—Nous avons reçu beaucoup de photos. Impossible de tout exposer[c]! Alors, nous avons écarté[d] les photos des gens que nous ne pouvions pas identifier.

—Ceux qui ont collaboré avec les Allemands?

—Pas seulement... Marseille a beaucoup souffert de la guerre. Des familles entières sont mortes. Des milliers de personnes.

[b]c'est... *Which means?* [c]*exhibit* [d]*set aside*

1. Cette scène se passe probablement dans un bar.
2. Il y a des photos dont (*of which*) personne ne sait l'origine.
3. On a exposé toutes les photos.
4. On a exposé des photos de ceux qui ont collaboré avec les Allemands.
5. Beaucoup de Marseillais ont souffert pendant la guerre.

Vocabulaire relatif à l'épisode

vous longez les quais	*you walk along the docks*
déçu(e)	*disappointed*
40 ter	*40c (in a street address)*
vous squattez ce local?	*are you squatters here?*
l'accord de la mairie	*approval of the mayor's office*
ce mec	*this guy*
une piste	*lead, clue*

Observez!

Dans cet épisode, Camille trouve l'adresse du garage de Fergus et de son père. Maintenant, regardez l'Épisode 21, et cherchez les réponses aux questions suivantes.

• Comment Camille trouve-t-elle le garage de Fergus?

• Où va-t-elle ensuite pour s'informer?

• Qu'est-ce que Camille apprend de plus sur Fergus?

• Est-ce qu'on établit l'identité de Fergus comme collaborateur?

Après le visionnement

A. De qui s'agit-il et quelle est la réponse? Lisez les extraits du dialogue et déterminez qui parle avec qui: Camille, le patron du bar, un musicien, la conservatrice du musée. Choisissez ensuite la réplique correcte.

1. _____: Vous voyez? Mon bar est ici. Vous prenez à gauche... Vous longez les quais. Vous tournez à droite... jusqu'au boulevard de la Corderie, et c'est là.

   _____: **a.** J'ai peur que vous soyez déçue, vous savez.
   b. Où est-ce?
   c. Je peux garder cette carte?

2. _____: Vous squattez ce local?

   _____: **a.** Il a travaillé dans la Résistance.
   b. Non, non. On a l'accord de la mairie...
   c. Le propriétaire? Personne ne l'a jamais vu.

3. _____: Alors, nous avons écarté les photos des gens que nous ne pouvions pas identifier.

   _____: **a.** Des familles entières sont mortes. Des milliers de personnes.
   b. Du Maroc. Il y a bien ce nom, Fergus.
   c. Ceux qui ont collaboré avec les Allemands?

4. ____: Mais c'est lui! C'est lui! C'est Roland Fergus. D'où vient cette photo?

____: **a.** Regardez ceci...

b. Du Maroc. Il y a bien ce nom, Fergus. Et il y a une adresse à Casablanca.

c. Nous avons reçu beaucoup de photos.

B. Réfléchissez. Les musiciens expliquent à Camille qu'ils squattent le garage avec la permission de la mairie. À votre avis, pourquoi veulent-ils utiliser le garage pour leur répétitions?

*R*egards sur la culture

*L*a notion du musée

Camille's search leads her to the **Musée de la Résistance**, a historical museum of the type that one could find anywhere in Europe or North America.

- The modern concept of the museum developed out of the Enlightenment and came into its own in the 19th century, when the notion of educating the masses for participation in democracy began to dominate the thinking of Euro-American intellectuals. The Louvre itself, originally made up of the confiscated collections of the monarchy, opened in 1793, in the middle of the French Revolution. It stood for the new order of things, where works of beauty could be admired not just by the wealthy, but by the common people as well.

Le musée d'Orsay à Paris

- The typical museum has thus aimed to provide examples of beauty and moments of instruction. In Marseille, there are museums that display works of art, archeological finds, and other historically significant objects. Larger museums, such as the Louvre, often display a combination of all three, with objects ranging from the Code of Hammurabi (18th c. B.C.E.) to **la Joconde** (*Mona Lisa*) by Leonardo da Vinci (16th c.) and the Crown Jewels of France.

- Over the two centuries since the founding of the Louvre, the notion of the museum has developed and expanded in many ways. Museums of technology and of natural history were developed very early on and continue to be popular. As time has gone by, more and more kinds of phenomena have found their way into specific sorts of museums, often for educational rather than aesthetic goals. Paris, for example, has a **Musée de la Contrefaçon** (*Counterfeiting*).

- For tourists, the many churches, palaces, and other historic buildings of France are museums in a sense, too. The Palace of Versailles is one of the most heavily visited buildings in Europe, and most people move through it and view it just as they would an art museum.

- There are even whole villages, towns, and cities in France that are thought of as **villes-musées**. For example, the walled city of Carcassonne, the ruins of Roman cities such as Vaison-la-Romaine, and the parts of Avignon that lie inside the medieval ramparts, are felt to be museum-like and are treated so by visitors.

La place Stravinsky à Paris

- European museums usually have an aesthetic and instructional goal, but American and Canadian museums have been particularly concerned about combining instruction and entertainment. Science museums in particular are usually more didactic in France than they are in North America. The point of view that the museum can be a place of entertainment is not particularly common in France.

Considérez

Most museums in France are publicly funded, whereas the majority of North American museums are private. How might this difference relate to the higher entertainment value found in North American museums? What are the advantages and disadvantages of the two systems?

Visionnement 2

La ville de Marseille. Marseille est la ville la plus ancienne de France. Fondée par les Grecs vers 600 avant J.-C.,* elle était célèbre pour son port magni-fique. Aujourd'hui on trouve des cafés et des restaurants autour du Vieux-Port. Il y a aussi un marché aux poissons tous les matins.

Marseille est très different de Paris: c'est une ville méditerranéenne qui ressemble un peu à Naples ou à Alger. Dans le quartier du Panier, on voit de petites rues étroites qui montent et qui descendent comme en Italie. La Canebière est la grande rue où les Marseillais aiment se promener. L'église Notre-Dame-de-la-Garde domine la ville et semble la protéger.

La ville de Marseille

*avant J.-C. = avant Jésus-Christ. En anglais, on écrit B.C. ou B.C.E. (*before the common era*). *600 B.C.*

La ville de Marseille

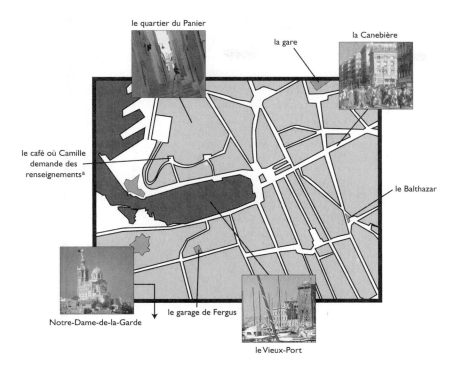

le quartier du Panier

la gare

la Canebière

le café où Camille demande des renseignements[a]

le Balthazar

Notre-Dame-de-la-Garde

le garage de Fergus

le Vieux-Port

Complétez le paragraphe à l'aide de la carte.

Camille a pris le train à Nîmes, et elle est arrivée dans la ville de Marseille à _____[1]. Elle est allée à pied jusqu'au grand boulevard qui s'appelle _____[2] et où tout le monde se promène. Elle a continué dans cette rue, et elle est arrivée au _____[3], où elle a vu le marché aux poissons. Mais elle était pressée. Dans le quartier du _____[4], elle est entrée dans un petit _____[5] pour demander des renseignements. Le patron du bar lui a dit de revenir le lendemain matin, alors le soir elle est peut-être allée s'amuser au _____[6].

Le lendemain, elle est retournée au _____[7] et le patron du bar lui a dit qu'il fallait chercher le boulevard de la Corderie de l'autre côté du _____[8]. Elle y est allée, mais le _____[9] avait disparu[b]: le bâtiment était vide.[c] Elle y a trouvé des musiciens qui jouaient de la musique raï. Est-elle montée sur la colline pour voir _____[10], qui domine la ville? Non, elle s'est dépêchée d'aller au musée de la Résistance.

[a]des… *information*   [b]avait… *had disappeared*   [c]*empty*

*O*bservez!

Considérez les aspects culturels expliqués dans **Regards sur la culture**. Ensuite, regardez l'Épisode 21 encore une fois, et répondez aux questions suivantes.

- Quelles expressions le patron du bar utilise-t-il pour expliquer à Camille comment aller au garage de Fergus? Quelles expressions utilisez-vous quand vous indiquez le chemin dans votre ville? Trouvez-vous des différences entre l'usage français et l'usage nord-américain?
- Dans le film, à quoi devine-t-on le mélange de cultures qui caractérise la ville de Marseille?

*É*crivez et explorez!

À explorer: **www.mhhe.com/debuts** pour trouver le sujet de composition et plus d'informations sur les thèmes de cet épisode.

Secrets dévoilés

Visionnement 1

A vant de visionner

Étude de vocabulaire. Parfois, on peut deviner (*guess*) la nouvelle signification d'un mot en analysant son emploi dans des contextes familiers. D'abord, lisez les phrases que vous avez déjà rencontrées dans le film. Ensuite, lisez la phrase où le nouvel emploi apparaît, et essayez de préciser le sens du nouvel usage.

1. **Famille** *prendre*

   Il rentre à Paris, il retrouve sa femme, *reprend* son travail...

   Mais tu peux en *reprendre* un peu! Une petite goutte?

   NOUVEL EMPLOI: Les Allemands **ont repris** cette rumeur à leur compte (*to their advantage*)!

2. **Famille** *lancer*

   Je *lance* une série de reportages sur la vie au Québec.

NOUVEAUX EMPLOIS: C'est lui qui *a lancé* la rumeur…
C'était un bon prétexte pour *lancer* des représailles.

3. Famille *rendre*

Dans quelle ville *s'est-il rendu*?

Donc, c'est nous qui l'avons découverte, formée et *rendue* célèbre.

Je sais qu'il est Marseillais et qu'il a quitté la ville au début de la guerre pour *se rendre* dans les Cévennes.

NOUVEAUX EMPLOIS: La Résistance avait *rendez-vous* avec Antoine et moi.
Mais aujourd'hui, croyez-vous qu'il est possible de *rendre justice* à… ?

4. Famille *mettre*

Quoi, le président me *met* à la porte?!

On y *met* de la tomme fraîche du Cantal.

Elle aussi, elle est désolée de vous *avoir mise* à la porte.

NOUVEAUX EMPLOIS: J'*avais mis* un uniforme…
La Résistance *a mis* des mois à *s'en remettre*.

Observez!

Dans l'Épisode 22, Camille rencontre Fergus, l'homme mystérieux qu'elle cherche depuis sa visite avec Jeanne Leblanc. Regardez l'épisode, et essayez de trouver les réponses aux questions suivantes.

• Comment l'histoire racontée par Fergus diffère-t-elle de celle racontée par Jeanne Leblanc? Quels détails ajoute-t-il?

• Pourquoi Fergus a-t-il quitté la France pour vivre à Casablanca?

Après le visionnement

A. Le récit de Fergus.   Dans cet épisode, Roland Fergus et son fils Thomas racontent les événements du 17 décembre 1943 du point de vue de Fergus père. Classez les actions dans l'ordre chronologique de 1 à 5.

_____ ROLAND FERGUS: Les Allemands ont repris cette rumeur à leur compte! Ils ont dit que nous travaillions pour eux et que c'est la Résistance qui avait tué[a] Antoine.

_____ ROLAND FERGUS: Antoine a vu que ses amis étaient tombés[b] dans un piège. Les Allemands les tuaient un à un, comme des lapins!

_____ THOMAS FERGUS (FILS): Un résistant, un certain Pierre Leblanc, les avait aperçus. Il avait vu votre grand-père, Antoine, avec mon père qui portait un insigne nazi. C'est lui qui a lancé la rumeur…

_____ ROLAND FERGUS: Antoine voulait rejoindre les résistants. Mais j'ai vu que ce combat était perdu.

_____ ROLAND FERGUS: C'était un bon prétexte pour lancer des représailles et pour commencer une campagne de désinformation! Ils ont pris vingt-cinq hommes au hasard,[c] dans la région, et ils les ont fusillés[d]! La Résistance a mis des mois à s'en remettre.

[a]avait… *had killed*   [b]étaient… *had fallen*   [c]au… *at random*   [d]les… *shot them*

B. De graves malentendus.   Qu'est-ce que Pierre Leblanc a vu qui l'a mené (*led*) à la conclusion que Fergus et Antoine étaient des traîtres? En quoi s'était-il trompé (*had he been mistaken*)?

La culture à Casablanca

When Camille decides to go to Casablanca, she does not seem bothered by the intercultural difficulties that such a trip will involve. It is true that the city has one of the largest populations of French citizens of any outside Europe. Still, Morocco is very different from Europe, despite its many historical connections with Spain and France.

La tradition et la modernité à Casablanca

- Morocco is only 8 miles (13 kilometers) from Europe and has had close historical links with both Spain and France. The country became a French protectorate in 1912. Although theoretically France was responsible only for maintaining order, it also directed foreign and economic policy. As Morocco became something very much like a French colony, it also underwent a process of modernization and Europeanization. During World War II, the sultan supported the Allies but met secretly with Churchill and Roosevelt in an attempt to build support for independence. Morocco finally did become independent in 1956. The French presence had an enormous impact, however, and is still a source of conflict and disagreement among Moroccans.

- The city of Dar el-Beida (*White House*)—best known abroad by its Spanish name, Casablanca—is the largest city in the entire Maghreb region (Morocco, Algeria, Tunisia) and the fourth largest city in Africa. The harbor of Casablanca, which was developed by the French in the early 20th century, has made the city the economic center of the country.

- Casa, as it is sometimes called in French, is considered a loud, aggressive, and cosmopolitan city. Parts of it look very modern and European, with restaurants, cafés, banks, and luxury stores. Other parts, like the Old Medina, resemble the traditional Muslim cities that have dominated the landscape of North Africa for centuries. On the outskirts are shantytowns, where country people, attracted by the economic dynamism of the city, often locate after moving to the city. Outsiders feel about Casablanca much as they do about Marseille or New York.

- Although it is situated on the Atlantic, Casablanca has a kind of Mediterranean climate. The weather is generally mild. Average temperatures range from 12 degrees Celsius (54 Fahrenheit) in January to 23 degrees C (73 F) in August.

- The official language in Morocco today is Arabic. But many Moroccan families have relatives living and working in France, and the constant communication back and forth maintains some knowledge of French at all levels of society.

- There has been a strong Jewish presence in the Maghreb since Roman times. In 1950, the Jewish population of Morocco was estimated at 300,000, but in recent years, many of the old Jewish communities have dwindled and disappeared, as their inhabitants moved to Israel or France. Today, there are only about 8,000 Moroccan Jews, and most of them live in Casablanca.

- Among the most important sights of Casablanca is the largest mosque and Islamic cultural center outside Saudi Arabia. The Hassan II Mosque, named for the late King of Morocco, was completed in 1988. It was built with contributions from Moroccans all over the world.

Considérez

If you were planning to go to Casablanca on business, what kinds of information and training would you want to have before going? Think about questions of language, religion, social customs, relations between the sexes, etiquette, work habits, food and drink, and so on.

Visionnement 2

Le Maroc.   Camille arrive à l'aéroport international Mohammed V de **Casablanca**, qui est la ville où vivent la majorité des juifs marocains et la plupart des Français. Mais le Maroc est très varié. Chacune (*Each one*) de ses villes a une réputation différente. **Rabat**, la capitale, est une ville élégante et calme. On y trouve des quartiers historiques, mais aussi des ambassades, le Palais Royal et l'université. **Marrakech**, la ville la plus importante du sud, a conservé un caractère traditionnel. C'est le point de rencontre des populations de la montagne de l'Atlas et du désert. **Fès** est le centre religieux et intellectuel traditionnel du Maroc, où des gens de toutes origines se rencontrent. La ville a la réputation d'être la plus raffinée du Maroc.

Le Maroc

Casablanca: une ruelle

Fès: une école islamique du XIVe siècle

Marrakech: la place Jemaa el Fna

Rabat: quartier des ambassades

Indiquez la ville que vous choisiriez pour faire les choses suivantes.

MODÈLE: voir la capitale → Si je voulais voir la capitale, j'irais à Rabat.

1. regarder l'océan   **2.** faire une promenade dans la montagne de l'Atlas
3. voir une école islamique médiévale   **4.** visiter une synagogue   **5.** aller à
l'ambassade américaine   **6.** voir un grand port   **7.** connaître les traditions
intellectuelles marocaines   **8.** voir le palais du roi (*king's palace*)

*O*bservez!

Considérez les aspects culturels expliqués dans **Regards sur la culture**. Ensuite,
regardez l'Épisode 22 encore une fois, et répondez aux questions suivantes.

• Comment conseille-t-on à Camille de s'habiller pour aller voir Fergus?
• Comment est-ce qu'on accueille Camille quand elle arrive chez Fergus?

*É*crivez et explorez!

À explorer: **www.mhhe.com/debuts** pour trouver le sujet de composition et plus
d'informations sur les thèmes de cet épisode.

Épilogue

Le Chemin du retour

Visionnement 1

Avant de visionner

A. Analyse. En visionnant *Le Chemin du retour* jusqu'ici, vous avez eu l'occasion d'analyser les actions et le caractère des personnages. En groupes de trois, discutez des questions suivantes.

1. Quel est le caractère de Camille? de Bruno? de Mado?
2. Quel est le rapport entre Camille et Bruno? entre Camille et Mado?

B. Changements. Maintenant, lisez les échanges suivants, extraits de l'Épilogue du film. D'après (*Based on*) ces dialogues, est-ce que le caractère de ces personnages a changé depuis qu'on les a rencontrés au début du film? Leurs rapports les uns avec les autres ont-ils changé?

1. Considérez d'abord Bruno.

BRUNO: Euh, excusez-moi. Quelqu'un sait où est Camille? (*vers la régie*) Euh, la régie? Quelqu'un peut me dire où se trouve Camille?

PRODUCTRICE: (*off*) Ne t'affole pas,[a] Bruno! Elle arrive!

BRUNO: Je suis sûr qu'elle est encore au maquillage!... C'est dingue,[b] ça! Non, mais qu'est-ce qu'on lui fait, un lifting[c] peut-être?

Et encore...

BRUNO: Excuse-moi, Camille. Excuse-moi. J'ai été ridicule, comme d'habitude. Au fond, je suis un type[d] banal, tu sais, un journaliste sans talent, sans avenir. Je comprends que tu ne veuilles pas de moi!

[a]*Ne... Don't get upset*   [b]*crazy*   [c]*facelift*   [d]*guy*

Est-ce le même Bruno dont (*of whom*) on a fait la connaissance au début du film ou est-ce un Bruno transformé par les événements de l'histoire?

2. Maintenant, lisez les réflexions de Mado.

MADO: J'ai été tellement stupide pendant toutes ces années, tellement lâche.° Maintenant, c'est fini, c'est trop tard... Je ne veux pas te perdre!

°*cowardly*

Le caractère de Mado a-t-il changé?

3. Finalement, lisez l'échange suivant.

MADO: Je n'ai pas le souvenir d'un seul jour où tu n'aies été impatiente avec moi, nerveuse.

CAMILLE: (*réfléchit une seconde*) C'est vrai. Mais maintenant, c'est fini. Ça va changer!

MADO: Vraiment? Tu ne pousseras plus de soupirs[a] à chaque fois que je parle?

CAMILLE: Non!

MADO: Tu ne lèveras plus les yeux au ciel?

CAMILLE: Jamais plus!

MADO: (*pour elle*[b]) Oh, c'est sûrement un rêve,[c] mais c'est tellement bon à entendre!

[a]*Tu... You won't sigh any more*   [b]*pour... to herself*   [c]*dream*

Le rapport entre Mado et Camille a-t-il changé? Expliquez.

*O*bservez!

Camille a découvert la vérité sur son grand-père, Antoine. Qu'est-ce qui va se passer maintenant? Pendant votre visionnement de l'Épilogue, essayez de trouver la réponse aux questions suivantes.

- Quel moment de l'épisode est le plus difficile pour Camille? le plus satisfaisant?
- À la fin de l'épisode, peut-on dire que Camille est une «nouvelle» femme? Justifiez votre réponse.

Vocabulaire relatif à l'épisode	
libérée d'un poids	*freed from a burden*
sa femme l'a pleuré	*his wife mourned him*
ils se réuniront	*they will be meeting*
décerné(e)	*awarded*
Ça, je vous fais confiance	*I trust you on that*
déranger	*to disturb*
me gronder	*scold me*
s'il y a bien une chose dont on n'a pas à avoir peur	*if there's anything one doesn't need to fear*

Après le visionnement

A. Avez-vous compris? Dites si les phrases suivantes sont vraies ou fausses et corrigez celles qui sont fausses.

1. En rentrant de son voyage, Camille téléphone immédiatement à Mado pour lui raconter les nouvelles.
2. À l'occasion de leur première rencontre, Camille et Bruno se disputent.
3. Bruno s'impatiente parce que Camille arrive en retard pour l'émission «Bonjour!».
4. David explique à Camille qu'un comité a refusé de revoir le cas d'Antoine.
5. Camille est très mécontente des nouvelles que David lui donne.
6. À la fin, Camille et Mado s'entendent bien.

B. Le passé... et l'avenir. Répondez aux questions suivantes.

1. Quelle est la réaction de Bruno quand il entend les nouvelles de Camille à propos d'Antoine? Comment Camille répond-elle aux remarques de Bruno?
2. Pourquoi David apporte-t-il des fleurs à Camille? A-t-il peut-être une autre motivation que celle qu'il annonce?
3. Selon vous, quel sera l'avenir de Camille et David? de Camille et Bruno? de Camille et Mado? de Camille et ses supérieurs? Est-ce que leurs rapports vont changer?

C. Hypothèses. Selon vous, pourquoi Camille a-t-elle persisté dans ses efforts pour trouver la vérité? Qu'est-ce qui l'a encouragée pendant les moments difficiles?

Regards sur la culture

Le cinéma français

Vous voilà arrivés maintenant à la fin du *Chemin du retour,* et c'est le moment de réfléchir au cinéma en général et à sa relation avec la culture française. Le cinéaste[1] de ce film est américain, mais le scénariste[2] et les acteurs sont français. Le film a donc[3] un caractère interculturel.

- Le cinéma, tel que[4] nous le connaissons aujourd'hui, est l'invention de deux Français: les frères Louis et Auguste Lumière. Ils ont organisé la première présentation publique du cinéma en 1895 au Grand Café de Paris. L'originalité

[1]*director* [2]*screenwriter* [3]*therefore* [4]*tel... as*

de leur conception (par rapport à celle de Thomas Edison, par exemple) se trouve dans l'idée d'une projection publique sur grand écran. C'est ce qui a déterminé le caractère social du cinéma, une caractéristique qui existe encore aujourd'hui, plus de cent ans plus tard.

- Le cinéma s'est développé rapidement en France. Le premier film de fiction a été créé[5] par Georges Méliès en 1897. C'est Méliès aussi qui a créé *Le Voyage dans la lune*[6] (1902), un film bien connu des amateurs du cinéma aujourd'hui. En réalité, la France a dominé le monde du cinéma jusqu'à la Première Guerre mondiale. Plus tard, c'est l'industrie américaine qui a pris la première place.

Une scène du *Voyage dans la lune* de Méliès

- En ce qui concerne le nombre de films produits par an, la France est en cinquième position (après l'Inde, les États-Unis, le Japon et la Chine). Mais l'influence du cinéma français est primordial.[7] Le Festival du film de Cannes symbolise le rôle important joué par la France dans cette industrie.

- Beaucoup de Français prennent le cinéma très au sérieux. Les jeunes assistent souvent à des séances[8] de ciné-club, où l'on[9] visionne et discute de films exceptionnels ou expérimentaux. De nombreux jeunes Français connaissent suffisament l'histoire du cinéma pour pouvoir comparer et évaluer les œuvres des grands cinéastes français et américains.

- La politique culturelle française prend le cinéma au sérieux aussi. L'État finance la Cinémathèque, qui conserve et restaure les films anciens et organise la projection de toutes sortes de films. L'État finance aussi la formation[10] des professionnels du cinéma et essaie de favoriser la promotion et la diffusion du cinéma français dans le monde.

- L'influence internationale du cinéma français a été particulièrement importante à la fin des années 50, quand la Nouvelle Vague (*New Wave*) est née. Ce mouvement, qui représentait une nouvelle spontanéité dans la création cinématographique, a accordé une grande importance au cinéaste en tant qu'«auteur»[11] de son film. Le caractère innovateur et expérimental des œuvres de la Nouvelle Vague—les films de François Truffaut et de Jean-Luc Godard, par exemple—a influencé des cinéastes dans le monde entier.

Le cinéaste François Truffaut au travail

- Puisque[12] les spectateurs nord-américains n'aiment pas beaucoup les films doublés[13] ou sous-titrés, il n'est pas rare qu'un film français soit refait en version américaine. Ces films, qu'on appelle «*remakes*» en anglais, ont souvent eu beaucoup de succès en Amérique du Nord, et quelquefois en France aussi, où le public peut donc voir la même histoire sous deux formes différentes. Mais les spécialistes du cinéma considèrent souvent que ces films américains n'ont pas la qualité artistique des versions d'origine. Quelques exemples de films français et de leurs versions américaines:

[5]*created* [6]*moon* [7]*paramount* [8]*meetings* [9]*one* [10]*training* [11]*en… as "author"* [12]*Seeing that, Since* [13]*dubbed*

Boudu sauvé des eaux (Renoir, 1932)	*Down and Out in Beverly Hills* (Mazursky, 1986)
Diabolique (Clouzot, 1955)	*Diabolique* (Chechik, 1996)
À bout de souffle (Godard, 1959)	*Breathless* (McBride, 1983)
Cousin Cousine (Tacchella, 1976)	*Cousins* (Schumacher, 1989)
La Cage aux folles (Molinaro, 1978)	*The Birdcage* (Nichols, 1996)
Trois Hommes et un couffin (Serreau, 1985)	*Three Men and a Baby* (Nimoy, 1987)
Les Visiteurs (Poiré, 1993)	*Just Visiting* (Gaubert, 2001)

La Cage aux folles de Molinaro

The Birdcage de Nichols

Considérez

Réfléchissez aux différences culturelles entre la France et l'Amérique du Nord que vous avez eu l'occasion d'observer dans ce cours. Ensuite, choisissez un de vos films nord-américains préférés et essayez de déterminer ce qu'on changerait pour en faire une version française. Considérez les éléments suivants:

- l'environnement (urbain ou rural, bâtiments, etc.)
- les relations familiales qui sont illustrées dans le film
- la conception de l'amitié dans le film
- le rôle de la nourriture, des voitures et d'autres objets
- les valeurs morales des personnages
- le ton ou le contenu moral du film
- la fin du film

Visionnement 2

À présent, regardez le film encore une fois, sans interruption. Vous allez voir que vous comprenez maintenant toute l'histoire et une grande partie du dialogue. Et après le visionnement, n'oubliez pas de vous offrir une petite récompense pour tous vos efforts. Bravo!

Lexique français-anglais

This end vocabulary provides contextual meanings of French words used in this text. It does not include proper nouns (unless the French equivalent is quite different in spelling from English), most abbreviations, exact cognates, most near cognates, past participles used as adjectives if the infinitive is listed, or regular adverbs formed from adjectives listed. Adjectives are listed in the masculine singular form; feminine endings or forms are included. An asterisk (*) indicates words beginning with an aspirate *h*.

Abbreviations

ab.	abbreviation	*indef.*	indefinite	*p.p.*	past participle
adj.	adjective	*inf.*	infinitive	*prep.*	preposition
adv.	adverb	*interj.*	interjection	*pron.*	pronoun
art.	article	*interr.*	interrogative	*Q.*	Quebec usage
colloq.	colloquial	*inv.*	invariable	*rel.*	relative
conj.	conjunction	*irreg.*	irregular	*s.*	singular
fam.	familiar or colloquial	*m.*	masculine noun	*s.o.*	someone
f.	feminine noun	*n.*	noun	*s.th.*	something
Gram.	grammatical term	*pl.*	plural	*v.*	verb

à *prep.* to; at; in; **à bientôt** see you soon; **à coté de** next to, beside; **à demain** see you tomorrow; **à droite (gauche)** to/on the right (left); **à haute voix** aloud; **à la campagne** in the country; **à la une** on the front page; **à l'heure** on time; **à mi-temps** part-time; **à nouveau** again; **à Paris** in Paris; **à pied** on foot; **à table** at the table; **à temps partiel** part-time; **à votre (ta) place** if I were you

abandonner to abandon, desert

abolition *f.* abolition

abonné(e) *m., f.* user, subscriber

abord: d'abord *adv.* first, first of all, at first

absence (de) *f.* absence (from)

absent(e) *adj.* absent

absolu(e) *adj.* absolute

abstrait(e) *adj.* abstract

absurde *adj.* absurd; silly

abus *m.* abuse, misuse

Académie Française *f.* French Academy (*official body that rules on language questions*)

accent *m.* accent; emphasis; accent mark; **accent aigu (grave, circonflexe)** acute (grave, circumflex) accent

accentuer to emphasize; **s'accentuer** to grow stronger

acceptable *adj.* acceptable

accepter (de) to accept (*to do s.th.*)

accès *m.* access

accessoire *m.* accessory

accident *m.* accident

accompagner to accompany, go along (with)

accord *m.* approval; agreement; **d'accord (je suis d'accord)** okay; agreed (I agree)

accorder to give

accordéon *m.* accordion

accordéoniste *m., f.* accordionist

accroître (*p.p.* **accru**) *irreg.* to grow, increase

accueil *m.* welcome, greeting; **famille** (*f.*) **d'accueil** host family; **page** (*f.*) **d'accueil** home page

accueillir (*like* **cueillir**) *irreg.* to welcome

accuser (de) to accuse (*of s.th.*); to blame

achat *m.* purchase; **faire des achats** to make purchases

acheter (j'achète) to buy; **acheter à quelqu'un** to buy for someone

acide *adj.* sour; tart

acrylique *adj.* acrylic

acte *f.* act; action

acteur/trice *m., f.* actor/actress

actif/ive *adj.* active

action *f.* action, deed

activité *f.* activity

actualités *f. pl.* news; news program

actuel(le) *adj.* current, present

acuponcture *f.* acupuncture

adapté(e) *adj.* adapted

addition *f.* check, bill (*in a restaurant*)

adéquat(e) *adj.* adequate

adhérer to join (*a political party*)

adjacent(e) *adj.* adjacent

adjectif *m., Gram.* adjective

administrateur/trice *m., f.* administrator; manager

administratif/ive *adj.* administrative

administration *f.* administration; management; **administration des affaires** business administration

admirer to admire

adolescence *f.* adolescence

adolescent(e) (*fam.* **ado**) *m., f.* adolescent, teenager

adopter to adopt; to take up

adorer to love, adore

adresse *f.* address

adresser: s'adresser à to address, speak to

adulte *m., f.* adult

adverbe *m., Gram.* adverb

adversité *f.* adversity

aérien(ne) *adj.* aerial

aéroport *m.* airport

affaire *f.* affair; subject; **affaires** (*f. pl.*) business; **homme (femme)** (*m., f.*) **d'affaires** businessman (woman)

affichage: tableau (*m.*) **d'affichage** bulletin board

affiche *f.* poster

affirmatif/ive *adj.* affirmative

affoler to panic; **ne t'affole pas** don't get upset

afin de *prep.* in order to

afin que *prep.* in order that, so that

africain(e) *adj.* African; **Africain(e)** *m., f.* African (*person*)

âge *m.* age; **au troisième âge** in old age; **quel âge avez-vous (as-tu) (a-t-il, etc.)?** how old are you (is he, etc.)?

âgé(e) *adj.* old; elderly

agence *f.* agency; **agence de location** car rental agency; **agence de voyages** travel agency

agent(e) *m., f.* agent; **agent(e) de police** police officer; **agent(e) de sécurité** security guard

agir to act; **il s'agit de** it's a question of, it's about

agneau *m.* lamb

agrandir to enlarge

agréable *adj.* pleasant, nice

agression *f.* aggression

agricole *adj.* agricultural

agriculteur/trice *m., f.* farmer

agriculture *f.* agriculture, farming

ah bien *interj.* well then

aide *f.* help, assistance; **à l'aide de** with the help of

aider to help

aigu: accent (*m.*) **aigu** acute accent (**é**)

ail *m.* garlic

ailleurs *adv.* elsewhere; **d'ailleurs** moreover, besides

aimable *adv.* lovable

aimer to like; to love; **aimer bien** to like; **aimer mieux** to prefer; **j'aimerais** I would like; **s'aimer** to love each other

ainsi *conj.* thus, in this way, like this; **ainsi que** as well as

air *m.* air; tune; **avoir l'air** to look, seem; **courant** (*m.*) **d'air** breeze, draft; **en plein air** outdoors

aisément *adv.* easily

ajouter to add

album-photo *m.* photo album

alcool *m.* alcohol

alcoolisé(e) *adj.* alcoholic (*beverage*)

Algérie *f.* Algeria

algérien(ne) *adj.* Algerian; **Algérien(ne)** *m., f.* Algerian (*person*)

algue *f.* seaweed

aligot *m.* regional potato-and-cheese soup

aliment *m.* food

alimentaire *adj.* alimentary, pertaining to food

Allemagne *f.* Germany

allemand(e) *adj.* German; **Allemand(e)** *m., f.* German (*person*)

aller *irreg.* to go; **aller + inf.** to be going (*to do s.th.*); **aller à la pêche** to go fishing; **billet** (*m.*) **aller-retour** roundtrip ticket; **billet** (*m.*) **aller simple** one-way ticket;

allez-y! go ahead!; **ça va?** how's it going?; **ça va bien** I'm fine; **comment allez-vous (vas-tu)?** how are you?

allergie *f.* allergy

allergique *adj.* allergic

alliance *f.* alliance, union

alliés *m. pl.* allies

allumer to light

allumette *f.* match

allusion *f.*: **faire allusion à** to make reference to

alors *adv.* so; then, in that case

alphabet *m.* alphabet

alsacien(ne) *adj.* Alsatian; **Alsacien(ne)** *m., f.* Alsatian (*person*)

amant(e) *m., f.* lover

amateur de *m.* fan of, enthusiast of

ambassade *f.* embassy

ambiance *f.* atmosphere, ambiance

ambitieux/euse *adj.* ambitious

ambition *f.* ambition

âme *f.* soul; **âme sœur** kindred spirit; **âmes perdues** lost souls

amère *adj.* bitter

américain(e) *adj.* American; **Américain(e)** *m., f.* American (*person*); **football** (*m.*) **américain** American football

Amérique (*f.*) **du Nord** North America

Amérique (*f.*) **du Sud** South America

ami(e) *m., f.* friend; **faux ami** false cognate; **petit(e) ami(e)** *m., f.* boyfriend (girlfriend); **se faire des amis** to make friends

amicalement *adv.* amicably

amitié *f.* friendship

amour *m.* love; **lettre** (*f.*) **d'amour** love letter

amoureux/euse *adj.* in love; **tomber amoureux/euse** to fall in love

amphithéâtre (*fam.* **amphi**) *m.* amphitheater, lecture hall

ampleur *f.* fullness

amusant(e) *adj.* amusing, funny

amuser: s'amuser (à) to have a good time

an *m.* year; **j'ai (il a, etc.) (vingt) ans** I am (he is, etc.) (twenty) years old; **nouvel an** New Year's Day

analyse *f.* analysis

analyser to analyze

ancêtre *m., f.* ancestor

ancien(ne) *adj.* ancient; old; former

anglais(e) *adj.* English; **anglais** *m.* English (*language*); **Anglais(e)** *m., f.* English person

Angleterre *f.* England

anglophone *adj.* English-speaking

animal *m.* animal

animateur/trice *m., f.* television anchor

animé(e) *adj.* animated; **dessin** (*m.*) **animé** animated cartoon

anis *m.* anise

année *f.* year; **année prochaine (dernière)** next (last) year

anniversaire *m.* birthday; **anniversaire de mariage** wedding anniversary

annonce *f.* advertisement; **petites annonces** classified ads

annoncer (nous annonçons) to announce; to state

annuaire *m.* telephone book

anonyme *adj.* anonymous

antagonisme *m.* antagonism

Antarctique *m.* Antarctica

anthropologie *f.* anthropology

antibiotique *m.* antibiotic

anticiper to anticipate, expect

antidote *m.* antidote

antillais(e) *adj.* West Indian; **Antillais(e)** *m., f.* West Indian (*person*)

antiquaire *m., f.* antiques dealer

août *m.* August

apaiser to appease

apercevoir (*like* **recevoir**) *irreg.* to see; to notice

apéritif *m.* cocktail

apostrophe *m.* apostrophe

apparaître (*like* **connaître**) *irreg.* to appear

appareil photo *m.* camera

apparent(e) *adj.* apparent

apparenté(e) *adj.* related, similar; **mots** (*m. pl.*) **apparentés** cognates

appartement *m.* apartment, flat

appartenir (*like* **tenir**) (*irreg.*) **à** to belong to

appel *m.* call

appeler (j'appelle) to call; **il (elle) s'appelle** his (her) name is; **je m'appelle** my name is; **s'appeler** to be named

appétit *m.* appetite; **bon appétit** enjoy your meal

applaudir to applaud

apporter to bring

appréciation *f.* appreciation

apprécier to appreciate

apprendre (*like* **prendre**) *irreg.* to learn

approcher to approach, draw near; **s'approcher (de)** to approach (*s.th.*)

approprié(e) *adj.* appropriate, fitting

après *prep.* after; **après que** after; **d'après** based on, according to

après-demain *adv.* day after tomorrow

après-midi *m. or f.* afternoon; **cet après-midi** this afternoon; **de l'après-midi** in the afternoon

aquarelle *f.* watercolor

aquatique *adj.* aquatic

arabe *adj.* Arab; **Arabe** *m., f.* Arab (*person*); **arabe** (*m.*) **littéraire** classical Arabic

arbre *m.* tree

arc *m.* arch
archéologie *f.* archeology
architectural(e) *adj.* architectural
archives *f. pl.* archives
arène *f.* arena
argent *m.* money
arithmétique *f.* arithmetic
armée *f.* army
arme *f.* arm, weapon
armistice *m.* armistice
armoire *f.* armoire, wardrobe (*furniture*)
arrestation *f.* arrest
arrêt *m.* (station) stop
arrêter (de) to stop, cease; to arrest; **des opinions** (*f. pl.*) **arrêtées** definite opinions; **s'arrêter** to stop (*oneself*)
arrière *adv.* (in the) back; **arrière-grand-parent** *m.* great-grandparent; **arrière plan** *m.* background
arrivée *f.* arrival
arriver (à) to arrive; to happen; to succeed in (doing); **qu'est-ce qui lui arrive?** what's going on with him?
arrondissement *m.* district
art *m.* art; **arts dramatiques** dramatic arts; **arts plastiques** visual arts (sculpture, painting, etc.); **beaux-arts** fine arts
arteriel(le) *adj.* arterial
article *m., Gram.* article
artifice: feux (*m. pl.*) **d'artifice** fireworks
artisan(e) *m., f.* craftsman, artisan
artisanal(e) *adj.* hand-crafted; **pain** (*m.*) **artisanal** hand-crafted bread
artiste *m., f.* artist
artistique *adj.* artistic
ascenseur *m.* elevator
asiatique *adj.* Asian; **Asiatique** *m., f.* Asian (*person*)
Asie *f.* Asia
asile *m.* asylum; **asile politique** political asylum
aspect *m.* aspect, feature
aspiré(e) *adj.* spoken, aspirated; **h aspiré** letter *h* not allowing liaison or elision
aspirine *f.* aspirin
asseoir (*p.p.* **assis**) *irreg.* to seat; **asseyez-vous (assieds-toi)** sit down; **s'asseoir** to sit down
assez *adv.* rather, somewhat, quite; **assez de** *adv.* enough; **assez jeune** quite young
assiette *f.* plate
assimilation *f.* assimilation
assimiler to assimilate
assistance *f.* assistance, help
assistant(e) *m., f.* assistant
assister à to attend (*an event*)
associer to associate
assorti(e) *adj.* matching; **bien assorti(e)** well-matched
assumer to take on

assurer to ensure
astronomique *adj.* astronomical
atelier *m.* workshop
athlète *m., f.* athlete
atmosphère *f.* atmosphere
attacher to attach; **s'attacher à** to become attached to (*s.th.*)
attaque *f.* attack
attaquer to attack
attendre to wait (for)
attention *f.* attention; **attention!** *interj.* watch out!; **faire attention (à)** to pay attention (to
attentivement *adv.* attentively
attitude *f.* attitude
attraper to trap
aubergine *f.* eggplant
au revoir *m.* good-bye
aucun(e): ne... aucun(e) *adj.* no, not one, not any
audacieux/euse *adj.* audacious
audience *f.* audience; **indices** (*m. pl.*) **d'audience** ratings
augmentation *f.* increase; rise
augmenter to increase
aujourd'hui *adv.* today; nowadays; **nous sommes le combien aujourd'hui?** What date is it?
auprès de *prep.* near, close to
aussi *adv.* also; as; so; **aussi... que** as . . . as; **aussi bien que** just as easily as
Australie *f.* Australia
autant; autant de + *noun* + **que** *adv.* as much/many + *noun* + as; **autant que** as much as
auteur (femme auteur) *m., f.* author; **en tant qu'auteur** as author
autocar *m.* (tour) bus
autographe *m.* autograph
automatique *adj.* automatic
automne *m.* autumn
automobile (*fam.* **auto**) *f.* automobile
autoritaire *adj.* authoritarian
autoroute *f.* highway
autour de *prep.* around
autre *adj., pron.* other, another; **autre chose?** something else?; **l'autre / les autres** the other(s)
autrefois *adv.* formerly, in the past
auxiliaire *m., Gram.* auxiliary (*verb*)
avance *f.* advance; **en avance** early; **retarder l'avance** to slow the advance
avancer (nous avançons) to advance
avant *adv.* before (in time); *prep.* before, in advance of; **avant de** before; **avant que** *conj.* before
avantage *m.* advantage, benefit
avantageux/euse *adj.* advantageous; profitable
avare *m., f.* miser

avec *prep.* with
avenir *m.* future
avenue *f.* avenue; **monter l'avenue** to go up the avenue
aveugle *adv.* blind
avion *m.* airplane; **billet** (*m.*) **d'avion** airplane ticket; **en avion** by airplane
avis *m.* opinion; **à votre (ton) avis** in your opinion; **changer d'avis** to change one's mind
avocat(e) *m., f.* lawyer
avoine *f.* oats
avoir (*p.p.* **eu**) *irreg.* to have; **avoir (vingt) ans** to be (twenty) years old; **avoir besoin (de)** to need; **avoir chaud** to feel hot; **avoir confiance en** to have confidence in; **avoir du mal (à)** to have a hard time (*doing s.th.*); **avoir envie de** to be in the mood for; **avoir faim** to be hungry; **avoir froid** to be cold; **avoir honte (de)** to be ashamed (of); **avoir horreur de** to hate, detest; **avoir l'air** to look, seem; **avoir lieu** to take place; **avoir l'occasion** to have the chance; **avoir mal à** to have pain, an ache in; to have a sore . . .; **avoir mal au cœur** to feel nauseated; **avoir peur (de)** to be afraid (of); **avoir raison** to be right; **avoir soif** to be thirsty; **avoir sommeil** to be sleepy; **avoir tort** to be wrong, to be mistaken
avril *m.* April

baccalauréat *m.* (*fam.* **bac**) high school diploma
baby-sitter *m., f.* babysitter
baguette *f.* French bread, baguette
baie *f.* bay
baignoire *f.* bathtub
bain *m.* bath; **bain thermal** spa bath (*spring water*); **maillot** (*m.*) **de bain** swimsuit; **salle** (*f.*) **de bains** bathroom
baiser *m.* kiss
baisser to lower
balle *f.* ball (*not inflated with air*)
ballon *m.* ball (*inflated with air*)
banal(e) *adj.* trite, superficial, banal
bande (*f.*) **dessinée** comic strip
bandé(e) *adj.:* **yeux** (*m. pl.*) **bandés** blindfolded
banlieue *f.* suburb
bancaire: carte (*f.*) **bancaire** bank (*debit*) card
banque *f.* bank; **banque de données** database
baptisé(e) *adj.* baptized, christened
bar *m.* bar, pub
base *f.* basis; base (*military*); **à base de** based on, from
base-ball *m.* baseball

baser to base; **baser sur** to base on

bassin *m.* basin

bataille *f.* battle

bateau *m.* boat; **bateau à voile** sailboat; **en bateau** by boat; **faire du bateau** to go sailing

bâtiment *m.* building

bavard(e) *adj.* talkative

bavarder to gossip; to talk a lot

beau (bel, belle [*pl.* **beaux, belles])** *adj.* handsome; beautiful; **beau temps** nice weather; **il fait beau** it's nice (weather) out

beaucoup (de) *adv.* much, many, a lot (of); **beaucoup plus** much more, many more

beau-frère *m.* stepbrother; brother-in-law

beau-père *m.* stepfather; father-in-law

beauté *f.* beauty; **institut** (*m.*) **de beauté** beauty parlor

bébé *m.* baby

belle-mère *f.* stepmother; mother-in-law

belle-sœur *f.* stepsister; sister-in-law

ben *interj. fam.* well

berbère *adj.* Berber

béret *m.* beret

besoin *m.* need; **avoir besoin de** to need

bêtise *f.* foolishness; **faire des bêtises** to make mistakes; to do silly things

betterave *f.* beet

beurre *m.* butter

bibliothèque *f.* library

bien *adv.* well, good; **bien payé** well paid; **bien que** although; **bien sûr que non** of course not; **bien sûr (que oui)** (yes), of course;; **ça va bien** I'm fine, I'm well; **s'entendre bien (avec)** to get along well (with); **très bien** very well; **vouloir bien** to be glad, willing (*to do s.th.*)

bientôt *adv.* soon; **à bientôt** *interj.* see you soon

bière *f.* beer

bijoux *m. pl.* jewelry

bilingue *adj.* bilingual

bilinguisme *m.* bilingualism

billiard *m.* billiards

billet *m.* ticket; **billet aller-retour** roundtrip ticket; **billet aller simple** one-way ticket; **billet d'avion** airplane ticket

biochimie *f.* biochemistry

biographique *adj.* bibliographical

biologie *f.* biology

bisou *m. fam.* kiss (*child's language*)

bizarre *adj.* weird, strange

blanc *m.* blank; space; **remplir les blancs** to fill in the blanks

blanc(he) *adj.* white

blé *m.* wheat

bled *m. fam.* small village

blesser to wound, injure

bleu(e) *adj.* blue; **carte** (*f.*) **bleue** bank card

bloc-notes *m.* pad of paper

blues *m.s. inv.* blues music

bœuf *m.* beef; **les bœufs** oxen

boire (*p.p.* **bu**) *irreg.* to drink

bois *m.* woods, wooded area

boisson *f.* beverage, drink

boîte *f.* box, can; **boîte aux lettres électronique** electronic mailbox; **boîte de nuit** nightclub

bol *m.* bowl

bombe *f.* bomb

bon(ne) *adj.* good; **bon appétit** enjoy your meal; **bon ben** *interj.* all right then; **bonne chance** good luck; **bonne humeur** good mood; **bonne journée** have a good day; **en bonne forme** in good shape

bonbon *m.* piece of candy

bonjour *interj.* hello, good day

bord *m.* edge; bank; **au bord de** on the banks (shore, edge) of

bordelais(e) *adj.* from Bordeaux (*region*)

botte *f.* boot

bouche *f.* mouth

boucher/ère *m., f.* butcher

boucherie *f.* butcher shop

bouddhisme *m.* Buddhism

bouddhiste *adj.* Buddhist

boue *f.* mud

bougie *f.* candle

bouillabaisse *f.* fish soup

bouillir (je bous) *irreg.* to boil; **faire bouillir** to boil (*food*)

boulanger/ère *m., f.* (bread) baker

boulangerie *f.* (bread) bakery

boule *f.* bowling ball; **jouer aux boules** to play lawn bowling

boulevard *m.* boulevard

bourgade *f.* village

bourgeois(e) *adj.* bourgeois, middle-class

bourguignon(ne) *adj.* from Burgundy (*region*)

bout *m.* end; **à bout de souffle** out of breath, breathless

bouteille *f.* bottle

boutique *f.* small shop, boutique

bowling *m.* bowling

boxe *f.* boxing; **match** (*m.*) **de boxe** boxing match

bras *m.* arm; **se croiser les bras** to cross one's arms

brebis *f.* ewe

breton(ne) *adj.* from Brittany (*region*)

brevet *m.* patent

bribes *f. pl.* snatches; bits

brie *m.* Brie cheese

briller to shine

brocoli *m.* broccoli

bronchite *f.* bronchitis; bad cough

brosser to brush; **se brosser (les cheveux, les dents)** to brush (one's hair, teeth)

bruit *m.* noise; **le bruit court** rumor has it

brûler to burn

brun(e) *adj.* brown

buffet *m.* buffet; sideboard

bureau *m.* desk; office; **bureau de poste** post office building

bus *m.* (city) bus

but *m.* goal

ça *pron.* this, that, it; **ça marche** that works for me; **ça me va?** does it suit me?; **ça va?** how's it going?; **ça va bien** I'm fine, I'm well; **c'est ça?** is that right?; **qu'est-ce que c'est que ça?** what is that?

cabine *f.* cabin; booth; **cabine téléphonique** telephone booth

cacahouète *f.* peanut

cacher to hide

cachemire *m.* cashmere

cadeau *m.* gift

cadre *m., f.* executive

café *m.* coffee; café; **café au lait** coffee with milk

caféteria *f.* cafeteria

cage *f.* animal cage

cahier *m.* notebook, workbook

caillé: lait (*m.*) **caillé** curdled milk (*similar to sour cream*)

caisse *f.* checkout; **caisse populaire** credit union

calcul *m.* calculus

calculatrice *f.* calculator

calendrier *m.* calendar

calme *adj.* calm

calmer to calm; **se calmer** to calm down

calorie *f.* calorie

camarade *m., f.* friend; **camarade de classe** classmate

camembert *m.* Camembert cheese

caméra *f.* movie camera

cameraman (*pl.* **cameramen**) *m.* cameraman

camion *m.* truck

camp *m.* camp

campagne *f.* country(side); campaign (*publicity, military*); **à la campagne** in the country; **pain** (*m.*) **de campagne** country-style wheat bread

camping *m.* campground; **faire du camping** to go camping

campus *m.* campus

Canada *m.* Canada

canadien(ne) *adj.* Canadian; **Canadien(ne)** *m., f.* Canadian (*person*)

canal *m.* channel

canapé *m.* sofa

canard *m.* duck; **canard laqué** Peking duck

candidat(e) *m., f.* candidate

candidature *f.* candidacy; **poser sa candidature** to submit one's application

canne (*f.*) **à sucre** sugarcane

cannelle *f.* cinnamon

canoë *m.* canoe; **faire du canoë** to go canoeing

cantate *f.* cantata

cantine *f.* cafeteria

capable *adj.* capable; **il en est capable** he can do it

capacité *f.* skill

capitale *f.* capital (city)

caprice *m.* caprice, whim

capuchon *m.* hood

car *conj.* for, because, since

caractère *m.* character (*personal quality*); **caractères gras** boldface type

caractériser to characterize; **se caractériser (par)** to be characterized (by)

caractéristique *f.* caracteristic

carbone *m.* carbon

carbonnade (*f.*) **flamande** regional meat stew

cardamome *f.* cardamom

cardiaque *adj.* cardiac; **crise** (*f.*) **cardiaque** heart attack

cardinal(e) (*pl.* **cardinaux**) *adj.* essential, cardinal

carême *m.* Lent

carnet *m.* notebook; **carnet de chèques** checkbook; **carnet du jour** society column

carotte *f.* carrot

carrière *f.* career

carte *f.* map; (greeting) card; menu; **carte bancaire** bank (*debit*) card; **carte bleue** bank card; **carte de crédit** credit card; **carte météorologique** weather map; **carte postale** postcard; **par carte de crédit** by credit card

cas *m.* case; **au cas où** in case, in the event that; **selon le cas** as the case may be

casser to break; **se casser** to break (*a limb*)

casserole *f.* saucepan

cassette *f.* cassette

catégorie *f.* category

cathédrale *f.* cathedral

catholicisme *m.* Catholicism

catholique *adj.* Catholic

cause *f.* cause; **à cause de** because of

causer to cause

CD *m.* compact disk (CD)

ce (cet, cette, *pl.* **ces)** *adj.* this, that, these, those; **ce (c')** *pron.* it, this, that; **ce matin** this morning; **ce soir** this evening; **c'est** this/that/it is; **cet après-midi** this afternoon; **n'est-ce pas?** isn't that right?

ceci *pron.* this

céder (je cède) to give in

cédille *f.* cedilla (**ç**)

cèdre *m.* cedar

ceinture *f.* belt

cela (ça) *pron.* that; **à part cela (ça)** besides that; **c'est pour cela seul** it's only for that reason; **cela (ne) vous regarde (pas)** that is (not) your problem

célèbre *adj.* famous

célébrer (je célèbre) to celebrate

célébrité *f.* fame; celebrity

célibataire *adj.* unmarried, single

celle *pron. f. s.* the/this/that one

celui *pron. m. s.* this/that one; **ceux** *pron. m., f. pl.* these/those (ones)

cellule *f.* nucleus

celte *adj.* Celtic; **Celte** *m., f.* Celtic (*person*)

censé(e) *adj.*: **être censé(e) faire** to be supposed to do (*s.th.*)

cent *adj.* hundred; **pour cent** percent

centimètre *m.* centimeter

central(e) *adj.* central; primary

centralisé(e) *adj.* centralized

centre *m.* center; **centre commercial** shopping center; **centre sportif** sports center; **centre-ville** (*m.*) downtown

cependant *adv.* nevertheless

céréale *f.* grain

cerf *m.* deer, stag

cerise *f.* cherry

certain(e) *adj.* certain; sure

certitude *m.* certainty

cerveau *m.* brain

cesser (de) to stop (*doing*)

c'est-à-dire *conj.* that is to say, I mean

ceux *pron. m. pl.* these/those ones

chacun(e) *pron.* each (one), every one

chagrin *m.* sorrow

chaîne *f.* (television, radio) station; network; **chaîne privée payante** private subscription channel

chaîne stéréo *f.* stereo system

chaise *f.* chair

chaleur *f.* warmth; heat

chambre *f.* bedroom; **camarade** (*m., f.*) **de chambre** roommate

chameau *m.* camel

champ *m.* field

champagne *m.* champagne

champignon *m.* mushroom

champion *m.* champion

chance *f.* luck; **avoir de la chance** to be lucky; **bonne chance** good luck

chancelier *m.* chancellor

chandelle *f.* candle

changer (nous changeons) to change; **changer d'avis** to change one's mind

changement *m.* change

chanson *f.* song

chant *m.* chant, song

chanter to sing

chanteur/euse *m., f.* singer

chapeau *m.* hat

chaque *adj.* each, every

charcuterie *f.* pork butcher shop; delicatessen; pork products

charcutier/ière *m., f.* butcher

chargé(e) *adj.* loaded (*weapon*)

charmant(e) *adj.* charming

charte *f.* charter; chart

chasser to hunt

chat *m.* cat

château (*pl.* **châteaux**) *m.* castle; **châteaux en Espagne** castles in the air

chaud(e) *adj.* warm, hot; **avoir chaud** to feel hot; **il fait chaud** it's hot (weather) out

chauffer to heat; **réchauffer** to reheat

chauffeur *m.* driver

chaussée *f.* pavement; **rez-de-chaussée** (*m.*) ground floor

chaussette *f.* sock

chaussure *f.* shoe; **chaussures de marche** walking shoes

chef *m.* chief; chef

chef-d'œuvre (*pl.* **chefs-d'œuvre**) *m.* masterpiece

chemin *m.* route, way; **chemin de fer** railroad; **est-ce que vous pourriez m'indiquer le chemin pour aller à… ?** could you show me the way to . . . ?; **voie** (*f.*) **de chemin de fer** railroad tracks

cheminée *f.* fireplace; chimney

chemise *f.* shirt

chemisier *m.* blouse

chèque *m.* check; **carnet** (*m.*) **de chèques** checkbook; **déposer un chèque** to deposit a check; **faire un chèque** to write a check; **par chèque** by check; **toucher un chèque** to cash a check

cher (chère) *adj.* dear; expensive

chercher to look for

chéri(e) *m., f.* dear, darling, honey

cheval (*pl.* **chevaux**) *m.* horse; **monter à cheval** to go horseback riding

cheveux *m. pl.* hair; **se brosser les cheveux** to brush one's hair

chèvre *m.* goat; goat cheese

chez *prep.* at the home (establishment) of; **chez moi** at my place

chic *adj.* chic

chiches: pois (*m.*) **chiches** chickpeas

chien *m.* dog; **nom** (*m.*) **d'un chien!** *interj.* darn it!

chiffon *m.* rag

chiffre *m.* number

chimie *f.* chemistry

chimique *adj.* chemical; **genie** (*f.*) **chimique** chemical engineering

Chine *f.* China

chinois(e) *adj.* Chinese; **Chinois(e)** *m., f.* Chinese person
chiropracteur/ticienne *m., f.* chiropractor
chiropractie *f.* chiropractic
chiropratique *f. Q.* chiropractic
chiropraxie *f.* chiropractic
chocolat *m.* chocolate; **mousse** (*f.*) **au chocolat** chocolate mousse
choisir to choose
choix *m.* choice; **à vous le choix** your choice; **premier choix** top quality
cholestérol *m.* cholesterol
chômage *m.* unemployment; **au chômage** *adj.* unemployed
chômeur/euse *m., f.* unemployed person
chose *f.* thing; **autre chose** something else; **quelque chose** something
choux de bruxelles *m. pl.* brussels sprouts
chrétien(ne) *adj.* Christian
christianisme *m.* Christianity
chronologie *f.* chronology
chronologique *adj.* chronological
cidre *m.* cider
ciel *m.* sky; **le ciel est couvert (clair)** the sky is cloudy (clear)
cimetière *m.* cemetery
cinéaste *m., f.* filmmaker
ciné-club *m.* film club
cinéma *m.* movie business; movie theater
cinémathèque *f.* film store, film library
cinématographe *m., f.* cinematographer
cinéphile *m., f.* movie lover
cinq *adj.* five
cinquantaine *f.*: **dans la cinquantaine** in one's fifties (*age*)
cinquante *adj.* fifty
cinquième *adj.* fifth
circonflexe: accent (*m.*) **circonflexe** *Gram.* circumflex accent (**â**)
circonstances *f. pl.* circumstances
circulation *f.* traffic
circulatoire *adj.* circulatory
circuler to travel around
cirque *m.* circus
ciseaux *m. pl.* scissors
cité *m.* area in a city; **cité universitaire** dormitory
citoyen(ne) *m., f.* citizen
citron *m.* lemon
citron vert *m.* lime
citronnelle *f.* lemongrass
civil *m.* general public; civilian; **civil(e)** *adj.* public; **état** (*m.*) **civil** civil status
clair(e) *adj.* clear; **le ciel est clair** the sky is clear
clandestin(e) *adj.* clandestine
clarifier to clarify
classe *f.* class; **camarade** (*m., f.*) **de classe** classmate; **classe moyenne** middle class; **salle** (*f.*) **de classe** classroom

classement *m.* classification
classer to classify
classique *adj.* classic; classical
clé *f.* key; **moments** (*m. pl.*) **clés** key moments; **mot-clé** *m.* key word; **sous clé** under lock and key
client(e) *m., f.* client
clientèle *f.* clientele
climat *m.* climate
climatique *adj.* pertaining to climate
cliquer (sur) to click (on)
clochard(e) *m., f.* hobo, tramp
clown *m.* clown
club *m.* club (*social*); **ciné-club** *m.* film club
coca *m.* Coca Cola
cochon *m.* pig; pork
coco: noix (*f.*) **de coco** coconut
code *m.* numerical code; **code civil** civil code, common law
cœur *m.* heart; **avoir mal au cœur** to feel nauseous; **savoir par cœur** to know by heart; **de tout cœur** with all one's heart; **greffe** (*f.*) **du cœur** heart transplant
coexistence *f.* coexistence
coexister to coexist
coffret *m.* little box
cognitif/ive *adj.* cognitive
cohabitation *f.* cohabitation
cohabiter to live together
coin *m.* corner; **les quatres coins du monde** the four corners (far reaches) of the world
coïncidence *f.* coincidence
colère *f.* anger
collaborateur/trice (*fam.* **collabo**) *m., f.* collaborator
collaborer to collaborate
collection *f.* collection
collègue *m., f.* colleague
colline *f.* hill
colonne *f.* column
coloris *m.* coloring
combat *m.* combat, fighting
combattre (*like* **battre**) *irreg.* to fight (*against*)
combien (de) *adv.* how much? how many?; **depuis combien de temps?** how long?; **nous sommes le combien aujourd'hui?** what date is it today?
combiné *m.* (telephone) receiver
combustion *f.* combustion
comédie *f.* comedy
comique *adj.* comic
comité *m.* committee
commander to give orders; to order (*in a restaurant*)
comme *adv.* as, like; **comme ça** this way; **comme d'habitude** as usual; **comme prévu** as expected
commémorer to commemorate

commencer (nous commençons) to begin
comment *adv.* how; **comment allez-vous (vas-tu)?; comment est/sont... ?** what is/are . . . like?
commentaire *m.* commentary
commerçant(e) *m., f.* tradesperson
commerce *m.* commerce; **commerce international** international commerce
commercial(e) *adj.* commercial; **centre** (*m.*) **commercial** shopping center
commun(e) *adj.* common
communauté *m.* community
communication *f.* communication
communiquer to communicate
communiste *m., f.; adj.* communist
commutateur *m.* switch
compagnie *f.* company, business
comparaison *f.* comparison
comparatif/ive *adj.* comparative
comparer to compare
compatissant(e) *adj.* caring
compétition *f.* competition
complément *m.* complement; **pronom complément d'objet direct (indirect)** *Gram.* direct (indirect) object pronoun
complet *m.* man's suit
complet/ète *adj.* full
compléter (*je* **complète**) to complete
compliment *m.* compliment
compliqué(e) *adj.* complicated
comportement *m.* behavior
comporter to involve, include
composé(e) *adj.* composed; **passé** (*m.*) **composé** compound past tense
composer to compose; **composer un numéro** to dial a (telephone) number
compositeur/trice *m., f.* composer
composter to punch (*a ticket*)
composteur *m.* dating stamp; ticket puncher
compréhension *f.* understanding
comprendre (*like* **prendre**) *irreg.* to understand; to include
comprimé *m.* tablet
compris(e) *adj.* included
compromis *m.* compromise
comptable *m., f.* accountant
compte *m.* account; **à leur compte** to their advantage; **compte en banque** bank account **compte rendu** report; **se rendre compte (de)** to realize
conception *f.* conception
concerner to concern; **en ce qui concerne** concerning (*s.o. or s.th.*)
concert *m.* concert
conclure to conclude
conclusion *f.* conclusion
concours *m.* competitive examination
conçu(e) *adj.* conceived, designed
condensateur *m.* condenser

condiments *m. pl.* condiments
condition *f.* condition
conditionnel *m., Gram.* conditional (*verb tense*)
condoléances *f. pl.* condolences
conducteur/trice *m., f.* driver
conduire (*p.p.* **conduit**) *irreg.* to drive
conférence *f.* lecture
confiance *f.* confidence; **avoir confiance en** to have confidence in; **faire confiance (à)** to trust (*s.o.*)
configuration *f.* configuration
confirmation *f.* confirmation
confiture *f.* jam
conflit *m.* conflict; dispute
confortable *adj.* comfortable
confrontation *f.* confrontation
congé *m.* holiday, time off; **prendre du congé** to take time off
congrès *m.* congress
conjonction *f., Gram.* conjunction
conjugaison *f., Gram.* conjugation
conjuguer to conjugate
connaissance *f.* knowledge; acquaintance; **faire la connaissance de** to meet (*a new person*)
connaître (*p.p.* **connu**) *irreg.* to know, be acquainted with
conquête *f.* conquest
consacré(e) *adj.* devoted
conscient(e) *adj.* aware
conseil *m.* advice; **donner des conseils** to give advice
conseiller to advise; **conseiller/ère** *m., f.* counselor
conséquence *f.* consequence
conservateur/trice *m., f.* curator; *adj.* (politically) conservative
conservation *f.* conservation
conservatoire *m.* conservatory
conserver to conserve
considérable *adj.* considerable
considérer (**je considère**) to consider; **se considérer** to believe oneself to be
console *f.* console
consommation *f.* consumption
consommer to consume, use
consonne *f.* consonant
constitution *f.* constitution
constructeur *m.* manufacturer
construction *f.* construction
construire (*like* **conduire**) *irreg.* to construct
consultation *f.* consultation
consulter to consult
contacter to contact
conte *m.* short story
contemporain(e) *adj.* contemporary
contenir (*like* **tenir**) *irreg.* to contain
content(e) *adj.* happy
contenu *m.* content

contexte *m.* context
continent *m.* continent
continuer to continue
contraceptive *adj.*: **pilule** (*f.*) **contraceptive** contraceptive pill
contraire *m.* opposite; **au contraire** on the contrary
contrat *m.* contract
contre *prep.* against; **le pour et le contre** pros and cons
contredire (*like* **dire**) *irreg.* to contradict
contrée *f.* homeland; region
contrefaçon *f.* counterfeiting
contrefait(e) *adj.* counterfeit
contribuer to contribute
contrôler to control
contrôleur/euse *m., f.* ticket collector; conductor
convaincre (*p.p.* **convaincu**) *irreg.* to convince
convaincant(e) *adj.* convincing
convenable *adj.* fitting, appropriate
convenir (*like* **venir**) *irreg.* to suit, be suitable for
conversation *f.* conversation
convoqué(e) *adj.* summoned
copain (copine) *m., f. fam.* friend, pal
corde *f.* rope
cordialement *adv.* cordially
cordialité *f.* cordiality
coriandre *f.* coriander
corps *m.* body; **Corps de la paix** Peace Corps; **extrémité** (*m.*) **du corps** limb; **partie** (*f.*) **du corps** part of the body
correct(e) *adj.* correct
correspondance *f.* correspondence; transfer, change (of trains); **faire/prendre une correspondance** to transfer
correspondant(e) *m., f.* correspondent
correspondre to correspond
corse *adj.* Corsican; **Corse** *m., f.* Corsican (*person*)
costume *m.* man's suit
costumier/ière *m., f.* wardrobe-keeper
côte *f.* coast
côté *m.* side; **à côté de** beside; **d'un côté** on the one hand
coton *m.* cotton
coucher to put to bed; **se coucher** to go to bed
couler to flow; **avoir le nez qui coule** to have a runny nose
couleur *f.* color
couloir *m.* hallway; **siège** (*m.*) **couloir** aisle seat
country *f.* country music
coup *m.* blow; **coup de soleil** sunburn; **coup de téléphone** telephone call; **tout à coup** suddenly

couper to cut
couple *m.* couple
cour *f.* courtyard
courant *m.* current; **courant d'air** breeze, draft; **tenir au courant** to keep up to date
courge *f.* squash
courgette *f.* zucchini
courir (*p.p.* **couru**) *irreg.* to run; **le bruit court** rumor has it
courrier *m.* mail; **courrier des lecteurs** letters to the editor; **courrier électronique** e-mail
cours *m.* class; course; **au cours de** throughout (*time*); **au cours des siècles** through the centuries; **échouer à un cours** to fail a course; **quels cours est-ce que vous suivez (tu suis)?** what courses are you taking?; **sécher un cours** to cut a class
course *f.* errand; **course à pied** running race; **faire les courses** to do errands
court(e) *adj.* short
couscous *m.* couscous; **grains** (*m. pl.*) **de couscous** grains of couscous
cousin(e) *m., f.* cousin
coûter to cost; **combien est-ce que ça coûte?** how much does it cost?
couteau *m.* knife
couture *f.* sewing; **haute couture** high fashion
couvert(e) *adj.* covered; **le ciel est couvert** the sky is cloudy
couvrir (*like* **ouvrir**) *irreg.* to cover
craie *f.* chalk
cravate *f.* tie
crayon *m.* pencil
création *f.* creation
crédit *m.* credit; **carte** (*f.*) **de crédit** credit card
créer to create
crème *f.* cream
crémerie *f.* dairy store
créole *adj.* creole
crêpe *f.* crepe
crever (**je crève**) *fam.* to die
crevettes *f. pl.* shrimp
criée *f.* auction
crier to shout, yell; **crier au scandale** to call it a scandal
crise *f.* attack; **crise cardiaque** heart attack; **crise de foie** queasy feeling
critère *m.* criteria
critique *m., f.* critic; *f.* criticism
critiquer to criticize
crocodile *m.* crocodile
croire (*p.p.* **cru**) *irreg.* to believe; **croire à** to believe in (*s.th.*); **il faut croire** it looks as if, it seems like it

croiser to cross; **mots** (*m. pl.*) **croisés** crossword puzzle; **se croiser les bras** to cross one's arms

croissant *m.* croissant, crescent roll

croustillant(e) *adj.* crusty

crudités *f. pl.* raw vegetables

cruel(le) *adj.* cruel

cueillir *irreg.* to pick, collect (*flowers*)

cuillère *f.* spoon

cuir *m.* leather

cuire to cook; **faire cuire à la vapeur** to steam; **faire cuire au four** to bake

cuisine *f.* food; kitchen; **faire la cuisine** to cook

cuisiner to cook

cuisinier/ière *m., f.* cook

cuisinière *f.* stove

cuisson *f.* cooking; **méthodes** (*f. pl.*) **de cuisson** cooking methods

culinaire *adj.* culinary

culpabilité *f.* guilt

cultiver to cultivate, grow, raise

culture *f.* culture

culturel(le) *adj.* cultural; **manifestation** (*f.*) **culturelle** cultural event

curieux/euse *adj.* curious

curriculum vitæ *m.* resumé, CV

curry *m.* curry

cybercafé *m.* cybercafé

cycliste *m., f.* cyclist

cynique *adj.* cynical

d'abord *adv.* first, first of all, at first

d'accord *interj.* okay, agreed; **d'accord?** okay?; **je suis d'accord** I agree

d'ailleurs *adv.* moreover, besides

dame *f.* lady

dangereux/euse *adj.* dangerous

dans *prep.* in; within; **dans cinq ans** in five years; **dans la rue...** on . . . Street

danser to dance

danseur/euse *m., f.* dancer

date *f.* date (*time*)

dater de to date from

daube *f.; daube de veau* veal stew

de *prep.* of; from; **de... à** from . . . to; **de l'après-midi** in the afternoon; **de nouveau** again; **de plus en plus** more and more; **de temps en temps** from time to time

débarquement *m.* landing

débarquer to land

débat *m.* debate

début *m.* beginning; **au début (de)** in/at the beginning (of)

décembre *m.* December

déception *f.* disappointment

décerner to award

décevoir (*p.p.* **déçu**) *irreg.* to disappoint

déchirer to tear up

décider (de) to decide (to)

décision *f.* decision; **prendre une décision** to make a decision

déclaration *f.* declaration

déclarer to declare

déclin *m.* decline

décliner to decline

décolleté: en décolleté in low-cut clothing

décolonisation *f.* decolonization

déconseiller to advise against

décor *m.* decor; (stage) set

découper to cut (up)

découragé(e) *adj.* discouraged

découvrir (*like* **ouvrir**) *irreg.* to discover

décrire (*like* **écrire**) *irreg.* to describe

décrocher to pick up (*the telephone receiver*)

décroissant(e) *adj.* descending

dedans *adv.* inside (it)

défaite *f.* defeat

défaitiste *adj.* defeatist

défaut *m.* fault (*character*)

défendre to defend

défilé *m.* parade

défiler to walk in procession, march

défini: article (*m.*) **défini** *Gram.* definite article

définition *f.* definition

degré *m.* degree

déjà *adv.* already; ever; yet

déjeuner to have lunch; *m.* lunch; **petit déjeuner** *m.* breakfast

délabré(e) *adj.* dilapidated

délicat(e) *adj.* delicate

délicieux/euse *adj.* delicious; **cela a l'air délicieux** that looks delicious

demain *adv.* tomorrow; **à demain** see you tomorrow

demande *f.* demand

demander (si) to ask (if, whether)

démarche *f.* step

déménagement *m.* move (*to a new residence*)

déménager to move (*to a new residence*)

démesuré(e) *adj.* excessive

demi(e) *adj.* half; **et demie** half-past (*the hour*); **un an et demi** a year and a half

demi-kilo *m.* half-kilogram

démissioner to quit, resign

démocrate *adj.* democrat

démonstratif/ive *adj.* demonstrative; **pronom (adjectif)** (*m.*) **démonstratif** *Gram.* demonstrative pronoun (adjective)

dent *f.* tooth; **se brosser les dents** to brush one's teeth

dentelle *f.* lace

départ *m.* departure; **point** (*m.*) **du départ** starting point

département *m.* department; **département d'outre-mer (DOM)** overseas department

dépêcher: se dépêcher (de) to hurry up (*to do s.th.*)

déplacer: se déplacer (nous nous déplaçons) to move around; to travel

déplaire (*like* **plaire**) *irreg.* to displease

dépliant *m.* brochure

déportation *f.* deportation

déposer to deposit; **déposer un chèque** to deposit a check

dépression *f.* depression, low area

depuis *prep.* for; since; **depuis combien de temps?** how long?; **depuis quand?** since when?; **depuis six ans** for the past six years

déranger (nous dérangeons) to disturb, bother

dernier/ière *m., f.; adj.* last; latter; **ces deux derniers** the latter two; **la semaine dernière** last week

dérouler: se dérouler to unfold; to happen

derrière *adv.* in back of, behind

désaccord *m.* disagreement

désagréable *adj.* unpleasant

descendre (de) to descend; to get down (*from s.th.*); **descendre une rue** to go down a street

description *f.* description

désert *m.* desert

déserter to desert

désertification *f.* desertification

désigner to designate

désinformation *f.* misinformation

désir *m.* wish, desire

désirer to want, desire

désolé(e) *adj.* sorry

désordre *m.* disorder; **en désordre** disorderly

dessert *m.* dessert

desservir to serve

dessin *m.* drawing; **dessin** (*m.*) **animé** animated cartoon

dessiné(e): bande (*f.*) **dessinée** comic strip

dessiner to draw

dessous: au-dessous (de), en dessous (de) *prep.* below

dessus: au-dessus (de), en dessus (de) *prep.* above, over

déstabilisation *f.* destabilization

destination *f.* destination

destruction *f.* destruction

détail *m.* detail

déterminer to determine; to figure out

détester to detest, hate

détruire (*like* **conduire**) *irreg.* to destroy

deux *adj.* two

deuxième *adj.* second

deux-pièces *m.s.* one-bedroom apartment

devant *prep.* in front of

développement *m.* development

développer: se développer to develop; to expand

devenir (*like* **venir**) *irreg.* to become

deviner to guess

devise *f.* motto

dévoiler to reveal

devoir (*p.p.* **dû**) *irreg.* to have to, must; to owe; *m.* homework; duty; **faire les devoirs** to do homework

dévoué(e) *adj.* devoted

d'habitude *adv.* usually, normally; **comme d'habitude** as usual

diable *m.* devil

dialectal(e) *adj.* dialectal

dialecte *m.* dialect

dialogue *m.* dialogue

dictature *f.* dictatorship

dictionnaire *m.* dictionary

dieu *m.* god

différence *f.* difference

différent(e) *adj.* different

différer (je **diffère**) (**de**) to differ (from)

difficile *adj.* difficult

difficulté *f.* difficulty

diffusé(e) *adj.* broadcast

diffusion *f.* broadcasting

digestif/ive *adj.* digestive

dignement *adv.* with dignity

diligemment *adv.* diligently

dimanche *m.* Sunday

dimension *f.* dimension, size

diminuer to diminish

dîner to dine, eat dinner; *m.* dinner

dingue *adj., fam.* crazy

dinosaure *m.* dinosaur

diplôme *m.* diploma

dire (*p.p.* **dit**) *irreg.* to tell; to say; **c'est-à-dire** that is to say; **dire à quelqu'un** to tell someone; **vouloir dire** to mean

direct(e) *adj.* direct; **pronom** (*m.*) **complément d'object direct** *Gram.* direct object pronoun

directeur/trice *m., f.* director, manager

direction *f.* direction

discothèque *f.* discotheque

discours *m.* discourse, speech; **discours direct (indirect)** *Gram.* direct (indirect) speech

discret/ète *adj.* discreet; reserved

discussion *f.* discussion

discuter to discuss

disparaître (*like* **connaître**) *irreg.* to disappear

disparition *f.* disappearance

disponible *adj.* available

dispute *f.* dispute

disputer: se disputer to argue

disque *m.* record; **disques compacts** compact disks

distant(e) *adj.* distant

distinct(e) *adj.* distinct; separate

distinguer to distinguish, tell apart

distractions *f. pl.* leisure activities; entertainment, amusement

distribuer to distribute

distributeur (*m.*) **automatique** (ticket) vending machine

divers(e) *adj.* various; diverse

diversité *f.* diversity

diviser to divide; **se diviser (en)** to divide / be divided (into)

division *f.* division

divorce *m.* divorce

divorcé(e) *adj.* divorced

divorcer (nous divorçons) to get a divorce

dix *adj.* ten; **dix-huit** eighteen; **dix-neuf** nineteen; **dix-sept** seventeen

dixième *adj.* tenth

doctorat *m.* doctorate; **thèse** (*m.*) **de doctorat** doctoral dissertation

document *m.* document

documentaire *m.* documentary

domaine *m.* domain, field

dôme *m.* dome

domicile *m.* domicile, residence; **sans domicile fixe** homeless

domination *f.* domination

dominer to dominate

dommage *m.:* **il est dommage que** it's too bad that

dompter to overcome

donc *conj.* therefore; thus; so

donner to give; **donner des conseils** to give advice; **donner sur (le port)** to have a view of, overlook (the port)

dont *pron.* whose, of which; including

dormir (je **dors**) *irreg.* to sleep

dos *m.* back; **sac** (*m.*) **à dos** backpack

dossier *m.* resumé; papers

douane *f.* customs; **passer la douane** to go through customs

douanier/ière *m., f.* customs officer

double *adj.* double

doublé(e) *adj.* dubbed; **film** (*m.*) **doublé** dubbed film

douche *f.* shower; **douche au jet** high-pressure shower

doué(e) *adj.* talented, gifted

douleur *f.* ache, pain

doute *m.* doubt; **sans doute** probably; no doubt; **sans aucun doute** without a doubt

douter que to doubt that

douteux/euse *adj.* doubtful

doux (douce) *adj.* gentle; soft; sweet; **doux mots** (*m. pl.*) **d'amour** sweet nothings; **il fait doux** it's mild (weather) out; **médecine** (*f.*) **douce** alternative medicine

douzaine (de) *f.* dozen (of)

douze *adj.* twelve

dragueur *m.* flirt

dramatique *adj.* dramatic; **arts** (*m. pl.*) **dramatiques** performing arts

drame *m.* drama; **psycho-drame** psychological drama

droit *m.* law; (*legal*) right

droit(e) *adj.* right; straight; **tout droit** *adv.* straight ahead

droite *f.* right (side), right-hand side; **à droite** to/on the right

drôle *adj.* odd; comical, funny; **drôle d'idée** *f.* odd idea

du (de la) *art. Gram.* some; **du matin** in the morning; **du soir** in the evening

dû (due) à owing to

duo *m.* duet

dupé(e) *adj.* duped

dur(e) *adj.* hard; **œuf** (*m.*) **dur mayonnaise** hard-boiled egg with mayonnaise

durant *prep.* during

durer to last

dynamique *adj.* dynamic

eau *f.* water; **eau de source** spring water; **eau minérale gazeuse (plate)** carbonated (noncarbonated, flat) mineral water; **l'eau t'en viendra à la bouche** your mouth will water

eaux *f. pl.* bodies of water

ébahi(e) *adj.* dumbfounded

ébéniste *m., f.* cabinet maker

écart *m.:* **à l'écart de** apart from

écarter to set aside

échange *m.* exchange

échappement *m.* exhaust; **gaz** (*m.*) **d'échappement** exhaust fumes; **pot** (*m.*) **d'échappement** exhaust pipe

échapper: s'échapper to escape

écharpe *f.* scarf

échouer to fail; **échouer à un cours (à un examen)** to fail a course (an exam)

éclair *m.* eclair (*pastry*)

éclairagiste *m., f.* lighting engineer

éclaircir to shed light on

école *f.* (elementary) school; **école maternelle** preschool, nursery school; **école primaire** elementary school

écologie *f.* ecology

écologique *adj.* ecological

écologiste *m., f.* ecologist; *adj.* ecological

économe *adj.* thrifty, economical

économie *f.* economy; **économie de gestion** business economics

économique *adj.* economic

écouter to listen (to); **écouter la radio** to listen to the radio

écran *m.* screen (*film, computer*); **petit écran** television

écrire (*p.p.* **écrit**) *irreg.* to write; **comment s'écrit... ?** how do you spell . . . ?

écrit *m.* written examination

écriture *f.* penmanship

écrivain (femme écrivain) *m., f.* writer

édicter to enact

édifice *m.* building

éditeur/trice *m., f.* publisher

édition *f.* edition

éditorial *m.* editorial

éducatif/ive *adj.* educational

éducation *f.* training

effet *m.* effect; **effet de serre** greenhouse effect

efficace *adj.* effective; efficient

effort *m.* effort; **faire un effort** to try, make an effort

égal(e) *adj.* equal

égalité *f.* equality

église *f.* church

égocentrique *adj.* self-centered

égoïsme *m.* selfishness

égoïste *adj.* selfish; egotistical

élection *f.* election

électricité *f.* electricity; **panne** (*f.*) **d'électricité** power outage

électrique *adj.* electric; **genie** (*f.*) **électrique** electrical engineering; **plaque** (*f.*) **électrique** burner (*on a stove*)

électronique *adj.* electronic; **boîte** (*f.*) **aux lettres électronique** electronic mailbox; **courrier** (*m.*) **électronique** e-mail; **message** (*m.*) **électronique** e-mail message

électrostatique *adj.* electrostatic

élégant(e) *adv.* elegant

élément *m.* element

élémentaire *adj.* elementary

éléphant *m.* elephant

élevage *m.* animal breeding

élève *m., f.* pupil

élevé(e) *adj.* high

élision *f., Gram.* elision

élite *f.* elite

éloigner: s'éloigner to walk off, move away

elle *pron.* she, it; her; **elle-même** herself

elles *pron.* they; them

émanciper: s'émanciper to become independent

embarquement *m.*: **porte** (*f.*) **d'embarquement** (*airport*) gate

embauche: entretien (*m.*) **d'embauche** job interview

embaucher to hire

embellissant(e) *adj.* flattering

embêté(e) *adj.* upset

embouteillage *m.* traffic jam

embrasser: s'embrasser to kiss (each other)

émission *f.* program (*television*)

émotion *f.* emotion

empêcher to hinder, prevent

empereur *m.* emperor

empire *m.* empire

emploi *m.* work; employment; job; **emploi à mi-temps** part-time job; **mode** (*f.*) **d'emploi** directions for use

employé(e) *m., f.* employee; *adj.* employed; **employé(e) de fast-food** fast-food worker

employer to employ; to use; **s'employer** to be used

emprunter to borrow

en *prep.* in; by; while; *pron.* of/from it/them/there; some; any; **en avance** early; **en bonne (pleine) forme** in good (great) shape; feeling good; **en décolleté** in low-cut clothing; **en espèces** in cash; **en face de** opposite, facing; **en plein air** outdoors; **en plus** in addition; **en réalité** in fact, actually; **en retard** late; **en solde** on sale; **en train** by train; **être en train de** to be in the process of; **en vacances** on vacation

enchaîner: s'enchaîner to be linked

enchanté(e) *adj.* delighted; it's nice to meet you

encore *adv.* again; still; more; **encore une fois** once again; **ne... pas encore** not yet

encourager (nous encourageons) to encourage

endormir: s'endormir (*like* **dormir**) *irreg.* to fall asleep

endroit *m.* place, location

énergie *f.* energy

enfance *f.* childhood

enfant *m., f.* child

enfin *adv.* at last, finally; *interj.* well; in short

engager (nous engageons) to hire

ennemi(e) *m., f.* enemy

ennuyeux/euse *adj.* boring; annoying, tiresome

enquête *f.* investigation; survey

enregistrer to register, check (in); **enregister une valise** to check a suitcase

enseignement *m.* teaching, education; **enseignement des langues étrangères** foreign language teaching; **enseignement secondaire** secondary school teaching; **enseignement supérieur** higher education

enseigner to teach

ensemble *adv.* together; *m.* collection, group

ensuite *adv.* next, then

entendre to hear; **s'entendre (bien, mal) (avec)** to get along (well, badly) (with)

enterrement *m.* burial

enterrer to bury

enthousiasme *m.* enthusiasm

enthousiaste *adj.* enthusiastic

entier/ière *adj.* entire, whole

entraîner: s'entraîner to train, be in training

entre *prep.* between; among

entrée *f.* first course (*meal*); entrance (*to a building*)

entreposer to warehouse, store

entreprise *f.* business

entrer to enter

entretien *m.*: **entretien d'embauche** job interview

envahir to invade

enveloppe *f.* envelope

envers *prep.* toward

envie *f.*: **avoir envie de** to feel like, want

environ *adj.* about

environnement *m.* environment

environs *m., f.* surroundings

envisager to envisage, imagine

envoyer (j'envoie) to send

épais(e) *adj.* thick

épaule *f.* shoulder

épice *f.* spice; **quatre-épices** *m., f. s.* allspice

épicé(e) *adj.* spicy

épicerie *f.* grocery store

épicier/ière *m., f.* grocer

épilogue *m.* epilogue

épisode *m.* episode

éponge *f.* sponge; blackboard eraser

époque *f.* period; era; **à l'époque** at that time

épouser to marry

époux (épouse) *m., f.* husband (wife); **ex-époux (ex-épouse)** ex-husband (ex-wife)

équipe *f.* team

équipement *m.* equipment

équiper to equip

équivalent(e) *m.* equivalent

escalade *f.*: **faire de l'escalade** to go rock climbing

escalier *m.* flight of stairs

escargot *m.* snail

esclavage *m.* slavery

esclave *m., f.* slave

espace *m.* space; venue

Espagne *f.* Spain; **châteaux** (*m. pl.*) **en Espagne** castles in the air

espagnol(e) *adj.* Spanish; **Espagnol(e)** *m., f.* Spaniard

espèce *f.*: **en espèces** in cash

espérer (j'espère) to hope

espoir *m.* hope

esprit *m.* spirit; mind; **état** (*m.*) **d'esprit** state of mind; **ouvert(e) d'esprit** open-minded

essai *m.* essay, composition

essayer (j'essaie) to try

essence *f.* gasoline

essentiel(le) *adj.* essential

est *m.* east

esthéthique *adj.* esthetic

estival(e) *adj.* summertime

estomac *m.* stomach

et *conj.* and; **et demi(e)** half-past (*the hour*); **et quart** quarter past (*the hour*); **et toi?** (*fam. s.*) and you?; **et vous?** (*fam. pl.; formal s. and pl.*) and you?

établir to establish; **s'établir** to be established, evolve

étage *m.* floor (*of building*); **premier étage** first floor (*above ground floor*)

étagère *f.* shelf

étape *f.* stage

état *m.* state; **état civil** civil status; **état d'esprit** state of mind

États-Unis *m. pl.* United States

été *m.* summer

éternel(le) *adj.* eternal

étonné(e) *adj.* astonished, surprised

étonnant(e) *adj.* amazing, surprising, shocking

étrange *adj.* strange; odd

étranger/ère *adj.* foreign; unfamiliar *m., f.* foreigner; stranger; **à l'étranger** abroad; **langue** (*f.*) **étrangère** foreign language

être (*p.p.* **été**) *irreg.* to be, **ce ne sont pas** these/those/they are not; **ce n'est pas** this/that/it is not; **c'est...** this/that/it is . . .; **c'est ça?** is that right?; **comment est/sont... ?** what is/are . . . like?; **est-ce... ?** is this/that . . . ?; **est-ce que... ?** is it so (*true*) that . . . ?; **il est (cinq) heures** it is (five) o'clock; **être de passage** to be passing through; **être de retour** to be back

étroit(e) *adj.* narrow

études *f. pl.* studies; **faire des études en** to major in

étudiant(e) *adj.* (male/female) university student

étudier to study

euh... *interj.* uh . . .

euro *m.* euro

Europe *f.* Europe

européen(ne) *adj.* European

eux *pron., m. pl.* them; **eux-mêmes** themselves

évaluer to evaluate

événement *m.* event

éventuel(le) *adj.* possible

évidemment *adv.* evidently, obviously

évident(e) *adj.* evident

évier *m.* (kitchen) sink

éviter to avoid

évoluer to evolve

exact(e) *adj.* exact, accurate

exagérer (j'exagère) to exaggerate

examen (*fam.* **exam**) examination, test; **échouer à un examen** to fail an exam; **passer un examen** to take an exam; **réussir à un examen** to pass a test

examiner to examine

excellent(e) *adj.* excellent

exceptionnel(le) *adj.* exceptional

excès *m.* excess

exclusion *f.* exclusion; **mesure** (*f.*) **d'exclusion** segregation policy

excursion *f.* excursion, trip

excuser: s'excuser to excuse oneself; to apologize; **excusez-moi** excuse me

exemple *m.* example; **par exemple** for example

ex-époux (ex-épouse) *m., f.* ex-husband (ex-wife)

exercer (nous exerçons) to practice (*a profession*)

exiger (nous exigeons) to demand, require

exister to exist

exode *m.* exodus

exotique *adj.* exotic

expansion *f.* expansion

expérience *f.* experience; experiment

expérimental(e) *adj.* experimental

expert(e) *adj.* expert

explication *f.* explanation

expliquer to explain

exploiter to exploit

explorer to explore

exposer to exhibit

exposition (*f.*) **d'art** art exhibit

express *adj. inv.* express; **transport** (*m.*) **express régional** regional express train

expression *f.* expression

exprimer to express; **s'exprimer** to express oneself

extermination *f.*: **camp** (*m.*) **d'extermination** concentration camp

exterminer to exterminate

extrait *m.* extract

extraordinaire *adj.* extraordinary

extra-terrestre *m., f.* extraterrestrial

extraverti(e) *adj.* extroverted

extrème *adj.* extreme

extrémité *f.* extremity; **extrémité du corps** limb

fable *f.* fable

fabriquer to build

fabuleux/euse *adj.* fabulous; amazing

façade *f.* façade; side

face *f.* side; **en face de** opposite, facing; **face à** in the face of, facing; **faire face à** to face, confront

fâché(e) *adj.* angry

fâcher: se fâcher (contre) to become angry (with)

facile *adj.* easy

façon *f.* manner, way; **à sa façon** in his (her) own way; **de façon sérieuse** in a serious way; **de toute façon** in any case

facteur *m.* letter carrier

faculté (*fam.* **fac**) *f.* faculty (*university department for a specific field of study*)

faible *adj.* weak; low

faim *m.* hunger; **avoir faim** to be hungry

faire (*p.p.* **fait**) *irreg.* to make; to do; **faire allusion** to make reference to; **faire attention (à)** to pay attention (to); **faire beau (il fait beau)** to be nice out; **faire bouillir** to boil; **faire chaud (il fait chaud)** to be hot out; **faire confiance à** to trust (*s.o.*); **faire cuire à la vapeur** to steam; **faire cuire au four** to bake; **faire de la photographie** to take photographs; **faire de la planche à voile** to windsurf; **faire de la spéléologie** to go spelunking (explore caves); **faire de la voile** to go sailing; **faire de l'escalade** to go rock climbing; **faire des achats** to make purchases; **faire des bêtises** to make mistakes, do silly things; **faire des études (en)** to major in; **faire des recherches** to do research; **faire doux (il fait doux)** to be mild out; **faire du bateau** to go sailing; **faire du camping** to go camping; **faire du canoë** to go canoeing; **faire du jogging** to go jogging; **faire du parapente** to hang glide; **faire du patin à glace** to go ice skating; **faire du roller** to roller-skate; **faire du shopping** to go shopping; **faire du ski** to go skiing; **faire du ski de fond** to cross-country ski; **faire du ski nautique** to waterski; **faire du soleil (il fait du soleil)** it's sunny out; **faire du sport** to play sports; **faire du surf de neige** to snowboard; **faire du tourisme** to go sightseeing; **faire du tricot** to knit; **faire du vélo (du VTT)** to bike (mountain bike); **faire du vent (il fait du vent)** to be windy; **faire face à** to face, confront; **faire frais (il fait frais)** to be chilly; **faire frire** to fry; **faire froid (il fait froid)** to be cold out; **faire la connaissance** to meet (*a new person*); **faire la cuisine** to cook; **faire la fête** to have a party; **faire la lessive** to do the laundry; **faire la queue** to stand in line; **faire la vaisselle** to do the dishes; **faire le lit** to make the bed; **faire le ménage** to do housework; **faire les courses** to run errands; **faire les devoirs** to do homework; **faire mauvais (il fait mauvais)** to be bad weather; **faire partie de** to be a part of; to belong to; **faire peur (à)** to frighten; **faire sa toilette** to wash up; **faire un chèque** to write a check; **faire une correspondance** to transfer; **faire un effort** to try, make an effort; **faire une promenade** to take a walk; **faire une randonnée** to hike, go hiking; **faire un pique-nique** to have a picnic; **faire un reportage** to prepare/give a report (*TV*); **faire un stage** to do an internship; **faire un voyage** to take a trip; **je ne sais pas quoi faire** I don't know what to do; **se faire des amis** to make friends; **se faire mal (à)** to hurt (a part of one's body)

fait *m.* fact, **tout à fait** completely

falloir (*p.p.* **fallu**) *irreg.* to be necessary; **il fallait** it was necessary to; **il faut** it is necessary (to); one must, one should; **il ne faut pas** one must (should) not

familial(e) *adj.* relating to the family

familier/ière *adj.* familiar

famille *f.* family

famine *f.* famine

fanatique: fanatique (*m., f.*) **du sport** sports fan

fantaisie *f.* fantasy

fantaisiste *adj.* fanciful

fantastique *adj.* fantastic; **c'est fantastique** it's fantastic; **film** (*m.*) **fantastique** fantasy film

fascinant(e) *adj.* fascinating

fasciné(e) *adj.* fascinated

fast-food *m.* fast food

fatal(e) (*pl.* **fatal(e)s**) *adj.* fatal

fatigué(e) *adj.* tired

faut: il faut it is necessary (to); one must, one should

faute *f.* fault; mistake

fauteuil *m.* armchair

faux (fausse) *adj.* false; **c'est faux** that's wrong; **faux ami** *m.* false cognate; **vrai ou faux?** true or false?

favori(te) *adj.* favorite

favoriser to favor

fax *m.* fax

félicitations *f. pl.* congratulations

féliciter to congratulate

féminin(e) *adj.* feminine

femme *f.* woman; wife; **femme écrivain** (woman) writer; **femme ingénieur** (woman) engineer; **femme médecin** (woman) doctor; **femme peintre** (woman) painter; **femme poète** (woman) poet; **femme sculpteur** woman sculptor

fenêtre *f.* window; **siège** (*m.*) **fenêtre** window seat

fer *m.* iron; **chemin** (*m.*) **de fer** railroad; **voie** (*f.*) **de chemin de fer** railroad tracks

férié(e) *adj.*: **jour** (*m.*) **férié** legal holiday

ferme *f.* farm

fermer to close

fermier/ière *m., f.* farmer

fertile *adj.* fertile

festival (*pl.* **festivals**) *m.* festival

fête *f.* celebration; festival; Saint's day; party; **fête des mères** Mother's Day; **fête du travail** Labor Day; **faire la fête** to have a party; **fête nationale** national holiday

feu *m.* traffic light; fire; **feux d'artifice** fireworks

feuille *f.* leaf; **feuille (de papier)** sheet (of paper)

feuilleton *m.* soap opera

février *m.* February

fiançailles *f. pl.* engagement

fiancer: se fiancer (nous nous fiançons) to get engaged

ficher: je m'en fiche *fam.* I don't care

fiction *f.* fiction

fier (fière) *adj.* proud

fièvre *f.* fever

figurer (dans) to figure (in)

fille *f.* girl; daughter; **jeune fille** girl; unmarried woman; **petite-fille** granddaughter

filleul *m.* godson

film *m.* film

filmer to film

fils *m.* son; **fils unique** only son; **petit-fils** *m.* grandson

fixe *adj.*: **sans domicile fixe** homeless

fin *f.* end; **en fin de journée** at the end of the day; **mettre fin à** to put an end to

finalement *adv.* finally

financer (nous finançons) to finance

financier/ière *adj.* financial

finir to finish

flamand(e) *adj.* Flemish; **Flamand(e)** *m. f.* Flemish person; **carbonnade** (*f.*) **flamande** Flemish regional stew

flamenco *m.* flamenco

fleur *f.* flower

fleuve *m.* large river

flexible *adj.* flexible

flipper *m.*: **jouer au flipper** to play pinball

flirter to flirt

flou(e) *adj.* blurry

flûte *f.* flute

foie *m.* liver; **crise** (*f.*) **de foie** queasy feeling

fois *f.* time (*occasion*); **encore une fois** once again

folie *f.* madness

follement *adv.* madly, wildly

fonction *f.* function

fonctionnaire *m., f.* civil servant, government worker

fonctionnel(le) *adj.* functional, useful

fonctionner to function

fond *m.* bottom; back; background; **à fond** in depth; **au fond** basically; **faire du ski de fond** to cross-country ski

fontaine *f.* fountain

football (*fam.* **foot**) *m.* soccer; **football américain** football; **match** (*m.*) **de foot** soccer match

footing *m.* jogging, running

forces *f. pl.* (armed) forces

forêt *f.* forest

formation *f.* education, training; upbringing

forme *f.* form; **en bonne (pleine) forme** in good (great) shape; feeling good

former to train; to form

formidable *adj.* terrific, wonderful

formule *f.* formula

formuler to formulate

fort(e) *adj.* strong; significant; *adv.* with strength, with effort; **frapper plus fort** to strike harder

forum *m.* forum

fou (folle) *adj.* crazy, mad

foulard *m.* lightweight scarf

four *m.* oven; **faire cuire au four** to bake; **four à micro-ondes** microwave oven

fourchette *f.* fork

fragile *adj.* fragile

frais (fraîche) *adj.* cool; fresh; **il fait frais** it's chilly out)

franc (franche) *adj.* frank

français(e) *adj.* French; *m.* French (*language*); **Français(e)** *m., f.* French person

France *f.* France

francophone *adj.* French-speaking; **monde** (*m.*) **francophone** French-speaking world

frapper to strike, hit; **frapper plus fort** to strike harder

fraternité *f.* brotherhood

fréquence *f.* frequency

fréquent(e) *adj.* frequent

fréquenter to frequent

frère *m.* brother; **beau-frère** stepbrother, brother-in-law

frigo *m., fam.* fridge, refrigerator

frire: faire (*irreg.*) **frire** to fry

Frisbee *m.* Frisbee

frites *f. pl.* French fries; **poulet-frites** *m.* chicken with French fries; **steak-frites** *m.* steak with French fries

froid *m.* cold; **avoir froid** to feel cold; **il fait froid** it's cold out

fromage *m.* cheese

Front national *m.* National Front (*political party*)

frontière *f.* border

fruit *m.* fruit; **fruits de mer** seafood

fumer to smoke

fumeurs: wagon (*m.*) **fumeurs (non-fumeurs)** smoking (nonsmoking) train car

furieux/euse *adj.* furious

fusil *m.* gun

fusiller to execute (somebody) by shooting

futur(e) *adj.* future; **futur** *m., Gram.* future tense; **futur proche** *Gram.* near future

gagner to earn; to win

gai(e) *adj.* cheerful, happy

galerie *f.* (art) gallery

garage *m.* garage

garagiste *m., f.* garage owner

garçon *m.* boy

garde-malade *m., f.* nurse's aide

garder to guard; to keep

gardien(ne) *m., f.* attendant; **gardien(ne) d'immeuble** building superintendent

gare *f.* train station

garer to park

gastronomie *f.* gastronomy

gastronomique *adj.* gastronomical

gauche *adj.* left; *f.* left (side), left-hand side; **à gauche** to/on the left

gaz *m.* gas; **gaz d'échappement** exhaust fumes

gazeux/euse *adj.* carbonated; **eau** (*f.*) **minerale gazeuse** carbonated mineral water

général(e) *adj.* general; **en général** in general

générale *f.* dress rehearsal

généralisation *f.* generalization

généraliser to generalize

génération *f.* generation

généreux/euse *adj.* generous

générique *adj.* generic

génial(e) *adj.* brilliant, inspired; fantastic

génie *m.* engineering; **génie chimique (électrique, industriele, mécanique)** chemical (electrical, industrial, mechanical) engineering

genou *m.* knee

genre *m.* type

gens *m. pl.* people

gentil(le) *adj.* nice, kind; well-behaved

gentilhomme *m.* gentleman

gentillesse *f.* kindness

géographie *f.* geography

géographique *adj.* geographical

germanique *adj.* Germanic

gestapo *f.* Gestapo

gestion *f.* management; **économie** (*f.*) **de gestion** business economics

gifle *m.* slap

gingembre *m.* ginger

glace *f.* ice cream; ice; **faire du patin à glace** to ice skate

gloire *f.* glory

golf *m.* golf; **mini-golf** *m.* miniature golf

gorge *f.* throat; **avoir mal à la gorge** to have a sore throat

goût *m.* taste

goûter to taste

goutte *f.* little drop

gouvernement *m.* government

grâce à *prep.* thanks to

grain *m.* grain; **grains de couscous** couscous grains

graine *f.* seed

gramme *m.* gram

grand(e) *adj.* large, big; tall; **grandes vacances** *f. pl.* summer vacation; **grand magasin** *m.* department store; **grand-mère** *f.* grandmother; **grand-père** *m.* grandfather; **grands-parents** *m. pl.* grandparents; **train** (*m.*) **à grande vitesse (TGV)** French high-speed train

grange *f.* granary, barn

gras(se) *adj.* fatty; thick; **en caractères** (*m. pl.*) **gras** in boldface type; **matières** (*f. pl.*) **grasses** (*meat*) fat

gratuitement *adv.* for free

grave *adj.* serious, grave; **accent** (*m.*) **grave** *Gram.* grave accent (**è**)

graveur *m.* engraver

gravité *f.* gravity

greffe *f.* graft; **greffe du cœur** heart transplant

grièvement *adv.* gravely

grippe *f.* flu, influenza

gris(e) *adj.* grey

grisé(e) *adj.* intoxicated

grommeller (nous grommelons) to grumble

gronder to scold

gros(se) *adj.* large, big; fat; **gros titre** *m.* headline

grotte *f.* cave

groupe *m.* group

gruyère *m.* Gruyere (Swiss) cheese

guérir to cure; to heal

guerre *f.* war; **Deuxième Guerre mondiale** Second World War

guichet *m.* ticket window

guide *m.* guidebook

guider to guide

guitare *f.* guitar

guitariste *m., f.* guitar player

gymnase *m.* gymnasium

gymnastique *adj.* gymnastic

habillé(e) *adj.* dressed; **mal (bien) habillé(e)** badly (well) dressed

habiller: s'habiller (en) to get dressed (in)

habit *m.* clothing, dress

habitant(e) *m., f.* inhabitant

habitation *f.* dwelling, residence; **habitation à loyer modéré (HLM)** low-income housing

habiter to live (in a place), reside

habitude *f.* habit; **comme d'habitude** as usual; **d'habitude** usually, normally

haine *f.* hatred

haïr (je hais) to hate

halle *f.* covered market

hamburger *m.* hamburger

handicap *m.* handicap

Hannukah *m.* Hannukah

haricot *m.* bean; **haricots verts** green beans

hasard *m.* chance; **au hasard** by chance, accidentally

haut(e) *adj.* high; **à haute voix** aloud **haute couture** *f.* high fashion; **haute technologie** *f.* high tech

hauteur *f.* elevation, height

hein? *interj. fam.* eh?; all right?

hélas *interj.* alas

herbe *f.* grass; herb

héritage *m.* inheritance; heritage

hériter (de) to inherit (*s.th.*)

héroïsme *m.* heroism

hésiter (à) to hesitate (*to do s.th.*)

heure *f.* hour; time (*on a clock*); **à... heure(s)** at . . . o'clock; **à l'heure** on time; **à quelle heure?** at what time?; **à toute heure** at any time; **de bonne heure** early; **heures de pointe** rush hour; **il est... heure(s)** it is . . . o'clock; **kilomètres** (*m. pl.*) **à l'heure** kilometers per hour; **quelle heure est-il?** what time is it?

heureux/euse *adj.* happy

hier *adv.* yesterday

hiérarchie *f.* hierarchy

hiéroglyphe *m.* hieroglyphic

hip-hop *m.* hip-hop music

histoire *f.* story; history; **histoire naturelle** natural history

historien(ne) *m., f.* historian

historique *adj.* historical

hiver *m.* winter; **sports** (*m.*) **d'hiver** winter sports

hivernage *m.* rainy season

hockey *m.* hockey

homéopathie *f.* homeopathy

homme *m.* man; **homme d'affaires** businessman

honnête *adj.* honest

honneur *m.* honor

*****honte** *f.* shame; **avoir honte (de)** to be ashamed (of)

hôpital *m.* hospital

horaire *m.* schedule, timetable; **horaires d'ouverture** hours when open

horloge *f.* clock

horreur *f.* horror; **avoir horreur de** to hate, detest; **j'ai horreur de** I can't stand

*****hors (de)** *adj.* outside (of)

hospitalité *f.* hospitality

hostile *adj.* hostile

hôtel *m.* hotel

hôtesse *f.* hostess

huile *f.* oil; **huile d'olive (de sésame)** olive (sesame) oil

*****huit** eight

*****huitième** *adj.* eighth

humain(e) *adj.* human

humeur *f.* mood; **de bonne (mauvaise) humeur** in a good (bad) mood

humide *adj.* humid

hymne *m.* hymn

hypertension (*f.*) **artérielle** high blood pressure

hypothèse *f.* hypothesis

ici *adv.* here

icone *m.* computer icon

idéal(e) *adj.* ideal

idéaliste *adj.* idealistic

idée *f.* idea; **drôle d'idée** odd idea

identification *f.* identification

identifier to identify

identité *f.* identity

idiot(e) *adj.* idiot

il *pron.* he, it; **il y a** there is / there are (*for counting*); **il y a (dix ans)** (ten years) ago

île *f.* island

illustration *f.* illustration

illustrer to illustrate; to exemplify

ils *pron.* they; **ils vivent en union libre** they are living together (without marriage)

image *f.* picture; image

imaginaire *adj.* imaginary

imagination *f.* imagination

imaginer to imagine

immangeable *adj.* uneatable, inedible

immédiat(e) *adj.* immediate

immense *adj.* immense

immeuble *m.* apartment building; **gardien(ne)** (*m., f.*) **d'immeuble** building superintendant

immigration *f.* immigration

immigré(e) *m., f.* immigrant

immigrer to immigrate

imparfait *m., Gram.* imperfect (*verb tense*)

impatience *f.* impatience

impatient(e) *adj.* impatient

impatienter: s'impatienter to become impatient

impératif/ive *adj.* imperative; **impératif** *m., Gram.* imperative; command

impersonnel(le) *adj.* impersonal

implantation *f.* planting

impliquer to implicate

impoli(e) *adj.* impolite

importance *f.* importance

important(e) *adj.* important; big

impossible *adj.* impossible

impressionné(e) *adj.* impressed

impressionnisme *m.* impressionism

impressionniste *m., f.* impressionist

improvisation *f.* improvisation

improviste: à l'improviste *adv.* unexpectedly

impuissant(e) *adj.* helpless

impulsif/ive *adj.* impulsive

inactif/ive *adj.* inactive

incertain(e) *adj.* uncertain

incertitude *f.* indecision

inciter to prompt

inclure (*p.p.* **inclu**) *irreg.* to include

incomparable *adj.* incomparable

incomplet/ète *adj.* incomplete

inconnu(e) *adj.* unknown

inconscient(e) (de) *adj.* unaware (of)

inconvénient *m.* inconvenience

incorporer to include

incrédule *adj.* incredulous; **d'un ton incrédule** incredulously

incrédulité *f.* disbelief

incroyable *adj.* unbelievable

incrusté(e) *adj.* inlaid

Inde *f.* India

indécis(e) *adj.* indecisive

indéfini(e) *adj.* indefinite; **article** (*m.*) **indéfini** *Gram.* indefinite article

indépendance *f.* independence

indépendant(e) *adj.* independent

indépendantiste *adj.* separatist

indicateur/trice *adj.*: **poteau** (*m.*) **indicateur** signpost

indicatif *m., Gram.* indicative (*verb tense*)

indice *m.* indication; **indices d'audience** ratings

indien(ne) *adj.* Indian; **Indien(e)** *m., f.* Indian (*person*)

indifférence *f.* indifference

indifférent(e) *adj.* indifferent

indiquer to show, indicate; **est-ce que vous pourriez m'indiquer le chemin pour aller à... ?** could you show me the way to . . . ?

indirect(e) *adj.* indirect; **discours** (*m.*) **indirect** *Gram.* indirect speech; **pronom** (*m.*) **complément d'objet indirect** *Gram.* indirect object pronoun

indiscret/ète *adj.* indiscreet

indispensable *adj.* indispensable

industrie *f.* industry

industriel(le) *adj.* commercial; **genie** (*f.*) **industrielle** industrial engineering

inférieur(e) *adj.* inferior

infiltrer to infiltrate

infinitif *m., Gram.* infinitive

infirmier/ière *m., f.* nurse

inflation *f.* inflation

inflexible *adj.* inflexible

influence *f.* influence

influencer (nous influençons) to influence

information *f.* information; data

informations *f. pl.* news; news program

informatique *f.* computer science; **réseau** (*m.*) **informatique** computer network

informer: s'informer to find out, become informed

ingénieur (femme ingénieur) *m., f.* engineer

ingénieux/euse *adj.* ingenious

ingrédient *m.* ingredient

injuste *adj.* unjust, not right

innocence *f.* innocence

innocent(e) *adj.* innocent

innovateur/trice *adj.* innovating

inquiet (inquiète) *adj.* anxious, worried

inquiéter: s'inquiéter (de, pour) (je m'inquiète) to worry (about)

inquiétude *f.* worry, anxiety

inscription *f.* inscription; writing

inscrire: s'inscrire (*like* **écrire**) *irreg.* to register

insigne *m.* badge, insignia

insistance *f.* insistence, tenacity

insister to insist

inspiration *f.* inspiration

inspirer to inspire

installer: s'installer to settle, set up (*house*)

instant *m.* instant, moment

institut *m.* institute; **institut de beauté** beauty parlor

instituteur/trice *m., f.* elementary school teacher

instruction *f.* instruction, education

instrument *m.* (musical) instrument; **jouer d'un instrument** to play a musical instrument

intacte *adj.* intact

intégrant(e) *adj.* essential; **partie** (*f.*) **intégrante** essential/integral part

intégration *f.* integration

intellectuel(le) *adj.* intellectual

intelligent(e) *adj.* intelligent
intensif/ive *adj.* intensive
intensifier: s'intensifier to intensify
interculturel(le) *adj.* intercultural
interdire (*like* **dire,** *but* **vous interdisez**) *irreg.* to forbid
interdit(e) *adj.* prohibited
intéressant(e) *adj.* interesting
intéresser to interest; **s'intéresser à** to be interested in
intérêt *m.* interest; concern; **sans intérêt** of no interest
intérieur(e) *adj.* interior; **intérieur** *m.* interior; **à l'intérieur des terres** in the center of the country
interjection *f., Gram.* interjection
intermédiaire *m.* intermediary
international(e) *adj.* international
internaute *m., f.* Internet user
interne *adj.* internal
interpeller to call out to
interprétation *f.* interpretation
interprète *m., f.* interpreter
interrogatif/ive *adj., Gram.* interrogative
interroger (**nous interrogeons**) to question
interrompre (*like* **rompre**) *irreg.* to interrupt
interruption *f.* interruption
interview *f.* interview
interviewer to interview
intime *adj.* intimate; personal; **journal** (*m.*) **intime** diary
intolérable *adj.* intolerable
intonation *f.* intonation
intoxiqué(e) *adj.* intoxicated
introduction *f.* introduction
introduire (*like* **conduire**) *irreg.* to introduce
intrus(e) *m., f.* intruder
inutile *adj.* useless, no use
invasion *f.* invasion
inventer to invent
invention *f.* invention
inversion *f.* reversal
invitation *f.* invitation
inviter (à) to invite (*s.o.*) (to)
invoquer to invoke, call upon
ironique *adj.* ironic
irrégulier/ière *adj., Gram.* irregular
irremplaçable *adj.* irreplaceable
irrité(e) *adj.* irritated
islamique *adj.* Islamic
isoler to isolate
Israël *m.* Israel
israélien(ne) *adj.* Israeli; **Israélien(ne)** *m., f.* Israeli (*person*)
Italie *f.* Italy
italien(ne) *adj.* Italian; **Italien(ne)** *m., f.* Italian (*person*)

italique *m.*: **en italique** in italic type
itinéraire *m.* itinerary

jamais *adv.* never; **jamais plus** never again; **ne... jamais** never, not ever
jambe *f.* leg
jambon *m.* ham
janvier *m.* January
Japon *m.* Japan
japonais(e) *adj.* Japanese; **Japonais(e)** *m., f.* Japanese (*person*)
jardin *m.* garden; **jardin des plantes** botanical garden
jarret (*m.*) **de porc** ham hocks
jaune *adj.* yellow; **pages** (*f. pl.*) **jaunes** yellow pages
jazz *m.* jazz
je *pron.* I; **j'ai (vingt) ans** I'm (twenty) years old; **je m'appelle...** my name is . . .; **je ne sais pas** I don't know; **je (ne) suis (pas) d'accord** I (don't) agree; **je suppose** I suppose; **je voudrais** I would like
jean *m. s.* jeans
jeep *m.* jeep
jet *m.*: **douche** (*f.*) **au jet** high-pressure shower
jeter (**je jette**) to throw
jeu (*pl.* **jeux**) *m.* game; **jeu de rôle** role play
jeudi *m.* Thursday
jeune *adj.* young; **jeune fille** *f.* girl; unmarried woman
jeûner to fast
jeunesse *f.* youth
job *m.* job
Joconde: La Joconde *f.* Mona Lisa (*painting*)
jogging *m.* jogging; **faire du jogging** to go jogging; **piste** (*f.*) **de jogging** jogging trail
joie *f.* joy; **joie de vivre** joy in living
joindre (**je joins, nous joignons**) *irreg.* to join
joli(e) *adj.* pretty
jouer to play; to act; **jouer à un sport/un jeu** to play a sport/game; **jouer d'un instrument** to play a musical instrument
jouet *m.* toy
joueur/euse *m., f.* player
jour *m.* day; **carnet du jour** society column; **jour férié** legal holiday; **par jour** per day; **plat** (*m.*) **du jour** today's special; **quel jour sommes-nous?** what day is it today?; **tous les jours** every day
journal (*pl.* **journaux**) *m.* newspaper; **journal intime** diary; **journal universitaire** college newspaper
journalisme *m.* journalism

journaliste *m., f.* journalist
journée *f.* (*whole*) day; **bonne journée** have a good day; **en fin** (*f.*) **de journée** at the end of the day; **toute la journée** all day
jovien(ne) *m., f.* inhabitant of Jupiter
joyeux/euse *adj.* joyous, joyful
judaïsme *m.* Judaism
judas *m.* peephole
judéo-arabe *adj.* Judeo-Arab
juge *m.* judge
jugement *m.* judgment
juif (juive) *adj.* Jewish
juillet *m.* July
juin *m.* June
jumeau (jumelle) *m., f.* twin
jupe *f.* skirt
jus *m.* juice; **jus d'orange** orange juice
jusque (jusqu'à, jusqu'en) *prep.* up to; as far as; until; **jusqu'à** until; **jusqu'à ce que** until
juste *adj.* just; fair
justice *f.* justice; **rendre justice à** to do justice to
justifier to justify

kilo *m.* kilogram; **demi-kilo** half kilogram
kilomètre (km) *m.* kilometer; **kilomètres à l'heure** kilometers per hour
kinésithérapeute *m., f.* massage therapist
kinésithérapie *f.* massage therapy
kiosque *m.* kiosk

la (l') *art., f. s.* the; *pron., f. s.* her, it
là *adv.* there; **là-bas** over there
laboratoire *m.* laboratory
lac *m.* lake; **au bord d'un lac** on a lake shore
lâche *adj.* cowardly
laid(e) *adj.* ugly
laine *f.* wool
laisser to leave; to allow
laissez-passer *m.* security pass
lait *m.* milk; **café** (*m.*) **au lait** coffee with milk; **lait caillé** curdled milk (*similar to sour cream*)
laitier/ière *adj.* dairy; **produits** (*m. pl.*) **laitiers** dairy products
lampe *f.* lamp
lancer (**nous lançons**) to launch
langage *m.* language, speech
langue *f.* language; **langue étrangère** foreign language; **langue seconde** second/foreign language
lapin *m.* rabbit
large *adj.* wide
larme *f.* tear; **au bord des larmes** on the verge of tears
latin(e) *adj.* Latin; **Quartier** (*m.*) **latin** Latin quarter
lavabo *m.* bathroom sink

lave-linge *m.* washing machine

laver: se laver to get washed, wash up; **se laver les cheveux (les mains)** to wash one's hair (hands)

lave-vaisselle *f.* dishwasher

le (l') *art., m. s.* the; *pron., m. s.* him, it

leçon *f.* lesson

lecteur *m.* reader; **courrier des lecteurs** letters to the editor; **lecteur de CD** CD player

lecture *f.* reading

légende *f.* caption

leger/ère *adj.* light (*weight*)

légion (*f.*) **d'honneur** legion of honor

légume *m.* vegetable

lendemain *m.* next day

lent(e) *adj.* slow

lentilles *f. pl.* lentils

lequel (laquelle, lesquels, lesquelles) *pron.* who; whom; which

les *art., m., f., pl.* the; *pron., m., f., pl.* them

lessive *f.* laundry; **faire la lessive** to do the laundry

lettre *f.* letter; **boîte** (*f.*) **aux lettres electronique** electronic mailbox; **lettre d'amour** love letter

leur (*pl.* **leurs**) *adj.* their; **leur** *pron. m., f., pl.* to/for them; **le/la/les leur(s)** *pron.* theirs

levain *m.* yeast

lever: se lever (je me lève) to get up (*out of bed*); to stand up

lèvres *f. pl.* lips; **se maquiller les lèvres** to put on lipstick

lexique *m.* glossary

liaison *f., Gram.* liaison

libéral(e) *adj.* liberal

libération *f.* liberation

libéré(e) *adj.* liberated

liberté *f.* liberty

librairie *f.* bookstore

libre *adj.* free; **ils vivent en union libre** they are living together (without marriage); **zone** (*f.*) **libre** free zone

licenciement *m.* dismissal, firing (*from a job*)

licencier to fire (*from a job*)

lifting *m.* facelift

lier to link, join

lieu (*pl.* **lieux**) *m.* place, location; **au lieu de** instead of; **avoir lieu** to take place; **lieu de naissance** birthplace

lieue *f.* league (*unit of measure*)

ligne *f.* line; **ligne téléphonique** telephone line

limite *f.* limit; **limite de vitesse** speed limit

limiter to limit, restrict

linge *m.* laundry; **lave-linge** *m.* washing machine

linguistique *adj.* linguistic

lire (*p.p.* **lu**) *irreg.* to read

lit *m.* bed; **faire le lit** to make the bed

lithium *m.* lithium

littéraire *adj.* literary; **arabe littéraire** classical Arabic

littérature *f.* literature

livraison *f.* delivery

livre *m.* book

livre *f.* pound (*approx. half kilo*)

local (*pl.* **locaux**) *m.* premises; business; facility; **local de recherche** research facility

location *f.* rental; **agence** (*f.*) **de location** car rental agency

logement *m.* lodging; place of residence

logique *f.* logic; *adj.* logical

loi *f.* law

loin *adv.* far; **loin de** *prep.* far from

lointain *adj.* faraway, distant

loisirs *m. pl.* leisure activities

long(ue) *adj.* long

longer (nous longeons) to walk along

longtemps *adv.* (for) a long time

longueur *f.* length

lors de *prep.* at the time of

lorsque *conj.* when

lôtissement *m.* (housing) development

louer to rent

loyer *m.* rent; **habitation** (*f.*) **à loyer modéré (HLM)** low-income housing

lugubre *adj.* gloomy

lui *pron., m., f.* him; to/for him/her

lumière *f.* light; **mettre la lumière** turn on the light

lundi *m.* Monday

lune *f.* moon

lunettes *f. pl.* glasses; **lunettes de soleil** sunglasses

leurre *m.* deception

lutter to fight

luxueux/euse *adj.* luxurious

lycée *m.* secondary school

ma *adj.* my

machine (*f.*) **à laver** washing machine

madame (*ab.* **Mme**) (*pl.* **mesdames**) *f.* madam; ma'am (*ab.* Mrs.)

mademoiselle (*ab.* **Mlle**) (*pl.* **mesdemoiselles**) *f.* miss (*ab.* Miss)

magasin *m.* store; **grand magasin** department store

magazine *m.* magazine

Maghreb *m.* Maghreb (Morocco, Algeria, Tunisia)

maghrébin(e) *adj.* from the Maghreb

magie *f.* magic

magnétoscope *m.* videocassette recorder (VCR)

magnifique *adj.* magnificent, great

mai *m.* May

maillot (*m.*) **de bain** swimsuit

main *f.* hand; **sac** (*m.*) **à main** handbag

main-d'œuvre *f.* manpower, workforce

maintenant *adv.* now

mairie *f.* mayor's office

mais *conj.* but

maïs *m.* corn

maison *f.* house; **maison particulière** private home; **rentrer à la maison** to go home

maître (maîtresse) *m., f.* elementary school teacher

majeur(e) *adj.* major

majorité *f.* majority

majuscule *adj., Gram.* uppercase (*alphabet letter*)

mal *adv.* badly; **au plus mal** very ill; **avoir du mal (à)** to have a hard time (*doing s.th.*); **avoir mal (à)** to have pain / an ache (in); to have a sore...; **avoir mal au cœur** to feel nauseated; **avoir mal au ventre** to have a stomachache **se faire mal (à)** to hurt (a part of one's body)

malade *adj.* sick; *m., f.* sick person; patient; **garde-malade** *m., f.* nurse's aide; **tomber malade** to fall ill

maladie *f.* illness

malaise *m.* weakness, fainting spell

malentendu *m.* misunderstanding

malheur *m.* unhappiness, misery

malheureux/euse *adj.* unhappy, miserable

malhonnête *adj.* dishonest

malien(ne) *adj.* from Mali; **Malien(ne)** *m., f.* person from Mali

maman *f., fam.* mommy

mammifère *m.* mammal

manche *f.* sleeve; **La Manche** *f.* English Channel

manchette *f.* headline

mandarin(e) *adj.* Mandarin

manger (nous mangeons) to eat; **salle** (*f.*) **à manger** dining room

manifestation *f.* (*public, political*) demonstration; outward sign; **manifestation culturelle** cultural event

manquer à to be missed by (*s.o.*); **tu me manques** I miss you

manteau *m.* overcoat

mantille *f.* mantilla

manuscrit *m.* manuscript

maquillage *m.* makeup; makeup room

maquiller: se maquiller to put on makeup; **se maquiller les yeux (les lèvres)** to make up one's eyes (one's lips)

maquis *m.* scrub, bush; French Resistance

maquisard(e) *m., f.* French Resistance fighter

marathon *m.* marathon race

marchand(e) *m., f.* merchant

marché *m.* market; **bon marché** cheap; **supermarché** *m.* supermarket

marcher to walk; to work (properly); **ça marche** that works for me

mardi *m.* Tuesday

maréchal *m.* marshal, field marshal

mari *m.* husband

mariage *m.* marriage; **anniversaire** (*m.*) **de mariage** wedding anniversary

marié(e) *adj.* married

marier: se marier to get married

marine nationale *f.* Marines

maritime *adj.* maritime

marketing *m.* marketing

marmite *f.* large iron cooking pot

Maroc *m.* Morroco

marocain(e) *adj.* Moroccan; **Marocain(e)** *m., f.* Moroccan (*person*)

marque *f.* brand

marquer to mark

marraine *f.* godmother

marron *adj., inv.* chestnut brown

mars *m.* March

marseillais(e) *adj.* from Marseille; **Marseillais(e)** *m., f.* person from Marseille

martiniquais(e) *adj.* from Martinique; **Martiniquais(e)** *m., f.* person from Martinique

martyr *m.* martyr

masculin(e) *adj.* masculine

massacre *m.* massacre

massage *m.* massage

massif *m.* old rounded mountain range

match *m.* (**de foot, de boxe**) (soccer, boxing) match

matelot *m.* sailor

matérialiste *adj.* materialistic

maternel(e) *adj.* maternal; **école** (*f.*) **maternelle** nursery school, preschool

mathématiques (*fam.* **maths**) *f. pl.* mathematics

matière *f.* (school) subject; substance; **matières grasses** (*meat*) fat

matin *m.* morning; **ce matin** this morning; **du matin** in the morning

matinée *f.* morning (*duration*)

mauritanien(ne) *adj.* Mauritanian; **Mauritanien(ne)** *m., f.* Mauritanian (*person*)

mauvais(e) *adj.* bad; **de mauvaise humeur** in a bad mood; **il fait mauvais** it's bad weather

maxichaud(e) *adj., fam.* extremely warm

maxima *f.* maximum

maximal(e) *adj.* highest

maxime *f.* maxim, saying

maximum *m.* maximum

mayonnaise *f.* mayonnaise; **œuf** (*m.*) **dur mayonnaise** hard-boiled egg with mayonnaise

me *pron.* me; to/for me

mec *m., fam.* guy

mécanicien(ne) *m.* mechanic

mécanique *adj.* mechanical; **génie** (*f.*) **mécanique** mechanical engineering

méchant(e) *adj.* mean, nasty

méchoui *m.* whole lamb roasted on a spit over open coals

mécontent(e) *adj.* displeased

mecque: La Mecque *f.* Mecca

médaillon *m.* locket

médecin (femme médecin) *m., f.* doctor

médecine *f.* medicine (*profession*); **médecine douce** alternative medicine

média *m. pl.* media

médiathèque *f.* media library

médical(e) (*pl.* **médicaux, médicales**) *adj.* medical; **soins** (*m. pl.*) **médicaux** health care

médicament *m.* medicine, drug

médiéval(e) *adj.* medieval

médina *f.* old portion of an Arab city

médiocre *adj.* mediocre; dull

méditation *f.* meditation

méditerranéen(ne) *adj.* Mediterranean

méfiant(e) *adj.* suspicious

méfier: se méfier to distrust

meilleur(e) *adj.* (**que**) better (than); **le/la/les meilleur(e)(s)** the best

mél *m.* e-mail message

mélanésien(ne) *adj.* Melanesian; **Mélanésien(ne)** *m., f.* Melanesian (*person*)

mélange *m.* mixture

mélanger (nous mélangeons) to mix

mélodrame *m.* melodrama

membre *m.* member

même *adj.* same; **elle-même** herself; **même chose** *f.* same thing; **nous-mêmes** ourselves

mémoires *m. pl.* memoires

mémorial (*pl.* **mémoriaux**) *m.* memorial

ménage *m.* housekeeping; **faire le ménage** to do housework

mener (**je mène**) (**à**) to lead (to)

mensonge *m.* lie

mentalité *f.* mindset, attitude

menteur/euse *m., f.* liar

menthe *f.* mint; **thé** (*m.*) **à la menthe** mint tea

mentionné(e) *adj.* mentioned

mentir (*like* **sortir**) *irreg.* to lie

menu *m.* menu

mer *f.* sea; **département** (*m.*) **d'outre-mer (DOM)** overseas department; **fruits** (*m. pl.*) **de mer** seafood; **territoire** (*m.*) **d'outre-mer (TOM)** overseas territory

merci *interj.* thank you

mercredi *m.* Wednesday

mercure *m.* Mercury

mère *f.* mother; **belle-mère** *f.* stepmother; mother-in-law; **fête** (*f.*) **des mères** Mother's Day; **grand-mère** *f.* grandmother

mériter to deserve

mes *adj.* my

message *m.* message; **message électronique** e-mail message

messe *f.* mass

mesure *f.* measure; **mesure d'exclusion** segregation policy

mesurer to measure

métabolique *adj.* metabolical

métamorphoser to change

météo *f., fam.* weather report, forecast

météorologique *adj.* meteorological; **carte** (*f.*) **météorologique** weather map

méthode *f.* method; **méthodes de cuisson** cooking methods

métier *m.* skilled trade

métro *m.* subway; **plan** (*m.*) **du métro** subway map; **réseau** (*m.*) **du métro** subway system

métropolitain(e) *adj.* metropolitan

metteur en scène *m.* director (*theatrical*)

mettre (*p.p.* **mis**) *irreg.* to put (on); to turn on ; **mettre du temps à** to spend time on; **mettre en ordre** to put in order; **mettre fin à** to put an end to; **mettre la radio/télé/lumière** to turn on the radio/TV/light; **mettre la table** to set the table; **mettre un vêtement** to put on a piece of clothing

meuble *m.* piece of furniture

meurette: en meurette in wine sauce

mexicain(e) *adj.* Mexican; **Mexicain(e)** *m., f.* Mexican (*person*)

Mexique *m.* Mexico

micro-ondes: four à micro-ondes *m.* microwave oven

micro-ordinateur *m.* personal computer

microphone *m.* microphone

microscope *m.* microscope

midi *m.* noon; **cet après-midi** *m.* this afternoon; **de l'après-midi** in the afternoon; **il est midi** it is noon

mien: le/la/les mien(ne)(s) *pron.* mine

mieux *adv.* (**que**) better (than); **aimer mieux** to prefer; **ça va mieux?** are you feeling better?

migraine *f.* migraine (headache)

migration *f.* migration

mil *m.* millet

milice *f.* militia

milieu *m.* environment; middle; **au milieu de** in the middle of

militaire *adj.* military; *m. pl.* the military

mille *adj.* thousand

millénaire *m.* millennium

milliard *m.* one billion

millier *m.* (around) a thousand

millimètre *m.* millimeter
million *m.* one million
millionaire *m.* millionaire
mime *m., f.* mime
mince *adj.* thin
minérai *m.* ore; **exploitation** (*f.*) **du minérai** mining of the ore
minéral(e) *adj.* mineral; **eau** (*f.*) **minérale gazeuse (plate)** carbonated (noncarbonated, flat) mineral water
minéralogie *f.* mineralogy
minéraux *m. pl.* minerals
mini-golf *m.* miniature golf
minima *f.* minimum
minimal(e) *adj.* minimal
minimum *m.* minimum
ministère *m.* ministry
ministre *m.* minister; **premier ministre** prime minister
Minitel *m.* Minitel (*French personal communications system*)
minoritaire *adj.* minority
minorité *f.* minority
minuit *m.* midnight
minuscule *adj., Gram.* lowercase (alphabet letter)
minute *f.* minute
miroir *m.* mirror
misanthrope *m.* misanthrope
mise *f.* putting; placing; **mise en contexte** putting into context; **mise en scène** (theatrical) production
misérable *adj.* miserable
mi-temps *f. inv.*: **à mi-temps** part-time
mixte *adj.* mixed
mobile *adj.* mobile
moche *adj., fam.* awful; ugly
mode *f.* fashion
mode *m.* method; *Gram.* mood; **mode d'emploi** directions for use
modèle *m.* model
modéré(e) *adj.* moderate; **habitation** (*f.*) **à loyer modéré (HLM)** low-income housing
moderne *adj.* modern
moelleux/euse *adj.* smooth, velvety
moi *pron., s.* me; I (*emphatic*); **à moi** mine; **chez moi** at my place; **excusez-moi** excuse me
moindre *adj.*: **le moindre problème** the slightest problem
moins *adv.* less; minus; before (the hour); fewer; **au moins** at least; **de moins en moins** less and less; **le moins** + *adv.* the least + *adv.*; **le/la/les moins** + *adj.* the least + *adj.*; **le/la/les moins de** + *n.* the least/fewest + *n.*; **moins** + *adj./adv.* + **que** less + *adj./adv.* + than; **moins de** + *n.* + **que** less/fewer + *n.* + than; **moins le quart** quarter to (the hour) (5); *v.* + **le**

moins *v.* + the least; *v.* + **moins que** *v.* + less than
mois *m.* month
moitié *f.* half
moment *m.* moment; **moments clés** key moments
mon *adj.* my
monde *m.* world; **les quatre coins** (*m. pl.*) **du monde** the far reaches of the world, the four corners of the world; **monde du travail** work world; **monde francophone** French-speaking world; **tout le monde** everyone
mondial(e) *adj.* worldwide; **Deuxième Guerre** (*f.*) **mondiale** Second World War
monoculture *f.* monoculture
monoparental(e) *adj.* single-parent
monotone *adj.* monotonous
monsieur (*ab.* **M.**) (*pl.* **messieurs**) *m.* sir; mister (*ab.* Mr.)
mont *m.* mount; mountain
montagne *f.* mountain
montant *m.* amount (*of a check or sale*)
montée *f.* climb; ascendancy
monter to go up; to climb; **monter à cheval** to go horseback riding; **monter une rue** to go up a street
montréalais(e) *adj.* from Montreal; **Montréalais(e)** *m., f.* person from Montreal
montrer to show
monument *m.* monument
moral(e) *adj.* moral
morale *f.* moral (*philosophy*)
morceau *m.* piece
mort *f.* death
mosquée *f.* mosque
mot *m.* word; **doux mots d'amour** sweet nothings; **le mot juste** the right word; **mot-clé** *m.* key word; **mot apparenté** cognate; **mots croisés** crossword puzzle
motivation *f.* motivation
moto *f., fam.* motorcycle
mouchoir *m.* handkerchief; **mouchoir en papier** facial tissue
moules *f. pl.* mussels
moulin *m.* mill
mourir (*p.p.* **mort**) *irreg.* to die
mousse *f.* mousse; **mousse au chocolat** chocolate mousse
mouton *m.* sheep; mutton
mouvement *m.* movement
mouvementé(e) *adj.* lively
moyen *m.* means, method, mode; **moyen de transport** means of transportation
moyen(ne) *adj.* moderate, average; **classe** (*f.*) **moyenne** middle class; **en moyenne** on average
mulâtre *adj.* mulatto, of mixed race
multiplication *f.* multiplication

multiplicité *f.* multiplicity
municipal(e) (*pl.* **municipaux**) *adj.* municipal
mur *m.* wall
muscle *m.* muscle
musculaire *adj.* muscular
musculation *f.* weight training
musée *m.* museum; **conservateur/ trice** (*m., f.*) **de musée** museum curator; **musée d'art (de sciences naturelles)** art (natural science) museum
musical(e) (*pl.* **musicaux**) *adj.* musical
musicien(ne) *m., f.* musician
musique *f.* music
musts *m. pl.* things one must do or have
musulman(e) *adj.* Muslim
mystère *m.* mystery
mystérieux/euse *adj.* mysterious
mythe *m.* myth
mythique *adj.* mythical

nager (nous nageons) to swim
naissance *f.* birth; **anniversaire** (*m.*) **de naissance** birthday; **date** (*f.*) **de naissance** birth date; **lieu** (*m.*) **de naissance** birthplace
naître (*p.p.* **né**) *irreg.* to be born
nappe *f.* tablecloth
narrateur/trice *m., f.* narrator
narration *f.* narrative, account
natal(e) *adj.* native; **ville** (*f.*) **natale** birthplace
nation *f.* nation
national(e) (*pl.* **nationaux**) *adj.* national; **fête** (*f.*) **nationale** national holiday
nationalisme *m.* nationalism
nationalité *f.* nationality
nature *f.* nature
naturel(le) *adj.* natural; **histoire** (*f.*) **naturelle** natural history; **sciences** (*f. pl.*) **naturelles** natural science
nautique *adj.* nautical; **faire du ski nautique** to waterski
navet *m.* turnip; **c'est un navet** it's awful, terrible, a flop
naviguer to navigate; **naviguer le Web** to surf the Web
nazi *adj.* Nazi
ne (n') *adv.* no; not; **ce n'est pas** this/that/ it is not; **ce ne sont pas** these/those/ they are not; **il n'est pas nécessaire** it is not necessary; **ne... aucun(e)** not any; **ne... jamais** not ever, never; **ne... ni... ni...** neither . . . nor; **ne... pas** not; **ne... pas du tout** not at all, absolutely not; **ne... pas encore** not yet; **ne... personne** no one, nobody; **ne... plus** not anymore, no longer; **ne... point** absolutely not; **ne... que** only; **ne... rien** nothing; **n'est-ce pas?** isn't that right?

néandertal *m.*: **homme** (*m.*) **du Néandertal** Neanderthal man
nécessaire *adj.* necessary; **si nécessaire** if necessary
nécessité *f.* necessity
nécrologie *f.* obituary column; obituary
négatif/ive *adj.* negative
négation *f.*, *Gram.* negative
négliger (**nous négligeons**) to neglect
négocier to negotiate
neige *f.* snow; **faire du surf de neige** to snowboard; **planche** (*f.*) **à neige** snowboard
neiger to snow; **il neige** it's snowing
nerveux/euse *adj.* nervous, high-strung
neuf *adj.* nine; **dix-neuf** nineteen
neuf (**neuve**) *adj.* new
neuvième *adj.* ninth
neveu *m.* nephew
nez *m.* nose; **nez qui coule** runny nose
ni *conj.* neither, nor; **ne... ni... ni...** neither . . . nor
nièce *f.* niece
noces *f. pl.* wedding; **voyage** (*m.*) **de noces** honeymoon
Noël *m.* Christmas; **père** (*m.*) **Noël** Santa Claus
noir(e) *adj.* black; **pieds-noirs** *m. pl.* French people born in North Africa
noix *f.* nut; **noix de coco** coconut
nom *m.* name; **nom d'un chien!** *interj.* darn it!
nomade *m., f.* nomad
nombre *m.* number; **nombres ordinaux** ordinal numbers
nombreux/euse *adj.* numerous
nommer to name
non *interj.* no, not; **bien sûr que non!** of course not!; **non?** isn't that right?; **non plus** neither, not either
non-fumeur: wagon non-fumeur nonsmoking train car
non-polluant(e) *adj.* nonpolluting
nord *m.* north
normal(e) *adj.* normal; **il est normal** it's to be expected
nos *adj.* our
note *f.* grade (*on a school paper*); note; **bloc-notes** (*pl.* **blocs-notes** *m.* pad of paper; **prendre des notes** to take notes
noter to take note (of); to notice; to grade (*papers*); **notez bien** take note
notre *adj.* our
nôtre: le/la/les nôtre(s) *pron.* ours
nourrir to feed
nourriture *f.* food
nous *pron.* we; us; to/for us; **nous-mêmes** ourselves
nouveau (**nouvel, nouvelle** [*pl.* **nouveaux, nouvelles**]) *adj.* new; **à/de**

nouveau again; **le nouvel an** New Year's Day
nouveauté *f.* novelty; change
nouvelle *f.* piece of news
novembre *m.* November
nuage *m.* cloud
nuageux/euse *adj.* cloudy
nucléaire *adj.* nuclear
nue *f.* cloud
nuisible *adj.* harmful
nuit *f.* night; **boîte** (*f.*) **de nuit** nightclub; **bonne nuit** good night
numéro *m.* number; **composer un numéro** dial a (phone) number

obéir (à) to obey
obésité *f.* obesity
objectif *m.* objective
objectif/ive *adj.* objective
objection *f.* objection
objet *m.* object; **pronom** (*m.*) **complément d'objet direct (indirect)** *Gram.* direct (indirect) object pronoun
obligation *f.* obligation
obligatoire *adj.* obligatory
obligé(e) *adj.* obligated
observateur/trice *m., f.* observer
observation *f.* observation
observer to observe
obstacle *m.* obstacle
obtenir (*like* **tenir**) *irreg.* to obtain
occasion *f.* opportunity; occasion; **à l'occasion de** at the time of; **avoir l'occasion** to have the chance
occidental(e) (*pl.* **occidentaux**) *adj.* western
occitan(e) *adj.* of the Provençal language
occupation *f.* occupation
occuper to occupy; **s'occuper de** to take care of
océan *m.* ocean
octobre *m.* October
ode *f.* ode
odeur *f.* odor, smell
œil (*pl.* **yeux**) *m.* eye
œuf *m.* egg; **œuf dur mayonnaise** hard-boiled egg with mayonnaise; **œufs en meurette** eggs in wine sauce
œuvre *f.* work (of art, literature, music); body of work; **chef-d'œuvre** (*pl.* **chefs-d'œuvre**) *m.* masterpiece; **main d'œuvre** *f.* manpower, workforce
office *m.* office
officiel(le) *adj.* official
officier *m.* officer
offrir (*like* **ouvrir**) *irreg.* to offer; to give
oignon *m.* onion; **oignon vert** green onion; **soupe** (*f.*) **à l'oignon** French onion soup
oiseau *m.* bird
O.K.? *interj.* okay?

olive *f.* olive; **huile** (*f.*) **d'olive** olive oil
olympique *adj.* olympic
omelette *f.* omelet
on *pron.* one; we, they, people, you
oncle *m.* uncle
onde *f.* wave; **four** (*m.*) **à micro-ondes** microwave oven
onze *adj.* eleven
opéra *m.* opera
opération *f.* operation; tactic
opéré(e) *adj.* operated
opinion *f.* opinion
optimiste *adj.* optimistic
option *f.* option
orage *m.* thunderstorm
oral(e) *adj.* oral
orange *adj., inv.* orange; *m.* orange (*color*); *f.* orange (*fruit*); **jus** (*m.*) **d'orange** orange juice
orchestre *m.* orchestra; band
ordinaire *adj.* ordinary; regular
ordinal(e) *adj.* ordinal; **nombres** (*m. pl.*) **ordinaux** ordinal numbers
ordinateur *m.* computer
ordonnance *f.* prescription
ordre *m.* order; **mettre en ordre** to put in order
oreille *f.* ear
organe *m.* organ (*body part*)
organisation *f.* organization
organiser to organize; **s'organiser** to organize oneself
orge *f.* barley
oriental(e) (*pl.* **orientaux**) *adj.* oriental, eastern
originaire (*adj.*) **de** originating from
originalité *f.* originality
origine *f.* origin
orthographe *f.* spelling
otage *m., f.* hostage
ou *conj.* or
où *adv., pron.* where; when: in/on which; **où se trouve... ?** where is . . . ?
oublier to forget
ouest *m.* west; **sud-ouest** *m.* southwest
oui *interj.* yes; **bien sûr que oui!** yes, of course!
ours *m.* bear
outre *prep.* besides, over and above; **département** (*m.*) **d'outre-mer (DOM)** overseas department; **outre-mer** *adv.* overseas; **territoire** (*m.*) **d'outre-mer (TOM)** overseas territory
ouvert(e) *adj.* open; **ouvert(e) d'esprit** open-minded
ouverture *f.* opening; **horaires** (*m. pl.*) **d'ouverture** hours when open
ouvrier/ière *m., f.* manual laborer
ouvrir (*p.p.* **ouvert**) *irreg.* to open
oxygène *m.* oxygen

page *f.* page; **page d'accueil** home page; **page perso** personal home page; **pages jaunes** yellow pages

pain *m.* bread; **pain artisanal** hand-crafted bread; **pain de campagne** country-style wheat bread; **petit pain** bread roll

paire *f.* pair

paix *f.* peace; **Corps** (*m.*) **de la paix** Peace Corps

Pakistan *m.* Pakistan

pakistanais(e) *adj.* Pakistani; **Pakistanais(e)** *m., f.* Pakistani (*person*)

palais *m.* palace; **palais du roi** king's palace

pâle *adj.* pale

panier *m.* basket

panne *f.* breakdown (*mechanical*); **panne d'électricité** power outage

pantalon *m. s.* pants, trousers

papa *m., fam.* papa, daddy

papeterie *f.* stationery store

papier *m.* paper; **feuille** (*f.*) **de papier** sheet of paper; **mouchoir** (*m.*) **en papier** facial tissue

papy *m., fam.* grandpa

pâque *f.* Passover

paquebot *m.* ocean liner

Pâques *m. s., f. pl.* Easter

par *prep.* by; per ; **par chèque (carte de crédit)** by check (credit card); **par cœur** by heart; **par exemple** for example; **par jour (semaine,** *etc.***)** per day (week, etc.); **par rapport à** with respect to; **par train (avion,** *etc.***)** by train (plane, etc.); **passer par** to pass by

paragraphe *m.* paragraph

paraître (*like* **connaître**) *irreg.* to seem, appear

parallèlement *adv.* in parallel, at the same time

parapente *m.*: **faire du parapente** to hang glide

paraphrase *f.* paraphrase

parc *m.* park

parcourir (*like* **courir**) *irreg.* to scan

pardon *interj.* pardon me

pardonner to excuse

parenté *f.* kinship, relationship; **quelle parenté?** what's the relationship?

parenthèse *f.* parenthesis; **entre parenthèses** in parentheses

parents *m. pl.* relatives; parents; **arrière-grands-parents** great-grandparents; **grands-parents** grandparents

parfait(e) *adj.* perfect

parfois *adv.* sometimes

parfum *m.* perfume

parisien(ne) *adj.* Parisian; **Parisien(ne)** *m., f.* Parisian (*person*)

parking *m.* parking lot, parking garage

parler to talk; to speak; **se parler** to talk to oneself

parmi *prep.* among

parole *f.* word

part *f.*: **à part cela** besides that; **de ma part** on my behalf; as for me, in my opinion; **quelque part** *adv.* somewhere

partage *m.* sharing

partager (nous partageons) to share

partenaire *m., f.* partner

parti *m.*: **parti politique** political party

participation *f.* participation

participe *m., Gram.* participle

participer to participate

particularité *f.* particularity

particulier/ière *adj.* particular; **en particulier** in particular; **maison** (*f.*) **particulière** private home

partie *f.* part; **faire partie de** to be a part of, belong to; **partie du corps** part of the body; **partie intégrante** essential/integral part

partiel(le) *adj.* partial; **à temps partiel** part-time

partir (*like* **dormir**) *irreg.* to leave (*a place*); **à partir de** beginning, starting from; **partir en voyage (vacances)** to go on a trip (vacation)

partisan(e) *m., f.* partisan, follower

partitif/ive *adj., Gram.* partitive

partout *adv.* everywhere; **presque partout** almost everywhere

parvenir (*like* **venir**) *irreg.* to reach

pas: ne... pas *adv.* not; **ce n'est pas** this/that it is not; **ne... pas du tout** not at all, absolutely not; **ne... pas encore** not yet; **pas de problème** no problem; **pourquoi pas?** why not?

passablement *adv.* fairly well

passage *m.* passage; **être de passage** to be passing through

passager/ère *m., f.* passenger

passé *m.* past; **passé composé** *Gram.* compound past tense

passeport *m.* passport

passer to pass; to spend; to be showing (*a film*); **en passant** in passing; **laissez-passer** *m.* security pass; **passer la douane** to go through customs; **passer le week-end** to spend the weekend; **passer par** to pass by; **passer un examen** to take an exam; **qu'est-ce qui se passe?** what's going on?; **se passer** to take place, to happen

passionant(e) *adj.* fascinating, gripping, exciting

passionné(e) *adj.* crazy/mad about

pastelliste *m., f.* artist who works in pastels

pastille *f.* lozenge, cough drop

pastis *m.* aperitif made with anise

pâté *m.* liver paste; pâté

paternel(le) *adj.* paternal

pâtes *f. pl.* pasta

patience *f.* patience; **perdre patience** to lose patience

patient(e) *adj.* patient

patin *m.* ice skate; **faire du patin à glace** to ice skate

patiner to ice skate

patisserie *f.* pastry bakery; pastry

patissier/ière *m., f.* pastry baker

patrie *f.* one's country, homeland

patriotique *adj.* patriotic

patron(ne) *m., f.* owner; boss

pauvre *adj.* poor; *m., f.* poor person

pavillon *m.* large building; private house

payant(e) *adj.* for which one must pay, not free; **chaîne** (*f.*) **privée payante** private subscription channel

payer (je paie) to pay

pays *m.* country

paysage *m.* landscape; scenery

paysan(ne) *m., f.* country dweller; peasant, farmer

pêche *f.* fishing; **aller à la pêche** to go fishing

pêcher to fish

pédagogique *adj.* pedagogical

peigner: se peigner to comb one's hair

peine *f.* punishment; **à peine** hardly

peintre (femme peintre) *m., f.* painter

peinture *f.* painting

pèlerinage *m.* pilgrimage

pendant *prep.* during; while; **pendant (cinq) heures** for (five) hours; **pendant combien de temps... ?** for how long . . . ?; **pendant les vacances** during vacation

pénétrer to enter, penetrate

pénible *adj.* painful; difficult

penicilline *f.* penicillin

pense *f.* slope

penser to think; **penser à** to think about; **penser de** to think of, to have an opinion about; **penser que** to think that

perception *f.* perception

perché(e) *adj.* perched

perdre to lose; **perdre la tête** to lose one's mind; **perdre patience** to lose patience; **se perdre** to get lost

perdu(e) *adj.* lost; **âmes** (*f. pl.*) **perdues** lost souls

père *m.* father; **beau-père** *m.* father-in-law, stepfather; **grand-père** *m.* grandfather; **père Noël** Santa Claus

période *f.* period (*of time*); **en période de** during times of

périphérique *adj.* peripheral

permanent(e) *adj.* permanent

permettre (*like* **mettre**) *irreg.* to permit, allow

permis *m.* permit

permission *f.* permission

persil *m.* parsley

persistent(e) *adj.* persistent
persister to persist, perservere
perso: page (*f.*) **perso** personal home page
personnage *m.* character
personnalité *f.* personality
personne *f.* person; **ne... personne** *pron. indef.* nobody, no one
personnel(le) *adj.* personal
pessimiste *adj.* pessimistic
pétanque: jouer à la pétanque to play lawn bowling
pétillant(e) *adj.* sparkling; fizzy; **vin** (*m.*) **pétillant** sparkling wine
petit(e) *adj.* small; **petit(e) ami(e)** *m., f.* boyfriend (girlfriend); **petit déjeuner** *m.* breakfast; **petit écran** *m.* small screen (TV); **petite-fille** *f.* granddaughter; **petites annonces** *f. pl.* classified ads; **petit-fils** *m.* grandson; **petit pain** *m.* bread roll; **petits pois** *m. pl.* peas; **tout(e) petit(e)** very little; at a young age
peu *adv.* little; few; hardly; **à peu près** about, nearly; **il est peu probable que** it is unlikely that; **un peu(de)** a little (of), a few (of)
peur *f.* fear; **avoir peur (de)** to be afraid (of); **faire peur à** to frighten
peut-être *adv.* perhaps
pharmacien(ne) *m., f.* pharmacist
phénomène *m.* phenomenon
philosophie (*fam.* **philo**) *f.* philosophy
photographie (*fam.* **photo**) *f.* photograph; **album-photo** *m.* photo album; **appareil photo** *m.* camera; **faire de la photographie** to take photographs; **prendre une photo** to take a photograph
photographe *m., f.* photographer
phrase *f.* sentence
physique *f.* physics; *adj.* physical
piano *m.* piano
pièce *f.* room; **deux-pièces** *m. s.* one-bedroom apartment **pièce de théâtre** play
pied *m.* foot; **à pied** on foot; **course** (*f.*) **à pied** running race; **pieds-noirs** *pl.* French people born in North Africa
piège *m.* trap
piéton(ne) *m., f.* pedestrian; **rue** (*f.*) **piétonne** pedestrian street
pilule (*f.*) **contraceptive** contraceptive pill
piment *m.* pimento, hot pepper
pion *m.* assistant (*in a school*)
piquant(e) *adj.* spicy
pique-nique *m.* picnic; **faire un pique-nique** to have a picnic
piqueniquer to have a picnic
piscine *f.* swimming pool
piste *f.* trail, track; ski run; lead; **piste de jogging** jogging trail

pita *m.* pita (bread)
pittoresque *adj.* picturesque
pizza *f.* pizza; **pizza surgelée** frozen pizza
placard *m.* cupboard
place *f.* place; (reserved) seat; public square; **à votre (ta) place** if I were you
plage *f.* beach
plaindre: se plaindre (nous nous plaignons) to complain
plaine *f.* plain
plainte *f.* complaint
plaire (*p.p.* **plu**) *irreg.* to please; **s'il vous (te) plaît** *interj.* please
plaisance *f.*: **port** (*m.*) **de plaisance** marina
plaisanter to joke/kid around
plaisanterie *f.* joke
plaisir *m.* pleasure; **avec plaisir** with pleasure, gladly
plan *m.* map (*subway, city, region*); plane; **arrière plan** background; **plan du métro** subway map; **sur le plan linguistic** linguistically
planche *f.* board; **faire de la planche à voile** to windsurf; **planche à neige** snowboard
planète *f.* planet
planifier to plan
plantation *f.* planting
plante *f.* plant; **jardin** (*m.*) **des plantes** botanical garden
planter to plant
plaque *f.*: **plaque électrique** burner (*on a stove*)
plastique *m., adj.* plastic; **arts** (*m. pl.*) **plastiques** visual arts (sculpture, painting, etc.)
plat *m.* dish; **plat (chaud, principal)** (hot, main) dish; **plat du jour** today's special
plat(e) *adj.* flat; **eau** (*f.*) **minérale plate** noncarbonated (flat) mineral water
plateau (*pl.* **plateaux**) *m.* plateau; set, stage (*cinema, television*)
plein(e) *adj.* full; **à plein temps** full-time; **en plein air** outdoors; **en pleine forme** in great shape
pleut: il pleut it's raining
pleurer to cry
pleuvoir (*p.p.* **plu**) *irreg.* to rain; **il pleut** it's raining
plier to fold
pluie *f.* rain
plupart *f.*: **la plupart (de)** most (of), the majority (of)
pluriel *m., Gram.* plural
plus *adv.* more; **au plus mal** very ill; **beaucoup plus** much more; **de plus en plus** more and more; **de plus en plus tôt** earlier and earlier; **en plus** in addition; **le plus** + *adv.* the most + *adv.*; **le/la/les plus** + *adj.* the most + *adj.*; **le/la/les plus de** + *n.* the most + *n.*;

ne... plus not any more, no longer; **non plus** neither; **plus** + *adj./adv.* + **que** more + *adj./adv.* + than; **plus de** + *n.* + **que** more + *n.* + than; **plus rien** nothing more; **plus tard** later; *v.* + **le plus** *v.* + the most; *v.* + **plus que** *v.* + more than
plusieurs *adj., indef. pron.* several
plûtot *adv.* rather; instead
poche *f.* pocket
poème *m.* poem
poésie *f.* poetry
poète (femme poète) *m., f.* poet
poids *m.* weight
point *m.* point; **ne... point** *adv.* absolutely not; **point de départ** starting point; **point de repère** landmark; **point de vue** point of view
pointe: heures de pointe *f. pl.* rush hour
pois *m. pl.* peas; **petits pois** green peas; **pois chiches** chickpeas
poisson *m.* fish; **soupe** (*f.*) **de poisson** fish soup
poissonnerie *f.* fish store
poitrine *f.* chest
poivre *m.* pepper
poivron *m.* bell pepper
poli(e) *adj.* polite
police *f.* police; **agent(e)** (*m., f.*) **de police** police officer
policier/ière *m., f.* police officer
politesse *f.* courtesy, good manners
politique *f.* politics; policy; *adj.* political; **parti** (*m.*) **politique** political party
polluant(e) *adj.* polluting
polluer to pollute
pollution *f.* pollution
pomme *f.* apple; **pomme de terre** potato; **tarte** (*f.*) **aux pommes** apple pie
ponctuation *f.* punctuation
pont *m.* bridge
populaire *adj.* popular; **caisse** (*f.*) **populaire** credit union
population *f.* population
porc *m.* pork; pig; **jarret** (*m.*) **de porc** ham hocks
porcelaine *f.* porcelain
port *m.* port; **port de plaisance** marina; **port maritime** shipping port
portable *m.* laptop computer; portable (cell) phone
porte *f.* door; **porte d'embarquement** (*airport*) gate
porter to wear; to carry; **prêt-à-porter** off-the-rack/ready-to-wear clothing
portrait *m.* portrait
portugais(e) *adj.* Portuguese; **Portugais(e)** *m., f.* Portuguese (*person*)
poser: poser sa candidature to submit one's application; **poser une question** to ask a question

position *f.* position; place
posséder (je possède) to possess
possessif/ive *adj.* possessive
possession *f.* possession
possibilité *f.* possibility
possible *adj.* possible; **autant que possible** as much as possible; **il est possible (que)** it is possible (that); **le plus vite possible** as soon as possible
postal(e) *adj.* postal; **carte** (*f.*) **postale** postcard
poste *f.* mail; post office; **bureau** (*m.*) **de poste** post office building
poste *m.* position, job
pot *m.*: **prendre un pot** to have a drink; **pot d'échappement** exhaust pipe
poteau (*m.*) **indicateur** signpost
poubelle *f.* garbage can
poulet *m.* chicken (meat); **poulet-frites** *m.* chicken with French fries
poumon *m.* lung
poupée *f.* doll
pour *prep.* for; **c'est pour cela** it's for that reason; **le pour et le contre** the pros and cons; **pour cent** percent; **pour que** so that, in order that; **s'inquiéter pour** to worry about
pourcentage *m.* percentage
pourquoi *adv., conj.* why; **pourquoi pas?** why not?
pourri(e) *m., f.* rotten person
poursuivre (*like* **suivre**) *irreg.* to pursue
pousser to grow; to push; **pousser des soupirs** to sigh
pouvoir (*p.p.* **pu**) *irreg.* to be able, can; to be allowed; **est-ce que vous pourriez m'indiquer le chemin pour aller à... ?** could you show me the way to . . . ?; **il se peut que** it is possible that
pratiquant(e) *adj.* practicing
pratique *f.* practice; *adj.* practical
pratiquer to practice
précédent(e) *adj.* preceding
précieux/euse *adj.* precious
précipiter: se précipiter to happen quickly
précisément *adv.* precisely, to be precise
préciser to specify
précision *f.* clarification
prédiction *f.* prediction
préfecture *f.* prefecture
préférable *adj.* preferable
préférer (je préfère) to prefer
préférence *f.* preference
premier/ière *adj.* first; **le premier** *m.* the first of the month; **premier choix** *m.* top quality; **premier étage** *m.* first floor (*above ground level*)
prendre (*p.p.* **pris**) *irreg.* to take; to have (*something to eat/drink*); **prendre des**

notes to take notes; **prendre du temps** to take a long time; **prendre sa retraite** to retire; **prendre un congé** to take time off; **prendre une correspondance** to transfer; **prendre une décision** to make a decision; **prendre une photo** to take a photograph; **prendre un verre (un pot)** to have a drink; **prenez soin de vous** take care of yourself
préoccuper to preoccupy
préparatif *m.* preparation
préparation *f.* preparation
préparatoire *adj.* preparatory
préparer to prepare; **préparer (une leçon, un examen)** to study for (a lesson; a test); **se préparer** to get ready
préposition *f., Gram.* preposition
près (de) *adv.* near; **à peu près** about, nearly
présence *f.* presence
présent *m.* present (*time*); **à présent** now, currently
présentation *f.* presentation
présent(e) *adj.* present
présenter to present; to introduce; **se présenter** to introduce oneself
président(e) *m., f.* president
presque *adv.* almost, nearly; **presque partout** almost everywhere
presse *f.* news media; press
pressé(e) *adj.* in a hurry
prestigieux/euse *adj.* prestigious
prêt(e) *adj.* ready; **prêt-à-porter** *m.* off-the-rack/ready-to-wear clothing
prêter to lend
prétexte *m.* pretext
preuve *f.* proof
prévision *f.* forecast
prévoir (*like* **voir**) *irreg.* to foresee, anticipate; **comme prévu** as expected
primaire *adj.* primary; **école** (*f.*) **primaire** elementary school
primordial(e) *adj.* paramount
prince *m.* prince
principal(e) *adj.* principal, main; **plat** (*m.*) **principal** main course
principe *m.* principle
printemps *m.* spring
prison *f.* prison
prisonnier/ière *m., f.* prisoner
privé(e) *adj.* private; **chaîne** (*f.*) **privée payante** private subscription channel; **vie** (*f.*) **privée** private life
prix *m.* price; prize; **à tout prix** at all costs
probabilité *f.* probability
probable *adj.* probable
problème *m.* problem; **le moindre problème** the slightest problem; **pas de problème** no problem

prochain(e) *adj.* next; **la semaine (l'année, etc.) prochaine** next week (year, etc.)
proche (de) *adj., adv.* near, close; **futur** (*m.*) **proche** *Gram.* near future
proclamer to proclaim
producteur/trice *m., f.* producer
production *f.* production
productivité *f.* productivity
produire (*like* **conduire**) *irreg.* to produce
produit *m.* product; **produits laitiers** dairy products
professeur *m.* professor; **professeure** *f. Q.* female professor; **prof** *m., f. fam.* professor
profession *f.* profession
professionel(le) *adj., m., f.* professional
profit *m.* profit; **au profit de** at the expense of
profiter to take advantage of; to profit from
programme *m.* program
progressivement *adv.* progressively
projecteur *m.* projector
projection *f.* projection
projet *m.* project
promenade *f.* walk; **faire une promenade** to take a walk
promener: se promener (*like* **mener**) *irreg.* to take a walk
promettre (*like* **mettre**) *irreg.* to promise
promotion *f.* promotion
prompt(e) *adj.* prompt
pronom *m., Gram.* pronoun; **pronom complément d'objet direct (indirect)** direct (indirect) object pronoun; **pronom (démonstratif, possessif, relative)** (demonstrative, possessive, relative) pronoun
pronominal *adj., Gram.* pronominal; **verbe** (*m.*) **pronominal** *Gram.* pronominal (reflexive) verb
prononcer (nous prononçons) to pronounce
propager: se propager (nous nous propageons) to be disseminated, spread
proportion *f.* proportion
propos *m.*: **à propos de** about, concerning
proposer to propose, suggest
propre *adj.* own; **propre à** characteristic of; **sa propre opinion** *f.* his (her) own opinion
propriétaire *m., f.* owner
prospère *adj.* prosperous
prospérer (je prospère) to prosper
prospérité *f.* prosperity
protection *f.* protection
protéger (je protège, nous protégeons) to protect
protestant(e) *adj.* Protestant; **Protestant(e)**, *m., f.* Protestant (*person*)
protestantisme *m.* Protestantism

protester to protest

provenance *f.*: **de provenance** originating in/from

provençal(e) *adj.* from Provence (*region*)

provenir (*like* **venir**) *irreg.* to come from, to originate in

province *f.* province

provincial(e) *adj.* provincial

provision *f.* provision; *pl.* food (*supplies*)

provoquer to provoke

prudent(e) *adj.* careful

psychiatre *m., f.* psychiatrist

psychiatrique *adj.* psychiatric

psycho-drame *m.* psychological drama

psychologie *f.* psychology

public *m.* public; **en public** in public

public (publique) *adj.* public

publicitaire *adj.* commercial

publicité *f.* commercial, advertisement

publier to publish

puce *f.* flea; **ma puce** *fam.*sweetheart

puis *adv.* then

puisque *conj.* since, seeing that

puissant(e) *adj.* powerful

pull-over (*fam.* **pull**) *m.* pullover (*sweater*)

punk *m.* punk music

pur(e) *adj.* pure

purifier to purify

pyjama *m.* pyjamas

pyramide *f.* pyramid

quai *m.* platform; dock

qualification *f.* qualification

qualifier to characterize

qualité *f.* quality

quand *adv., conj.* when; **depuis quand?** since when?

quantité *f.* quantity

quarantaine *f.*: **dans la quarantaine** in one's forties (*age*)

quarante *adj.* forty

quart *m.* quarter, fourth; quarter of an hour; **et quart** quarter past (*the hour*); **moins le quart** quarter to (*the hour*)

quartier *m.* neighborhood, area of town; **Quartier latin** Latin Quarter

quatorze *adj.* fourteen

quatre *adj.* four; **quatre-vingt-dix** ninety; **quatre vingts** eighty

quatre-épices *m., f.* allspice

quatrième *adj.* fourth

que (qu') *conj.* that; than; as; *interr. pron.* what; *rel. pron.* whom, that, which; **ne... que** only; **pour que** in order to; **qu'est-ce que** what (*object*); **qu'est-ce que c'est?** what is it/this/that?; **qu'est-ce qui** what (*subject*)

Québec *m.* Quebec

québécois(e) *adj.* from Quebec; **Québécois(e)** *m., f.* person from Quebec

quel(le)(s) *interr. adj.* what?, which?; **quel âge avez-vous (as-tu)(a-t-il, *etc.*)?** how old are you (is he, etc.)?; **quel jour sommes-nous?** what day is it today?; **quel temps fait-it?** what's the weather like?; **quelle heure est-il?** what time is it?; **quels cours est-ce que vous suivez (tu suis)?** what courses are you taking?

quelque(s) *indef. adj.* several, some; **quelque chose** *indef. pron.* something; **quelque part** *adv.* somewhere

quelquefois *adv.* sometimes

quelques-uns/unes *indef. pron., pl.* some, a few

quelqu'un *indef. pron.* someone

question *f.* question; **poser une question** to ask a question

quête *f.* quest

queue *f.* queue, line; **faire la queue** to stand in line

qui *interr. pron.* who, whom; *rel. pron.* who, that, which; **qui est-ce?** who is it?; **qui est-ce que** whom (*object*); **qui est-ce qui** who (*subject*)

quinze *adj.* fifteen

quitter to leave (*s.o. or someplace*)

quoi *pron.* what; **à quoi tu joues?** are you playing games?; **de quoi parlez-vous (parles-tu)?** what are you talking about?; **je ne sais pas quoi faire** I don't know what to do

quotidien(ne) *adj.* daily

raccrocher to hang up (*the telephone receiver*)

race *f.* race (*ethnicity*)

racine *f.* root

racisme *m.* racism

raconter to tell (about)

radicalement *adv.* radically

radieux/euse *adj.* glorious, radiant

radio *f.* radio; **écouter la radio** to listen to the radio; **mettre la radio** to turn on the radio; **station** (*f.*) **de radio** radio station

radioactif/ive *adj.* radioactive

raffiné(e) *adj.* refined

ragoût *m.* stew

raï *m.* raï music

raisin *m.*: **du raisin** grapes; **raisin sec** raisin

raison *f.* reason; **avoir raison** to be right

raisonnable *adj.* reasonable

ralentir to slow down

ramadan *m.* Ramadan

ramasser to pick (up), gather (up); to dig up

randonnée *f.* hike; **faire une randonnée** to hike

rap *m.* rap music

rapide *adj.* fast, rapid

rapidité *f.* speed

rappeler: se rappeler (je me rappelle) to remember

rappeur *m.* rap musician

rapport *m.* relation; **par rapport à** with respect to

rapporter to report; to bring in; to bring back

rare *adj.* rare

rarement *adv.* rarely

raser: se raser to shave

rassurer to reassure, comfort

ratatouille *f.* ratatouille

ravi(e) *adj.* thrilled

ravissant(e) *adj.* beautiful, delightful

rayon *m.* department (*in a store*)

réaction *f.* reaction

réagir to react

réalisateur/trice *m., f.* director

réalisme *m.* realism

réaliste *adj.* realistic

réalité *f.* reality; **en réalité** in fact, actually

rébellion *f.* rebellion

récent(e) *adj.* recent

recette *f.* recipe

recevoir (*p.p.* **reçu**) *irreg.* to receive

réchauffer to reheat

recherche *f.* research; **à la recherche de** in search of; **faire des recherches** to do research; **local** (*m.*) **de recherche** research facility

rechercher to search for; to research

récit *m.* narrative, story

récolte *f.* harvest, crop

récolter to harvest

recommander to recommend

récompense *f.* recompense

reconforter to comfort

reconnaissance *f.* gratitude

reconnaître (*like* **connaître**) *irreg.* to recognize

reconstituer to restore

recoucher: se recoucher to go back to bed

recueillir (*like* **cueillir**) *irreg.* to collect

recyclable *adj.* recyclable

recyclage *m.* recycling

recycler to recycle

rédacteur/trice *m., f.* editor

rédaction *f.* composition; **salle** (*f.*) **de rédaction** editing room

rédiger (nous rédigeons) to write, compose

redoutable *adj.* fearsome

redresser to rebuild

réduire (*like* **conduire**) *irreg.* to reduce

refait(e) *adj.* remade (*movie*)

référer: se référer (je me réfère) to refer (back) to

refermer to close again

réfléchi(e) *adj.* thoughtful

réfléchir à to reflect (on), think (about)

refléter (je reflète) to reflect, mirror

réflexion *f.* reflection; thought

réfrigérateur (*fam.* **frigo**) *m.* refrigerator (fridge)

réfugié(e) *m., f.* refugee

réfugier: se réfugier to take refuge

refuser (de) to refuse (*to do s.th.*)

regard *m.* look, glance

regarder to watch, look at; **cela (ne) vous regarde (pas)** that is (not) your problem; **regarder la télé** to watch TV

reggae *m.* reggae music

régie *f.* control room

régime *m.* regime; diet

région *f.* region

régional(e) *adj.* regional

régler (je règle) to resolve, settle

réglisse *m.* licorice

regret *m.* regret, remorse

regretter to regret, be sorry; **regretter que** to be sorry that

régulier/ière *adj.* regular

rejoindre (*like* **craindre**) *irreg.* to join; to meet

relatif/ive *adj.* relative; **pronom** (*m.*) **relatif** *Gram.* relative pronoun

relation *f.* relationship

relativement *adv.* relatively

relief *m.* topography, relief

religieux/euse *adj.* religious

religion *f.* religion

relire (*like* **lire**) *irreg.* to reread

remarquable *adj.* remarkable

remarque *f.* remark, comment

remarquer to notice

rembrunir: se rembrunir to become somber/disgruntled/darker, to cloud over

remède *m.* remedy, treatment, fix

remercier to thank

remettre: se remettre (*like* **mettre**) *irreg.* to recover

remonter to go back (up)

remplaçant(e) *m., f.* replacement

remplacer (nous remplaçons) to replace

remplir to fill out (*a form*); **remplir les blancs** to fill in the blanks

renaissance: la renaissance *f.* the Renaissance

rencontre *f.* meeting, encounter

rencontrer to meet; to run into, encounter

rendez-vous *m.* meeting; appointment

rendre to return (*s.th.*); to render, make; **rendre justice** (*f.*) **à** to do justice to;

rendre visite à to visit (*s.o.*); **se rendre à** to go to; **se rendre compte (de)** to realize

renforcer (nous renforçons) to reinforce

rénovation *f.* renovation

renseignements *m. pl.* information

rentrée *f.* back-to-school day

rentrer to come/go back (home); **rentrer à la maison** to go home

renvoyer (je renvoie) to send back, return

répandre: se répandre to spread

repartir (*like* **partir**) *irreg.* to leave again

repas *m.* meal; **commander un repas** to order a meal

repère: point (*m.*) **de repère** landmark

repérer (je repère) to locate

répéter (je répète) to repeat

répétition *f.* rehearsal

réplique *f.* response

répondeur *m.* answering machine

répondre to answer, respond

réponse *f.* response

reportage *m.* report; **faire un reportage** to prepare/give a report (*TV*)

reporter *m.* reporter

repos *m.* rest

reposé(e) *adj.* rested

reposer: se reposer to rest

reprendre (*like* **prendre**) *irreg.* to take up again, continue; to take more (*food*)

représailles *f. pl.* reprisals

représenter to represent

reproduire (*like* **conduire**) *irreg.* to reproduce

républicain(e) *m., f.* Republican

république *f.* republic

réputation *f.* reputation

réputé(e) *adj.* well known

réseau *m.* network; system; **réseau du métro** subway system; **réseau informatique** computer network

réserver to reserve

résidence *f.* residence; **résidence universitaire** dormitory building

résidentiel(le) *adj.* residential

résistance *f.* resistance

résistant(e) *m., f.* French Resistance fighter

résister to resist

résoudre (*p.p.* **résolu**) *irreg.* to resolve

respecter to respect

respectif/ive *adj.* respective

respectueux/euse *adj.* respectful

respiration *f.* breathing

responsabilité *f.* responsibility

responsable *adj.* responsible

ressemblance *f.* resemblance

ressentir (*like* **dormir**) *irreg.* to feel

resservir (*like* **dormir**) *irreg.* to serve again (*food*)

ressource *f.* resource; **ressources naturelles** natural resources

restaurant (*fam.* **restau**) *m.* restaurant

rester to stay

résultat *m.* result

résulter (en) to result in

résumé *m.* summary

résumer to summarize

rétablir to reestablish

retard *m.* delay; **en retard** late

retarder to slow; **retarder l'avance** to slow the advance

retour *m.* return; **être de retour** to be back

retourner to return; to turn around

retraite *f.* retirement; **prendre sa retraite** to retire

retraité(e) *m., f.* retiree

retroprojecteur *m.* overhead projector

retrouver to find (again); **se retrouver** to find oneself

réunion *f.* meeting

réunir to gather together; **se réunir** to get together

réussir (à) to succeed; to pass (*a course or an exam*)

rêve *m.* dream

réveiller to wake (*s.o.*); **se réveiller** to wake up

réveillon *m.* Christmas Eve; New Year's Eve

révéler (je révèle) to reveal

revenir (*like* **venir**) *irreg.* to come back, return

révision *f.* review

revoir (*like* **voir**) *irreg.* to see again; **au revoir** good-bye

révolte *f.* revolt

révolution *f.* revolution

rez-de-chaussée *m.* ground floor

rhubarbe *f.* rhubarb

rhume *m.* common cold

rhythme *m.* rhythm

rhythmé(e) *adj.* rhythmic

riche *adj.* rich

richesse *f.* wealth

ridicule *adj.* ridiculous

ridiculiser to make fun of, mock

rien; ne... rien *indef. pron.* nothing; **plus rien** nothing more

ringard(e) *adj.* out-of-date

risque *m.* risk

risquer to risk

rivière *f.* small river

riz *m.* rice

robe *f.* dress

rocher *m.* rock

rocheux/euse *adj.* rocky

rock *m.* rock music

roi *m.* king; **palais** (*m.*) **du roi** king's palace
rôle *m.* role; **jeu** (*m.*) **de rôle** role play
roller *m.* roller skating; **faire du roller** to roller-skate
romain(e) *adj.* Roman
roman *m.* novel
romancier/ière *m., f.* novelist
romantique *adj.* romantic
rompre (*p.p.* **rompu**) *irreg.* to break
roquefort *m.* Roquefort cheese
rose *adj.* pink
rosé(e) *adj.* rosy; **vin** (*m.*) **rosé** rosé wine
rôti *m.* roast; **rôti(e)** *adj.* roasted
rouge *adj.* red
rougir to blush
rouler to travel (*in a car*); to roll (*along*)
route *f.* road, highway; **en route** on the way
routier/ière *adj.* pertaining to the road; **signalisation** (*f.*) **routière** road signs
routine *f.* routine
royal(e) *adj.* royal
rubrique *f.* section, column (*in a newspaper*)
rue *f.* street; **dans la rue...** on . . . Street; **descendre une rue** to go down a street; **monter une rue** to go up a street; **rue piétonne** pedestrian street
ruelle *f.* alleyway
ruine *f.* ruin
rumeur *f.* rumor
rural(e) *adj.* rural
russe *adj.* Russian; **Russe** *m., f.* Russian (*person*)
Russie *f.* Russia

sa *adj.* his, her, its, one's
sac *m.* bag; **sac à dos** backpack; **sac à main** handbag
sacré(e) *adj.* sacred
sacrifice *m.* sacrifice
sage *adj.* well-behaved
saint(e) *m., f.* saint
saisir to seize; to grasp
saison *f.* season
salade *f.* lettuce; salad; **salade verte** green salad
salaire *m.* salary
salarié(e) *m., f.* full-time employee
sale *adj.* dirty
salle *f.* room; **salle à manger** dining room; **salle de bains** bathroom; **salle de classe** classroom; **salle de rédaction** editing room; **salle de séjour** living room
saluer to greet
salut *interj.* hi; bye
salutations *f.* greetings
samedi *m.* Saturday
sandwich *m.* sandwich

sans *prep.* without; **sans aucun doute** without a doubt; **sans domicile fixe** homeless; **sans doute** probably, no doubt; **sans intérêt** of no interest; **sans que** unless; without
santé *f.* health
satisfaisant(e) *adj.* satisfying
sauce *f.* sauce; **sauce de soja** soy sauce
saucisse *f.* sausage link
saucisson *m.* sausage
sauf *prep.* except
saumon *m.* salmon
sauna *m.* sauna
sauter to jump
sauver to save
savoir (*p.p.* **su**) *irreg.* to know (*a fact*); **je ne sais pas** I don't know; **je ne sais pas quoi faire** I don't know what to do
scandale *m.* scandal; **crier au scandale** to call it a scandal
scanner *m.* scanner
scénario *m.* script; scenario
scénariste *m., f.* screenwriter
scène *f.* scene; **metteur en scène** director (*theatrical*); **mise** (*f.*) **en scène** (*theatrical*) production
science *f.* science; **sciences naturelles** natural science
scientifique *adj.* scientific
scoop *m.* scoop (*news*)
scripte *m.* script
script *m., f.* script coordinator
sculpteur (femme sculpteur) *m., f.* sculptor
sculpture *f.* sculpture
se (s') *pron.* oneself; himself; herself, itself, themselves; to oneself, etc.; each other
séance *f.* meeting; showing (*of a film*)
sec (sèche) *adj.* dry; **raisin** (*m.*) **sec** raisin
sécher (je sèche) to dry; **sécher un cours** to cut a class
sécheresse *f.* drought
séchoir *m.* dryer
secondaire *adj.* secondary; **enseignement** (*m.*) **secondaire** secondary school teaching
seconde *f.* second (*sixtieth of a minute*); **second(e)** *adj.* second; **langue** (*f.*) **seconde** second/foreign language
secret *m.* secret
secrétaire *m., f.* secretary
secrètement *adv.* secretly
sécurité *f.* security; **agent (e)** (*m., f.*) **de sécurité** security guard
sédentaire *adj.* sedentary
séduire (*like* **conduire**) *irreg.* to seduce, charm
seize *adj.* sixteen
séjour *m.* stay; trip; **salle** (*f.*) **de séjour** living room

séjourner to stay (*in a place*)
sel *m.* salt
self-sélect *m.* self-service restaurant
selon *prep.* according to; **selon le cas** depending on the case; **selon vous** in your opinion
semaine *f.* week; **par semaine** per week; **la semaine dernière (prochaine)** last (next) week
sembler to seem
semer (je sème) to sow
semestre *m.* semester
sénégalais(e) *adj.* Senegalese; **Sénégalais(e)** *m., f.* Senegalese (*person*)
sens *m.* meaning
sentiment *m.* sentiment, emotion
sentimental(e) *adj.* sentimental
sentir (*like* **dormir**) *irreg.* to smell, to feel; **se sentir** to feel (*an emotion*)
séparer to separate
sept *adj.* seven
septembre *m.* September
septième *adj.* seventh
serf *m.* serf
série *f.* series
sérieux/euse *adj.* serious
serre *f.* greenhouse; **effet** (*m.*) **de serre** greenhouse effect
serré(e) *adj.* tight
serrure *f.* latch
serveur/euse *m., f.* waiter/waitress
serviable *adj.* willing (*to do s.th.*)
service *m.* service; department; **station** (*f.*) **service** service station
serviette *f.* napkin
servir (*like* **dormir**) *irreg.* to serve
ses *adj.* his, her, its, one's
sésame *m.* sesame; **huile** (*f.*) **de sésame** sesame oil
seul(e) *adj.* alone; sole; **c'est pour cela seul** it's only for that reason
seulement *adv.* only
sévère *adj.* severe
sexe *m.* sex
shopping *m.* shopping; **faire du shopping** to go shopping
short *m.* shorts
si *adv.* so (very); so much; yes (*response to negative question*); **si (s')** *conj.* if, whether; **s'il vous (te) plaît** *interj.* please
SIDA *m.* AIDS
siècle *m.* century; **au cours des siècles** through the centuries
siège *m.* seat; **siège couloir (fenêtre)** aisle (window) seat
sien: le/la/les sien(ne)(s) *pron.* his, hers
signaleur *m.* signalman; **timonier** (*m.*) **signaleur** helmsman-signalman

signalisation *f.* signage; **signalisation routière** road signs
signe *m.* sign
signer to sign
signet *m.* bookmark
signification *f.* significance
signifier to mean, signify
silence *f.* silence
silencieux/euse *adj.* silent
silencieusement *adv.* silently
similaire *adj.* similar
similarité *f.* similarity
simple *adj.* simple
sincère *adj.* sincere
sincérité *f.* sincerity
singulier/ière *adj.* singular; *m., Gram.* singular (*form*)
sinon *prep.* if not, otherwise
site *m.* site; **site touristique** tourist site; **site web** website
situation *f.* situation; placement
situer to situate; **se situer** to be located
six *adj.* six
sixième *adj.* sixth
ska *m.* ska music
skate *m.* skateboarding
ski *m.* skiing; ski; **faire du ski** to go skiing; **faire du ski de fond (ski nautique)** to cross-country ski (waterski)
skier to ski
snob *m.* snob
sociable *adj.* friendly
social(e) *adj.* social
socialiste *adj.* socialist
société *f.* company; society, organization
socio-économique *adj.* socioeconomic
sœur *f.* sister; **âme** (*f.*) **sœur** kindred spirit; **belle-sœur** *f.* sister-in-law, stepsister
soi (soi-même) *pron.* oneself, herself, himself, itself; **sûr de soi** self-confident
soie *f.* silk
soif *f.* thirst; **avoir soif** to be thirsty
soigner to take care of, nurse
soin *m.* care, treatment; **prenez soin de vous** take care of yourself; **soins médicaux** health care
soir *m.* evening; **ce soir** this evening; **du soir** in the evening
soirée *f.* evening; party
soixantaine *f.*: **dans la soixantaine** in one's sixties (*age*)
soixante *adj.* sixty
soixante-dix *adj.* seventy
soja *m.* soy; **sauce** (*f.*) **de soja** soy sauce
sol *m.* ground; **sous-sol** *m.* basement
soldat *m.* soldier
solde *f.* sale; **en solde** on sale
soleil *m.* sun; **coup** (*m.*) **de soleil** sunburn; **il fait du soleil** it's sunny out; **lunettes** (*f. pl.*) **de soleil** sunglasses

solitaire *adj.* solitary
solitude *f.* solitude
solution *f.* solution
sombre *adj.* dark
sommeil *m.* sleep; **avoir sommeil** to be sleepy
somptueux/euse *adj.* sumptuous
son *adj.* his, her, its, one's
sondage *m.* survey
sonner to ring (*telephone, bell*)
sorte *f.* sort, type
sortie *f.* exit
sortir (*like* **dormir**) *irreg.* to go out; **sortir avec** to go out with (*s.o.*)
soucier: se soucier de to care about
souci *m.* worry, concern
soudain *adv.* suddenly; **soudain(e)** *adj.* sudden
souffle *m.* breath; **à bout de souffle** out of breath, breathless
souffrir (*like* **ouvrir**) *irreg.* to suffer
souhaiter (que) to wish, hope (that)
soumettre (*like* **mettre**) *irreg.* to hand in; to submit
soupe *f.* soup; **soupe à l'oignon** French onion soup; **soupe de poisson** fish soup
soupir *m.* sigh; **pousser des soupirs** to sigh
source *f.* source; **eau** (*f.*) **de source** spring water
sourd(e) *adj.* deaf; *m., f.* deaf person
sourire to smile
souris *f.* mouse; computer mouse
sous *prep.* under; **sous clé** under lock and key; **sous-préfecture** *f.* subprefecture; **sous-sol** *m.* basement; **sous-titre** *m.* subtitle
souterrain(e) *adj.* underground
soutien *m.* support
souvenir *m.* memory
souvenir: se souvenir (*like* **venir**) *irreg.* **de** to remember
souvent *adv.* often
spaghettis *m. pl.* spaghetti
spécial(e) *adj.* special
spécialisation *f.* (*educational*) major
spécialiser: se spécialiser en to major in
spécialiste *m., f.* specialist, expert
spécialité *f.* specialty
spectacle *m.* entertainment; show
spectateur/trice *m., f.* spectator
spéléologie *f.* spelunking; **faire de la spéléologie** to go spelunking (explore caves)
splendide *adj.* splendid, wonderful
spontanéité *f.* spontaneity
sport *m.* sports; **faire du sport** to play sports; **fanatique** (*m., f.*) **du sport** sports fan; **sports d'hiver** winter sports; **voiture** (*f.*) **de sport** sportscar

sportif/ive *adj.* athletic; **centre** (*m.*) **sportif** sports center
squatter to squat (*claim a residence*)
stabiliser: se stabiliser to become stable
stade *m.* stadium
stage *m.* internship; **faire un stage** to do an internship
standard *m.* standard
star *f.* star (*celebrity*)
station *f.* station; **station de radio** radio station; **station service** service station; **station thermale** spa, health resort
stationner to park
statistique *f.* statistics
statuettes *f.* statuette
statut *m.* statute
steak-frites *m.* steak with French fries
stéréo *adj.* stereo; **chaîne** (*f.*) **stéréo** stereo system
stéréotype *m.* stereotype
stratégie *f.* strategy
stress *m.* stress
stressé(e) *adj.* stressed
structure *f.* structure
studio *m.* studio; studio apartment
stupéfait(e) *adj.* stupefied, dumbfounded
stupide *adj.* stupid
style *m.* style
stylo *m.* pen
subjonctif *m., Gram.* subjunctive (*mood*)
substantif *m., Gram.* noun
subtilité *f.* subtlety
succès *m.* success
sucre *m.* sugar; **canne** (*f.*) **à sucre** sugarcane
sucré(e) *adj.* sweet
sucrerie *f.* sweets
sud *m.* south; **sud-ouest** southwest
suffisamment *adv.* sufficiently
suffire to suffice; **ça suffit** that's enough; **il suffit** it's enough
suggérer (je suggère) to suggest
suggestion *f.* suggestion
suicider: se suicider to commit suicide
suite *f.* outcome; **tout de suite** right away
suivant(e) *adj.* following
suivre (*p.p.* **suivi**) *irreg.* to follow; to take (*a class*)
sujet *m.* subject; **au sujet de** concerning
super *adj.* super, great
supérieur(e) *adj.* superior; **enseignement** (*m.*) **supérieur** higher education
superlatif *m., Gram.* superlative
supermarché *m.* supermarket
supplémentaire *adj.* supplementary, extra
supposer to suppose; **je suppose?** I suppose?
supprimer to eliminate, abolish

sur *prep.* on, on top of; **donner sur** to overlook, have a view of; **sur Internet** on the Internet; **tirer sur** to fire on, to shoot at

sûr(e) *adj.* sure, certain; **bien sûr, bien sûr que oui (non)!** of course (not)!; **sûr de soi** self-confident

surf de neige *m.* snowboarding; **faire du surf de neige** to snowboard

surfer (le Web) to surf (the Web)

surgelé(e) *adj.* frozen; **pizza** (*f.*) **surgelée** frozen pizza

surmonter to overcome

surnommer to name, call; to nickname

surprendre (*like* **prendre**) *irreg.* to surprise

surpris(e) *adj.* surprised

surprise *f.* surprise

surtout *adv.* especially; above all; **surtout pas** definitely not

surveillé(e) *adj.* managed

survivre (*like* **vivre**) *irreg.* to survive

susceptible *adj.* susceptible

sweatshirt (*fam.* **sweat**) *m.* sweatshirt

symbole *m.* symbol

symboliser to symbolize

sympathie *f.* friendliness, liking

sympathique (*fam.* **sympa**) *adj.* nice

symphonie *f.* symphony

symptôme *m.* symptom

synagogue *f.* synagogue

syndicat *m.* union

syntaxe *f.* syntax

synthèse *f.* synthesis

système *m.* system

ta *adj.* your

table *f.* table; **à table** at the table; **mettre la table** to set the table

tableau (*pl.* **tableaux**) *m.* blackboard; painting (*picture*); **tableau d'affichage** bulletin board

tâche *f.* task

tailleur *m.* woman's suit

talent *m.* talent

tant *adj.* so much; so many; **en tant qu'auteur** as author; **tant de spectateurs** so many spectators

tante *f.* aunt

tapis *m.* rug

taquiner to tease

tard *adv.* late; **plus tard** later

tarte *f.* pie; **tarte aux pommes** apple pie

tartine *f.* bread with butter and jam

tasse *f.* cup

taxi *m.* taxi

te (t') *pron., s., fam.* you; to/for you; **combien te faut-il?** how much do you need?; **s'il te plaît** please

technicien(ne) *m., f.* technician

technique *adj.* technical

technologie *f.* technology; **haute technologie** high tech

technophobe *m., f.* technophobe

tee-shirt *m.* T-shirt

tel(le) *adj.* such; like; **tel(le) ou tel(le)** this or that; **tel que** like, such as

télé *fam.* TV **téléphone** *m.* telephone; **coup** (*m.*) **de téléphone** phone call; **téléphone portable** mobile (cell) phone

téléphoner (à) to phone (*s.o.*)

téléphonique *adj.* telephone; **annuaire** (*f.*) **téléphonique** phone book; **cabine** (*f.*) **téléphonique** phone booth; **ligne** (*f.*) **téléphonique** telephone line

télévisé(e) *adj.* televised

télévision (*fam.* **télé**) *f.* television (TV); **mettre la télé** to turn on the TV; **regarder la télé** to watch TV

tellement *adv.* so (very), so much

température *f.* temperature

temps *m.* time; weather; *Gram.* tense; **à mi-temps** part-time; **à temps partiel** part-time; **beau temps** nice weather; **dans le temps** in the past; **de temps en temps** from time to time; **depuis combien de temps?** how long?; **il fait un temps splendide** it's a gorgeous day; **mettre du temps à** to spend time on; **prendre du temps** to take a long time; **quel temps fait-il?** what's the weather like?

tenir (*p.p.* **tenu**) *irreg.* to hold; to keep; **je tiens à toi** I care about you; **tenir au courant** to stay up to date

tennis *m.* tennis

tension *f.* tension

tente *f.* tent

terme *m.* term

terminal *m.*: **terminal Minitel** Minitel (*French personal communication system*) terminal

terminal(e) *adj.* terminal, final

terminer to finish; **c'est terminé?** are you finished?

terminus *m.* terminus, last stop

terrain *m.* ground; **terrain de golf** golf course; **vélo** (*m.*) **tout terrain** (*fam.* **VTT**) mountain bike

terre *f.* earth; soil; land; **à l'intérieur des terres** in the center of the country; **pomme** (*f.*) **de terre** potato; **par terre** to/on the ground

terrestre *adj.* earthly; **extra-terrestre** *m., f.* extraterrestrial

terrible *adj.* terrible, awful

territoire *m.* territory; **territoire d'outre-mer (TOM)** overseas territory

tes *adj.* your

test *m.* test

tête *f.* head; **avoir mal à la tête** to have a headache; **perdre la tête** to lose one's mind

têtu(e) *adj.* stubborn

texte *m.* text

TGV (train à grande vitesse) *m.* French high-speed train

thaïlandais(e) *adj.* Thai; **Thaïlandais(e)** *m., f.* Thai (*person*)

thé *m.* tea; **thé à la menthe** mint tea

théâtre *m.* theater; **pièce** (*f.*) **de théâtre** play

théière *f.* teapot

thème *m.* theme, subject

thérapeutique *adj.* therapeutic

thermal(e) *adj.* thermal; **bain** (*m.*) **thermal** spa bath (*hot spring water*); **station** (*f.*) **thermale** spa, health resort

thermalisme *m.* science of therapeutic baths

thèse *f.* thesis, dissertation; **thèse de doctorat** doctoral dissertation

thon *m.* tuna

tien: le/la/les tien(ne)(s) *pron.* yours

tiers *m.* third; **deux-tiers** two-thirds

tigre *m.* tiger

timbre *m.* stamp

timonier-signaleur *m.* helmsman-signalman

tiré(e) *adj.* **de** taken from, excerpted from

tirer sur to fire on, shoot at

tissu *m.* fabric

titre *m.* title; **gros titre** headline; **sous-titre** *m.* subtitle

tofu *m.* tofu

toi *pron., s., fam.* you; **et toi?** and you?

toilette *f.*: **faire sa toilette** to wash up, get ready to go out; *pl.* restroom

tomate *f.* tomato

tomber to fall; **ça tombe un mardi** that falls on a Tuesday; **tomber amoureux/euse** to fall in love; **tomber malade** to fall ill

tomme *f.* regional cheese

ton *adj.* your

ton *m.* tone

tonalité *f.* dial tone

torse *m.* torso

tort *m.* wrong; **avoir tort** to be wrong, to be mistaken

torture *f.* torture

tôt *adv.* early; **de plus en plus tôt** earlier and earlier

totalitaire *adj.* totalitarian

touché(e) *adj.* touched; moved

toucher to touch; **toucher un chèque** to cash a check

toujours *adv.* always; still; **est-ce qu'il vit toujours?** is he still living?

tour *f.* tower; *m.* walk; turn; **c'était mon tour** it was my turn

tourisme *m.* tourism; **faire du tourisme** to go sightseeing

touriste *m., f.* tourist

touristique *adj.* tourist; **site** (*m.*) **touristique** tourist site

tourmenté(e) *adj.* tormented

tourner to turn; to film (*a movie*); **tournez** (**tourne**) **à droite** turn right

Toussaint *f.* All Saints' Day

tousser to cough

tout(e) (*pl.* **tous, toutes**) *adj., indef. pron.* all, every (one), the whole; very; **à toute heure** at any time; **à tout prix** at all costs; **ne... pas du tout** not at all, absolutely not; **tous les jours** every day; **tout à coup** suddenly; **tout à fait** completely; **tout de suite** right away; **tout droit** straight ahead; **tout heureux/euse** very happy; **toute la journée** all day; **tout le monde** everyone

trace *f.* trace

tradition *f.* tradition

traditionnel(le) *adj.* traditional

traduction *f.* translation

traduire (*like* **conduire**) *irreg.* to translate

tragédie *f.* tragedy

tragique *adj.* tragic

trahir to betray

trahison *f.* treason

train *m.* train; **en train** by train; **en train de** to be in the process of; **par train** by train; **train à grande vitesse** (*fam.* **TGV**) French high-speed train

traîner: se traîner to move slowly, with difficulty; to crawl

trait *m.* trait, feature; **trait d'union** hyphen

traitement *m.* treatment

traiter to treat, behave toward

traître/tresse *m., f.* traitor

trajet *m.* journey

tramway *m.* tramway, trolley car

tranquille *adj.* calm, peaceful

tranquillité *f.* calm, tranquillity

transformation *f.* transformation

transformer to change, transform

transport *m.* transportation; **moyen** (*m.*) **de transport** means of transportation; **transport express régional** regional express train

travail *m.* work; job; **au travail** at work; **fête** (*f.*) **du travail** Labor Day; **monde** (*m.*) **du travail** work world

travailler to work

travailleur/euse *adj.* hardworking

travers: à travers *prep.* through

traverser to cross

treize *adj.* thirteen

tréma *m.* umlaut (**ë**)

trentaine *f.:* **dans la trentaine** in one's thirties (*age*)

trente *adj.* thirty

très *adv.* very; **très bien** very well

tricot *m.* knitting; **faire du tricot** to knit

tricoter to knit

trilogie *f.* trilogy

trimestre *m.* trimester

triomphe *f.* triumph

triple *adj.* triple

triste *adj.* sad

trivial(e) *adj.* commonplace

trois *adj.* three

troisième *adj.* third; **au/du troisième âge** elderly, in old age

tromper to deceive, trick; **se tromper** to make a mistake, be mistaken

trop (de) *adv.* too much (of), too many (of); **trop tard** too late

tropical(e) *adj.* tropical

troublant(e) *adj.* troubling

troupe *f.* group; troop

troupeau *m.* herd; flock

trouver to find; to consider; **où se trouve... ?** where is . . . ?; **se trouver** to be located (situated; found)

tu *pron.* you

tuer to kill

tunisien(ne) *adj.* Tunisian; **Tunisien(ne)** *m., f.* Tunisian (*person*)

turc (turque) *adj.* Turkish; **Turc (Turque)** *m., f.* Turk (*person*)

type *m.* type, kind; *fam.* guy

typique *adj.* typical

un(e) (*pl.* **des**) *indef. art.* a, an; *inv. adj.* one; *pron.* one; **à la une** on the front page; **les uns avec les autres** with each other; **un peu (de)** a little (of); a few (of)

uni(e) *adj.* united

unième: vingt et unième *adj.* twenty-first

uniforme *m.* uniform

union *f.* union; **ils vivent en union libre** they're living together (without marriage); **trait** (*m.*) **d'union** hyphen

unique *adj.* sole, only; **fils** (*m.*) **unique** only son

unir to unite

univers *m.* universe

universitaire *adj.* (*of or belonging to the*) university; **cité** (*f.*) **universitaire** dormitory; **journal** (*m.*) **universitaire** college newspaper; **résidence universitaire** dormitory building

université *f.* university

urbain(e) *adj.* urban; **vie** (*f.*) **urbaine** city life

urinaire *adj.* urinary

usage *m.* use; *Gram.* usage

utile *adj.* useful

utilisation *f.* use

utiliser to use

vacances *f. pl.* vacation; **grandes vacances** summer vacation; **partir en vacances** to go on vacation; **pendant les vacances** during vacation; **vacances de Noël** Christmas vacation

vache *f.* cow

vachement *adv., fam.* very, tremendously

vague *f.* wave; **Nouvelle Vague** New Wave (*films*)

vaisselle *f.* dishes; **faire la vaisselle** to do the dishes; **lave-vaisselle** *f.* dishwasher

valeur *f.* value

valise *f.* suitcase; **enregistrer une valise** to check a suitcase

vallée *f.* valley

valse *f.* waltz

vapeur *f.* steam; **faire cuire à la vapeur** to steam (*food*)

varié(e) *adj.* varied, diverse

varier to vary

variété *f.* variety show

vaste *adj.* vast

veau *m.* veal; calf; **daube** (*f.*) **de veau** veal stew

vedette *f.* star (*of a show, movie*)

végétarien(ne) *adj.* vegetarian

véhicule *m.* vehicle

vélo *m.* bicycle; **faire du vélo (du VTT)** to bike (mountain bike); **vélo tout terrain (VTT)** mountain bike

vendeur/euse *m., f.* sales clerk

vendre to sell

vendredi *m.* Friday

venir (*p.p.* **venu**) *irreg.* to come; **venir de +** *inf.* to have just (*done s.th.*)

vent *m.* wind; **il fait du vent** it's windy

ventre *m.* belly; stomach; **avoir mal au ventre** to have a stomachache

verbe *m.* verb; **verbe pronominal** *Gram.* pronominal (reflexive) verb

verger *m.* orchard

vérifier to check; to verify

vérité *f.* truth

vernissage *m.* opening; preview

verre *m.* glass; **prendre un verre** to have a drink; **verre d'eau** glass of water

verrouillé(e) *adj.* locked

vers *prep.* toward

verser to pour

version *f.* version; **version originale** original-language version, not dubbed (*film*); **version française** French-language version (*film*)

vert(e) *adj.* green; **citron** (*m.*) **vert** lime; **haricots** (*m. pl.*) **verts** green beans; **oignon** (*m.*) **vert** green onion; **salade** (*f.*) **verte** green salad

vertébré *m.* vertebrate

veste *f.* sports coat

vêtement *m.* piece of clothing; *pl.* clothes; **mettre un vêtement** to put on a piece of clothing

veuf (veuve) *adj.* widowed

viande *f.* meat

vice-versa *adv.* vice versa

victime *f.* victim (*male or female*)

victoire *f.* victory

vide *adj.* empty

vidéo *f.* videotape; *adj.* video

vidéotext *adj.* on-screen text

vie *f.* life; **étape** (*f.*) **de la vie** stage of life; **vie privée** private life; **vie urbaine** city life

vieillesse *f.* old age

Viêtnam *m.* Vietnam

vietnamien(ne) *adj.* Vietnamese; **Vietnamien(ne)** *m., f.* Vietnamese (*person*)

vieux (vieil, vieille [*pl.* **vieux, vieilles**]**)** *adj.* old; *m., f.* old man, old woman; *m. pl.* the elderly

vif (vive) *adj.* lively; spirited; intense

vigne *f.* vine

vignoble *m.* vineyard

vilain *m.* brutish peasant

villa *f.* single-family house; villa

village *m.* village

ville *f.* city; **centre-ville** *m.* downtown; **en ville** in the city; **ville natale** birthplace

vin *m.* wine; **vin pétillant** sparkling wine; **vin rouge (blanc, rosé)** red (white, rosé) wine

vingt *adj.* twenty; **vingt et un (vingt-deux,** etc.**)** twenty-one (twenty-two, etc.); **vingt et unième** twenty-first

vingtième *adj.* twentieth

violence *f.* violence

violent(e) *adj.* violent

violet(te) *adj.* purple

violoniste *m., f.* violinist

virgule *m.* comma

vis-à-vis *adv.* with respect to

visa *m.* visa

visage *m.* face

visionnement *m.* viewing

visionner to watch, view

visite *f.* visit; **rendre visite à** to visit (*s.o.*)

visiter to visit (*a place*)

visiteur/euse *m., f.* visitor

vite *adv.* fast, quickly

vitesse *f.* speed; **limite** (*f.*) **de vitesse** speed limit; **train** (*m.*) **à grande vitesse (TGV)** French high-speed train

viticulture *f.* wine growing

vitre *f.* pane of glass; windowpane

vivant(e) *adj.* alive, living

vivre (*p.p.* **vécu**) *irreg.* to live, be alive; **est-ce qu'il vit toujours?** is he still living; **joie** (*f.*) **de vivre** joy in living; **ils vivent en union libre** they're living together (without marriage)

vocabulaire *m.* vocabulary

voici *prep.* here is/are

voie *f.* road, lane; **voie de chemin de fer** railroad tracks

voilà *prep.* there is/are, here is/are (*for pointing out*)

voile *f.* sail; **bateau à voile** sailboat; **faire de la planche à voile** to windsurf; **faire de la voile** to sail

voir (*p.p.* **vu**) *irreg.* to see

voisin(e) *m., f.* neighbor

voiture *f.* car; **voiture de sport** sportscar

voix *f.* voice; **à haute voix** aloud

vol *m.* flight

volaille *f.* poultry; group of chickens

volcanique *adj.* volcanic

volley-ball *m.* volleyball

volonté *f.* will

volontiers *adv.* willingly, gladly

vos *adj.* your

vote *m.* vote

voter to vote

votre *adj.* your

vôtre: le/la/les vôtre(s) *pron.* yours

vouloir (*p.p.* **voulu**) *irreg.* to want; **je voudrais** I would like; **vouloir bien** to be glad, to be willing (*to do s.th.*); **vouloir dire** to mean

vous *pron.* you; to/for you; **comment allez-vous?** how are you?; **et vous?** and you?; **quel âge avez-vous?** how old are you?

voyage *m.* trip; **agence** (*f.*) **de voyages** travel agency; **faire un voyage** to take a trip; **partir en voyage** to go on a trip; **voyage de noces** honeymoon

voyager to take a trip, travel

voyageur/euse *m., f.* traveler

voyelle *f.* vowel

vrai(e) *adj.* true; **c'est vrai** that's true; **vrai ou faux?** true or false?

vraiment *adv.* truly

VTT (vélo tout terrain) *m.* mountain bike

vue *f.* view; panorama; **point** (*m.*) **de vue** point of view

wagon *m.* (train) car; **wagon fumeurs (non-fumeurs)** smoking (nonsmoking) train car

Web *m.* World Wide Web; **site** (*m.*) **Web** website; **sur le Web** on the Web; **surfer le Web** to surf the Web; **webmestre** *m.* webmaster

week-end *m.* weekend; **passer le week-end** to spend the weekend

world music *f.* world music

y *pron.* there, to/about it/them; **il y a** there is / there are (*for counting*); **il y a (dix ans)** (ten years) ago

yaourt *m.* yogurt

yeux (*pl. of* **œil**) *m. pl.* eyes; **les yeux bandés** blindfolded; **se maquiller les yeux** to put on eye makeup

yoga *m.* yoga

zéro *m.* zero

zone *f.* zone; **zone libre** free zone

zoo *m.* zoo

zut! *interj.* rats!

Lexique anglais-français

See the introduction to the *Lexique français-anglais* for a list of abbreviations used.

abdomen ventre *m.*

able: to be able pouvoir *irreg.*

above au-dessus de

absolute absolu(e)

absolutely: absolutely not ne... pas du tout

accept accepter (de)

according to selon

account: bank account compte *m.* en banque

accountant comptable *m., f.*

accurate exact(e)

accuse accuser

ache: douleur *f.*; **to have an ache in** avoir (*irreg.*) mal à

acquaintance: to make the acquaintance of faire (*irreg.*) la connaissance de

active actif/ive

actor acteur/trice *m., f.*

ad: classified ad petit annonce *f.*

add ajouter

adolescence adolescence *f.*

adolescent adolescent(e) (*fam.* ado) *m., f.*

adore adorer

adult adulte *m., f.*

advertisement publicité *f.*

advise against déconseiller

afraid: to be afraid of avoir (*irreg.*) peur de

Africa Afrique *f.*

after après; après que

afternoon après-midi *m., f.*; **in the afternoon** de l'après-midi; **this afternoon** cet après-midi

again encore

age âge (*m.*); **in old age** au/du troisième âge; **old age** vieillesse *f.*

ago: ten years ago il y a dix ans

agree: I (don't) agree je (ne) suis (pas) d'accord

agriculture agriculture *f.*

airplane avion *m.*

airport aéroport *m.*

aisle seat siège (*m.*) couloir

Algeria Algérie *f.*

Algerian *adj.* algérien(ne)

alive: to be alive vivre

all tout, toute, tous, toutes; **all it takes is** il suffit de; **All Saints' Day** Toussaint *f.*

alleyway ruelle *f.*

allow permettre *irreg.*; laisser; **to be allowed** pouvoir

allspice quatre-épices *m., f.*

almost presque

alone seul(e)

already déjà

also aussi

although bien que

always toujours

amazing étonnant(e)

American *adj.* américain(e); **American football** football (*m.*) américain

amount (*of check or sale*) montant *m.*

amusing amusant(e)

and; and you? et vous (toi)?

angry fâché(e); **to get angry** se fâcher

animal animal *m.* (*pl.* animaux); **animal breeding** élevage *m.*

animated cartoon dessin (*m.*) animé

anniversary (*wedding*) anniversaire (*m.*) de mariage

answer *v.* répondre

answering machine répondeur *m.*

Antarctica Antarctique *m.*

antique dealer antiquaire *m., f.*

anxious inquiet (inquiète)

any *pron.* en; **there is/are not any** il n'y en a pas (de)

apart from à l'écart de

apartment appartement *m.*; **apartment building** immeuble *m.*

apparent apparent(e)

appear apparaître *irreg.*; paraître *irreg.*

applaud applaudir

apple pomme *f.*

April avril *m.*

Arab *adj.* arabe; **old portion of an Arab city** médina *f.*

argue se disputer

arm bras *m.*; (*weapon*) arme *f.*

armchair fauteuil *m.*

armoire armoire *f.*

arrival arrivée *f.*

arrive arriver

artisan artisan(e) *m., f.*

as comme; **as . . . as** aussi... que; **as many/much (. . .) as** autant (de...) que

ashamed: to be ashamed (of) avoir (*irreg.*) honte (de)

Asia Asie *f.*

ask demander

asleep: to fall asleep s'endormir *irreg.*

aspirin aspirine *f.*

astonished: to be astonished that être (*irreg.*) étonné(e) que

at à; **at . . . o'clock** à... heure(s); **at first** d'abord; **at last** enfin; **at the home of** chez; **at what time?** à quelle heure?

athletic sportif/ive

attack *v.* attaquer

attend (*an event*) assister à

attention: to pay attention faire (*irreg.*) attention

August août *m.*

aunt tante *f.*

Australia Australie *f.*

author auteur / femme auteur *m., f.*

automobile voiture *f.*

autoroute autoroute *f.*

autumn automne *m.*

average *adj.* moyen(ne)

baby bébé *m.*

babysitter baby-sitter *m., f.*

back dos *m.*; **to go back home** rentrer; **in back of** derrière

backpack sac à dos *m.*

bad mauvais(e); **it's bad weather** il fait mauvais; **it is too bad that** il est dommage que

badly mal

bake faire (*irreg.*) cuire au four

baker (*of bread*) boulanger/ère; **pastry baker** patissier/ière

bakery (*for bread*) boulangerie *f.*; **pastry shop** patisserie *f.*

ball (*inflated with air*) ballon *m.*; (*not inflated with air*) balle *f.*

bank banque *f.*; **bank account** compte (*m.*) en banque **bank (debit) card** carte (*f.*) bancaire

banks: on the banks of au bord de
bar bar *m.*
barn grange *f.*
baseball base-ball *m.*
basin bassin *m.*; **bathroom basin**
　lavabo *m.*
basket panier *m.*
bathing suit maillot (*m.*) de bain
bathroom salle (*f.*) de bains; **bathroom**
　basin lavabo *m.*
bay baie *f.*
be être *irreg.*; **there is/are** (*counting*) il y
　a; **there is/are, here is/are** (*pointing*
　out) voilà; **these/those/they are**
　(not) ce (ne) sont (pas); **to be alive**
　(*to live*) vivre; **to be mistaken**
　(about) se tromper (de); **to be**
　named s'appeler; **to be (twenty)**
　years old avoir (vingt) ans
beach plage *f.*
beans: green beans haricots (*m. pl.*)
　verts
bear ours *m.*
beautiful beau (bel, belle, beaux,
　belles)
because parce que
become devenir *irreg.*; **to become angry**
　(with) se fâcher (contre); **to become**
　sick tomber malade
bed lit *m.*); **to go to bed** se coucher;
　to make the bed faire (*irreg.*) le lit
bedroom chambre *f.*
beef bœuf *m.*
beet betterave *f.*
before avant; avant de ; avant que;
　before (*the hour*) moins
begin commencer
behaved: well-behaved gentil(le)
behind derrière
believe croire *irreg.*
belly ventre *m.*
belong to appartenir (*irreg.*) à
below au-dessous de
belt ceinture *f.*
Berber berbère
beside à côté de
best: the best *adj.* le/la/les meilleur(e)(s);
　adv. le mieux
better *adj.* meilleur(e); *adv.* mieux
between entre
bicycle vélo *m.*; **to go bicycling (to**
　bike) faire (*irreg.*) du vélo; **to**
　mountain bike faire (*irreg.*) du VTT
big grand(e)
billiards billiard *m.*
billion milliard *m.*
biochemistry biochimie *f.*
biology biologie *f.*
bird oiseau *m.*
birth naissance *f.*

birthday anniversaire *m.*
black noir(e)
blackboard tableau *m.* (*pl.* tableaux);
　blackboard eraser éponge *f.*
blouse chemisier *m.*
blue bleu(e); **blues** (*music*) blues *m.*
board: blackboard tableau *m.* (*pl.*
　tableaux); **bulletin board** tableau
　d'affichage
boat bateau *m.*; **sailboat** bateau à
　voile
body corps *m.*; **body of work**
　œuvre *f.*
boil faire (*irreg.*) bouillir
book livre *m.*
bookmark signet *m.*
bookstore librairie *f.*
boot botte *f.*
booth: telephone booth cabine
　téléphonique
boring ennuyeux/euse
born: to be born naître *irreg.*
boss patron(ne) *m., f.*
bottle bouteille *f.*
bowling bowling *m.*
box boîte *f.*
boy garçon *m.*
brain cerveau *m.*
bread pain *m.*; **bread roll** petit pain *m.*;
　bread with butter and jam
　tartine *f.*
break (*a limb*) se casser
breakfast petit déjeuner *m.*
breeding: animal breeding (*farming*)
　l'élevage *m.*
bridge pont *m.*
brother frère *m.*; **brother-in-law,**
　stepbrother beau-frère *m.*
　(*pl.* beaux-frères)
brown brun(e); **chestnut brown**
　marron *inv.*
brush (one's teeth, hair) se brosser (les
　dents, les cheveux)
buffet buffet *m.*
building bâtiment *m.*; **apartment**
　building immeuble *m.* **building**
　superintendent gardien(ne) (*m., f.*)
　d'immeuble
bulletin board tableau (*m.*)
　d'affichage
burial enterrement *m.*
bus: short distance, city bus bus *m.*;
　long distance, tour bus autocar *m.*
business affaires *f. pl.*; **business**
　administration administration (*f.*) des
　affaires; **business economics** économie
　(*f.*) de gestion
but mais
butcher boucher/ère *m., f.*; **butcher shop**
　boucherie *f.*

butter beurre *m.*
buy *v.* acheter
by par
'bye salut

café café *m.*
calculator calculatrice *f.*
call *v.* appeler
camera appareil photo *m.*
campground camping *m.*
camping: to go camping faire (*irreg.*) du
　camping
can (to be able) pouvoir *irreg.*
can (*container*) boîte *f.*
Canada Canada *m.*
Canadian *adj.* canadien(ne)
canoeing: to go canoeing faire (*irreg.*) du
　canoë
car voiture *f.*; **train car** wagon *m.*
carbonated *adj.* gazeux/euse
card carte *f.*; **credit card** carte de crédit;
　bank (debit) card carte bancaire
cardamom cardamome *m.*
carrot carotte *f.*
cartoon: animated cartoon dessin (*m.*)
　animé
case: in case au cas où; **in that case**
　alors
cash: in cash en espèces; **to cash a check**
　toucher un chèque
cat chat *m.*
cave: to explore caves faire (*irreg.*) de la
　spéléologie
CD player lecteur (*m.*) de CD
celebration fête *f.*
cell phone portable *m.*
century siècle *m.*
certain certain(e); sûr(e)
chair chaise *f.*
chalk craie *f.*
champagne champagne *m.*
change *v.* changer
character (*in a story*) personnage *m.*
check chèque *m.*; **to cash a check**
　toucher un chèque; **to check a**
　suitcase enregistrer une valise; **to**
　deposit a check déposer un chèque;
　to write a check faire (*irreg.*) un
　chèque
checkbook carnet (*m.*) de chèques
checkout caisse *f.*
cheese fromage *m.*
chemistry chimie *f.*
cherry cerise *f.*
chest poitrine *f.*
chestnut brown marron *inv.*
chicken poulet *m.*); **chicken with french**
　fries poulet frites *m.*; **poultry, group**
　of chickens volaille *f.*
chick peas pois (*m. pl.*) chiches

child enfant *m., f.*
childhood enfance *f.*
chimney cheminée *f.*
China Chine *f.*
Chinese chinois(e) *adj.*
chiropractic chiropraxie *f.*
chocolate chocolat *m.*; **chocolate mousse** mousse (*f.*) au chocolat
choose choisir
Christmas Noël *m.*
church église *f.*
cinnamon cannelle *f.*
circus cirque *m.*
city ville *f.*; **city life** vie (*f.*) urbaine; **old portion of an Arab city** médina *f.*
civil servant fonctionnaire *m., f.*
class classe *f.*; **to cut a class** sécher un cours
classified ad petite annonce *f.*
classmate camarade (*m., f.*) de classe
classroom salle (*f.*) de classe
clear clair(e); **the sky is clear** le ciel est clair
click (on) cliquer (sur)
client client(e) *m., f.*
climb *v.* monter
clock horloge *f.*
close *v.* fermer
clothing (*article*) vêtement *m.*; **to put on a piece of clothing** mettre (*irreg.*) un vêtement
cloudy nuageux/euse; **the sky is cloudy** le ciel est couvert
coast côte *f.*
coat: overcoat manteau (*m.*); **sports coat** veste *f.*
Coca Cola coca *m.*
coconut noix (*f.*) de coco
coffee café *m.*; **coffee with an equal amount of milk** café au lait
cold: to be cold avoir (*irreg.*) froid; **it's cold out** il fait froid; **common cold** rhume *m.*
collection ensemble *m.*
column (*newspaper*) rubrique *f.*; **society column** carnet (*m.*) du jour
comb (**one's hair**) se peigner (les cheveux)
come venir *irreg.*; **to come back** revenir *irreg.*, rentrer; **to come home** rentrer
comic strip bande (*f.*) dessinée
commerce commerce *m.*
commercial publicité *f.*
company société *f.*
compose composer
composer compositeur/trice *m., f.*
composition (*literary, artwork, musical*) œuvre *m.*

computer ordinateur *m.*; **computer mouse** souris *f.*; **computer science** informatique *f.*; **laptop computer** portable *m.*
concert concert *m.*
conservation conservation *f.*
consider (*s.o., s.th.*) **to be** trouver
construct *v.* construire
consume consommer
consumption consommation *f.*
contain contenir *irreg.*
contemporary contemporain(e)
continue continuer
contract contrat *m.*
control room régie *f.*
cook cuisinier/ière *m., f.*; **to cook** (*s.th.*) faire (*irreg.*) cuire **to cook (make) a meal** faire (*irreg.*) la cuisine
cooking pot (*large, iron*) marmite *f.*
cool: it's cool out il fait frais
coriander coriandre *f.*
corn maïs *m.*
corner coin *m.*
cough *v.* tousser; **cough drop** pastille *f.*
could you show me the way to . . . ? est-ce que vous pourriez m'indiquer le chemin pour aller à... ?
country pays *m.*; **country dweller** paysan(ne) *m., f.*; **country music** country *f.*; **in the country** à la campagne
course cours *m.*; **first course** (*meal*) entrée *f.*; **of course** bien sûr (que oui); **of course not** bien sûr que non; **to fail a course** échouer à un cours; **to pass a course** réussir à un cours; **to take a course** suivre un cours; **What courses are you taking?** Quels cours est-ce que tu suis?
couscous couscous *m.*; **couscous grains** grains (*m. pl.*) de couscous
cousin cousin(e) *m., f.*
cover *v.* couvrir *irreg.*
cow vache *f.*
craftsperson artisan(e) *m., f.*
crazy fou (folle)
cream crème *f.*
credit: credit card carte (*f.*) de crédit; **credit union** caisse (*f.*) populaire
croissant croissant *m.*
crop récolte *f.*
cross *v.* traverser
cross-country: to cross-country ski faire du ski de fond
crossword puzzle mots (*m. pl.*) croisés
cultivate cultiver
cup tasse *f.*
curator (**of a museum**) conservateur/trice *m., f.* (de musée)

current *adj.* actuel(le)
curry curry *m.*
customs douane *f.*; **to go through customs** passer la douane

dairy product store crémerie *f.*
dark *adj.* sombre
daughter fille *f.*
day jour *m.*
dear cher (chère)
death mort *f.*
December décembre *m.*
decide (to do) décider (de) **decision: to make a decision** prendre (*irreg.*) une décision
deer cerf *m.*
delicatessen charcuterie *f.*
demand *v.* exiger
demonstration (*public, political*) manifestation *f.*
department (*in a store*) rayon *m.*; **department store** grand magasin *m.*
departure départ *m.*
deposit *v.*: **deposit a check** déposer un chèque
descend descendre
describe décrire *irreg.*
desire *v.* désirer
desk bureau *m.* (*pl.* bureaux)
dessert dessert *m.*
destroy détruire *irreg.*
detest détester
dial (a phone number) composer un numéro; **dial tone** tonalité *f.*
dictionary dictionnaire *m.*
die *v.* mourir *irreg.*
difficult difficile
dignity: with dignity dignement
dilapidated délabré(e)
dine dîner
dining room salle (*f.*) à manger
dinner dîner *m.*; **to eat dinner, to dine** dîner
diploma diplôme *m.*
direction direction *f.*
disappear disparaître *irreg.*
discover découvrir *irreg.*
discreet discret/ète
discuss discuter
dish: hot dish plat (*m.*) chaud; **main dish** plat (*m.*) principal; **to do the dishes** faire (*irreg.*) la vaisselle
dissertation thèse *m.*
district arrondissement *m.*
diverse divers(e)
divorce *v.* (**to get divorced**) divorcer; **divorced** divorcé(e)

do faire *irreg.*; **to do errands** faire les courses; **to do homework** faire les devoirs; **to do housework** faire le ménage; **to do the dishes** faire la vaisselle; **to do the laundry** faire la lessive

doctor médecin / femme médecin *m., f.*

doctorate doctorat *m.*

documentary documentaire *m.*

dog chien *m.*

door porte *f.*

doubt *v.* douter; **it is doubtful that** il est douteux que; **no doubt** sans doute

down: **to get/go down** descendre; **to go down a street** descendre une rue

dozen douzaine *f.*

dramatic arts arts (*m. pl.*) dramatiques

dress robe *f.*; **to get dressed (in)** s'habiller (en)

drink boisson *f.*; **to drink** boire *irreg.*; **to have a drink** prendre un verre

drive conduire *irreg.*

driver conducteur/trice *m., f.*

drug (**medicine**) médicament *m.*

during pendant

dynamic dynamique

each chaque

ear oreille *f.*

early en avance; tôt

earth terre *f.*

east est *m.*

Easter Pâques *m. s., f. pl.*

easy facile

eat manger; **to eat dinner** dîner

economics: **business economics** économie (*f.*) de gestion

edge: **on the edge of** au bord de

editor: **letters to the editor** courrier (*m.*) des lecteurs

editorial éditorial *m.* (*pl.* éditoriaux)

efficient efficace

effort: **with effort** fort

egg œuf *m.*; **hard-boiled egg with mayonnaise** œuf dur mayonnaise

eggplant aubergine *f.*

eight huit

eighteen dix-huit

eighth huitième

eighty quatre-vingts

elderly au/du troisième âge

electronic mailbox boîte (*f.*) aux lettres électronique

elegant élégant(e)

elevation (*height*) hauteur *f.*

eleven onze

e-mail courrier (*m.*) électronique; **e-mail message** mél *m.*

employ *v.* employer

encounter rencontre *f.*

encourage encourager

engineer ingénieur / femme ingénieur *m., f.*

engineering génie *m.*; **chemical (electrical, industrial, mechanical) engineering** génie chimique (électrique, industriel, mécanique)

England Angleterre *f.*

English *adj.* anglais(e); (*language*) anglais *m.*

English Channel Manche *f.*

enough assez (de); **it is enough** il suffit

enter entrer

entertainment (*show*) spectacle *m.*

envelope enveloppe *f.*

environment environnement *m.*

eraser gomme *f.*; **blackboard eraser** éponge *f.*

errands: **to do errands** faire (*irreg.*) les courses

escape *v.* s'échapper

especially surtout

essential: **it is essential** il est essentiel

Europe Europe *f.*

evening soir *m.*; soirée *f.*; **in the evening** du soir; **this evening** ce soir

event événement *m.*; **cultural event** manifestation (*f.*) culturelle; **in the event that** au cas où; **special event** spectacle *m.*

ever déjà

every tout, toute, tous, toutes; **every day** tous les jours

everyone tout le monde

everywhere partout

evident évident(e)

ewe brebis *f.*

exact exact(e)

exam examen *m.*; **to fail an exam** échouer à un examen; **to pass an exam** réussir à un examen; **to study for an exam** préparer un examen; **to take an exam** passer un examen

execute (s.o.) **by shooting** fusiller

executive cadre *m., f.*

exhibit: **art exhibit** exposition (*f.*) d'art

exit sortie *f.*

expensive cher (chère)

explore caves faire de la spéléologie

eye œil *m.* (*pl.* yeux)

face visage *m.*

facial tissue mouchoir (*m.*) en papier

facility local *m.* (*pl.* locaux)

facing en face de

fail échouer; **to fail a course (an exam)** échouer à un cours (à un examen)

fall *v.* tomber; (*season*) automne *m.* **to fall asleep** s'endormir *irreg.*

false faux (fausse); **that's (it's) false (wrong)** c'est faux

famous célèbre

far (from) loin (de)

farm ferme *f.*

farmer agriculteur/trice *m., f.*; fermier/ière *m., f.*

fast *adj.* rapide; *adv.* vite; **fast food** fast-food *m.*; **fast-food worker** employé(e) (*m., f.*) de fast-food

father père *m.*; **father-in-law, stepfather** beau-père *m.* (*pl.* beaux-pères)

February février *m.*

feel: **to feel like** (*doing*) avoir envie de; **to feel nauseated** avoir mal au cœur

festival festival *m.* (*pl.* festivals); fête *f.*

fever fièvre *f.*

few peu (de); **a few** quelques; un peu (de)

fewer (. . .) than moins (de...) que

fewest: **the fewest** le moins (de)

field champ *m.*

fifteen quinze

fifth cinquième

fifty cinquante; **in one's fifties** (*age*) dans la cinquantaine

film film *m.*

finally enfin

find *v.* trouver

fine: **I'm fine** ça va bien

finish *v.* finir

fire feu *m.*; **to fire** licencier; **to fire on** tirer sur

fireplace cheminée *f.*

first *adj.* premier/ière; **at first, first (of all)** *adv.* d'abord; **first course** (*meal*) entrée *f.*; **first of the month** premier *m.*

fish poisson *m.*; **fish store** poissonnerie *f.*; **to go fishing** aller (*irreg.*) à la pêche

five cinq

flight vol *m.*

flower fleur *f.*

flu grippe *f.*

follow suivre *irreg.*

food aliment *m.*

foot pied *m.*; **on foot** à pied

football (**American**) football (*m.*) américain

for pour; (*time*) depuis

forest forêt *f.*

foreign *adj.* étranger/ère; **foreign language** langue (*f.*) étrangère

forget oublier
fork fourchette *f.*
form *v.* former
formerly autrefois
forty quarante; **in one's forties** *(age)* dans la quarantaine
four quatre
fourteen quatorze
fourth quatrième
France France *f.*
frank franc(he)
French français(e); *(language)* français *m.*; **French fries** frites *f. pl.*; **French-speaking** francophone
Friday vendredi *m.*
friend ami(e) *m., f.*
Frisbee Frisbee *m.*
from de; **from . . . to . . .** de... à...; **from time to time** de temps en temps
front: in front of devant; **on the front page** *(newspaper)* à la une
fruit fruit *m.*
fry faire *(irreg.)* frire
full complet/ète; **full-time** à plein temps
funny amusant(e)
furious furieux/euse
furniture (piece of) meuble *m.*
future avenir *m.*

gallery galerie *f.*
game jeu *m.* *(pl.* jeux)
garden jardin *m.*
garlic ail *m.*
gasoline essence *f.*
gate *(airport)* porte *(f.)* d'embarquement
gather *(flowers)* cueillir *irreg.*; **to gather up (toys, etc.)** ramasser
gentle doux (douce)
geography géographie *f.*
German *adj.* allemand(e)
Germany Allemagne *f.*
get: to get along well (poorly) (with) s'entendre bien (mal) (avec); **to get around** circuler; **to get down** descendre; **to get dressed (in, as)** s'habiller (en); **to get up** se lever
ginger gingembre *m.*
girl jeune fille *f.*
give *v.* donner; **to give a gift** offrir un cadeau
glad: to be glad to vouloir *(irreg.)* bien
glass verre *m.*
go aller *irreg.*; **to go back (home)** rentrer; **to go camping** faire *(irreg.)* du camping; **to go canoeing** faire *(irreg.)* du canoë; **to go down** descendre; **to go down (up) a street** descendre (monter) une rue; **to go fishing** aller à la pêche; **to go horseback riding** monter à cheval; **to go out** sortir *irreg.*; **to go rock climbing** faire de l'escalade; **to go shopping** faire *(irreg.)* du shopping; **to go through customs** passer la douane; **to go to bed** se coucher **to go up** monter
golf: to play golf jouer au golf
good bon(ne); **good-bye** au revoir; **good-looking** beau (bel, belle, beaux, belles); **good luck** bonne chance; **to have a good time** s'amuser
grade *(on a paper)* note *f.*
grain céréale *f.*
granddaughter petite-fille *f.* *(pl.* petites-filles)
grandfather grand-père *m.* *(pl.* grandspères)
grandmother grand-mère *f.* *(pl.* grandsmères)
grandparents grands-parents *m. pl.*
grandson petit-fils *m.* *(pl.* petits-fils)
grape raisin *m.*
great super; magnifique
green vert(e); **green beans** haricots *(m. pl.)* verts
greenhouse effect effet *(m.)* de serre
greeting accueil *m.*
gray gris(e)
grocer épicier/ière *m., f.*; **grocery store** épicerie *f.*
ground floor rez-de-chaussée *m.*
group ensemble *m.*
grow pousser
guard *v.* garder; **security guard** agent(e) *m., f.* de sécurité
guitar guitare *f.*
gymnasium gymnase *m.*

hair cheveux *m. pl.*
half: half-kilogram demi-kilo *m.,*; **half-past** *(the hour)* et demi(e); **half-time** à mi-temps
ham jambon *m.*
hamburger hamburger *m.*
hand main *f.*
handkerchief: paper handkerchief mouchoir *(m.)* en papier
handsome beau (bel, belle, beaux, belles)
hang glide faire *(irreg.)* du parapente
hang up *(the telephone receiver)* *v.* raccrocher
Hannukah Hannukah
happen se passer
happy heureux/euse
harvest récolte *f.*; **to harvest** récolter

hat chapeau *m.*
hate *v.* détester
have avoir *(irreg.)*; **to have** *(s.th. to eat)* prendre *(irreg.)*; **to have a drink** prendre un verre; **to have a good time** s'amuser; **to have a party** faire la fête; **to have a picnic** faire un pique-nique, piqueniquer; **to have a stomachache** avoir mal au ventre; **to have a view of (the port)** donner sur (le port); **to have lunch** déjeuner; **to have pain, an ache in, to have a sore . . .** avoir *(irreg.)* mal à; **to have to** *(must)* devoir *irreg.*
head tête *f.*
headline gros titre *m.*; manchette *f.*
health santé *f.*
hear entendre
heart cœur *m.*
heat *v.* chauffer; *n.* chaleur *f.*
height *(elevation)* hauteur *f.*
hello bonjour
here ici; là; **here is (here are)** voici
hesitate *(to do)* hésiter (à)
hi salut
hide se réfugier
high-speed train train à grande vitesse *(fam.* TGV) *m.*
highway autoroute *f.*
hike *v.* faire *(irreg.)* une randonnée
hill colline *f.*
hip-hop music hip-hop *m.*
hire engager
history histoire *f.*
hit *v.* frapper
hockey: to play hockey jouer au hockey
hold *v.* tenir *(irreg.)*
holiday congé *m.*; fête *f.*; **legal holiday** jour *(m.)* férié
home: at the home of chez; **home page** page *(f.)* d'accueil; **personal home page** page *(f.)* perso; **to come home** rentrer
homeland patrie *f.*
homework devoir *m.*; **to do homework** faire *(irreg.)* les devoirs
hope *v.* espérer; souhaiter
horse cheval *m.*; **to go horseback riding** monter à cheval
hospital hôpital *m.*
hostage otage *m.*
hot: to feel hot avoir *(irreg.)* chaud; **it's hot out** il fait chaud
hotel hôtel *m.*
hour heure *f.*; **rush hour** heures *(f. pl.)* de pointe
house maison *f.*

housework: to do the housework faire (*irreg.*) le ménage
how comment; **how are you?** comment allez-vous? (vas-tu?); **how many, how much** combien de; **how old are you (is he, etc.)?** quel âge avez-vous (a-t-il, *etc.*)?; **How's it going?** Ça va?
hundred cent
hungry: to be hungry avoir (*irreg.*) faim
hunt *v.* chasser
hurry *v.* se dépêcher; **in a hurry** pressé(e)
husband mari *m.*

ice cream glace *f.*
ice skate *n.* patin *m.*; *v.* patiner; faire (*irreg.*) du patin à glace
icon (computer) icone *m.*
if si; **if I were you** à ta (votre) place
immediate immédiat(e)
immigrant immigré(e) *m., f.*
important important(e)
impossible impossible
in dans; **in a hurry** pressé(e); **in back of** derrière; **in case, in the event that** au cas où; **in cash** en espèces; **in front of** devant; **in good (great) shape** en bonne (pleine) forme; **in old age** au troisième âge; **in one's thirties** (*age*) dans la trentaine; **in order to/that** afin de/que, pour que; **in short** *interj.* enfin; **in that case** alors; **in the afternoon** de l'après-midi; **in the country** à la campagne; **in the evening** du soir; **in the middle of** au milieu de; **in the morning** du matin; **in the past** autrefois; **in your place** à ta (votre) place
incredible incroyable
India Inde *f.*
Indian *adj.* indien(ne)
indicate indiquer
inhabitant habitant(e) *m., f.*
intellectual intellectuel(le)
interesting intéressant(e); **to be interested in** s'intéresser à
Internet: Internet user internaute *m., f.*; **on the Internet** sur Internet
internship stage *m.*
interpreter interprète *m., f.*
invite inviter
is: to be être; **is it so** (*true*) **that . . .** Est-ce que...; **isn't that right?** n'est-ce pas?; non?; **is that right?** c'est ça?; **is this (that, it) . . . ?** est-ce... ?; **it could be that, it is possible that** il se peut que
island île *f.*
Israel Israël *m.*

Israeli *adj.* israélien(ne)
it: it could be that il se peut que; **it is . . .** c'est...; **it is not . . .** ce n'est pas...; **it's (ten) o'clock** il est (dix) heures; **It's a pleasure** (*to meet you*). Enchanté(e).
Italian italien(ne) *adj.*
Italy Italie *f.*

jam confiture *f.*
January janvier *m.*
Japan Japon *m.*
Japanese *adj.* japonais(e)
jeans jean *m., s.*
job emploi *m.*; poste *m.*; travail *m.*
jogging jogging *m.*; **jogging trail** piste (*f.*) de jogging
journalist journaliste *m., f.*
joyful, joyous joyeux/euse; **joyful attitude** (*toward life*) joie (*f.*) de vivre
juice (orange) jus *m.* (d'orange)
July juillet *m.*
June juin *m.*
just: to have just (*done something*) venir (*irreg.*) de + *inf.*

keep garder
kill *v.* tuer
kilogram kilo *m.*; **half kilogram** demi-kilo *m.*
kind *adj.* gentil(le)
kiss (each other) *v.* s'embrasser
kitchen cuisine *f.*
knee genou *m.*
knife couteau *m.*
know: to be acquainted with connaître (*irreg.*); **I don't know** je ne sais pas; **to know** (*a fact*) savoir (*irreg.*)

Labor Day fête (*f.*) du travail
laboratory laboratoire *m.*
laborer: manual laborer ouvrier/ière *m., f.*
lake lac *m.*
language langue *f.*; **foreign language** langue étrangère; **foreign language teaching** enseignement (*m.*) des langues étrangères
laptop computer portable *m.*
last *adj.* dernier/ière; **at last** enfin; **last stop** terminus *m.*
late en retard; tard
later plus tard
launch *v.* lancer
laundry: to do the laundry faire (*irreg.*) la lessive
law droit *m.*
lawn bowling: to play lawn bowling jouer à la pétanque (aux boules)

lawyer avocat(e) *m., f.*
leaf feuille *f.*
learn apprendre (*irreg.*)
least: the least le/la/les moins
leave partir *irreg.*; **to leave** (*s.o., a place*) quitter; **to leave** (*s.th. somewhere*) laisser
lecture conférence *f.*
left: to/on the left à gauche
leg jambe *f.*
legal holiday jour (*m.*) férié
leisure activities distractions *f. pl.*; loisirs *m. pl.*
lemon citron *m.*
lemongrass citronnelle *f.*
lentil lentille *f.*
less moins; **less (. . .)** moins (de...); **less (than)** moins (que)
lesson leçon *f.*; **to study for a lesson** préparer une leçon
let laisser
letter lettre *f.*; **letters to the editor** courrier (*m.*) des lecteurs
lettuce salade *f.*
library bibliothèque *f.*
lie *v.* mentir (*irreg.*)
life vie *f.*; **city life** vie urbaine
light: to turn on the light mettre (*irreg.*) la lumière; **traffic light** feu *m.*
light (*weight*) léger (légère)
like *prep.* comme; *adj.* tel(le)
like: *v.* aimer; **I would like** je voudrais
likely: it is (un)likely that il est (peu) probable que
line: to stand in line faire (*irreg.*) la queue
listen (to) écouter
literary littéraire
little peu (de); **a little** un peu (de)
live *v.* (*reside*) habiter; **live** (*to be alive*) vivre; **they are living together (without marriage)** ils vivent en union libre
living: joy in living joie (*f.*) de vivre; **living room** salle (*f.*) de séjour
location endroit *m.*; lieu *m.* (*pl.* lieux)
long time: for a long time longtemps
look (at) regarder; **to look for** chercher; **to look (like)** avoir (*irreg.*) l'air
lose perdre; **to lose one's mind** perdre la tête; **to lose patience** perdre patience
lot: a lot (of) beaucoup (de)
love *v.* aimer
low-cut: in low-cut clothing en décolleté
lozenge (*cough drop*) pastille *f.*

lunch déjeuner *m.*; **to have lunch** déjeuner *v.*
lung poumon *m.*

madam (Mrs.) madame (Mme)
magazine magazine *m.*
Maghreb Maghreb *m.*; **from the Maghreb** maghrébin(e)
magnificent magnifique
mail *n.* poste *f.*; (*letters, etc.*) courrier *m.*
major in se spécialiser en; faire (*irreg.*) des études en
make faire *irreg.*, rendre; **to make a decision** prendre (*irreg.*) une décision; **to make a meal** faire (*irreg.*) la cuisine; **to make a mistake (about)** se tromper (de); **to make the acquaintance of** faire (*irreg.*) la connaissance de; **to make the bed** faire (*irreg.*) le lit; **to make up one's eyes (one's lips)** se maquiller les yeux (les lèvres)
makeup: to put on makeup se maquiller
man homme *m.*
management gestion *f.*
manual laborer ouvrier/ière *m., f.*
many beaucoup (de); **how many** combien de; **too many** trop (de)
map carte *f.*; (*subway, city, region*) plan *m.*
March mars *m.*
market marché *m.*
marketing marketing *m.*
marriage mariage *m.*
married marié(e)
match (soccer, boxing) match *m.* (de foot, de boxe)
mathematics (math) mathématiques (maths) *f. pl.*
May mai *m.*
meal repas *m.*; **to cook a meal** faire la cuisine
mean *v.* vouloir (*irreg.*) dire
means moyen *m.*
meat viande *f.*
medicine médicament *m.*
media média *m. pl.*
meet *v.* rencontrer **Nice to meet you** Enchanté(e)
meeting rencontre *f.*; (*business*) réunion *f.*
merchant marchand(e) *m., f.*
method moyen *m.*
Mexican mexicain(e)
Mexico Mexique *m.*
microwave oven four (*m.*) à micro-ondes
middle: in the middle of au milieu de

midnight minuit *m.*
mild: it's mild out il fait doux
milk lait *m.*
million million *m.*
mind: to lose one's mind perdre la tête
mineral water eau (*f.*) minérale
minus moins
mirror miroir *m.*
miserable malheureux/euse
Miss mademoiselle (Mlle)
miss: to be missed by (*s. o.*) manquer à; **I miss you** tu me manques
mistake: to make a mistake, be mistaken (about) se tromper (de)
mix *v.* mélanger
mode moyen *m.*
moderate moyen(ne)
Monday lundi *m.*
money argent *m.*
month mois *m.*
more: more (. . .) plus (de); **more (than)** plus (que)
morning matin *m.*; **in the morning** du matin; **this morning** ce matin
Moroccan *adj.* marocain(e)
Morocco Maroc *m.*
mosque mosquée *f.*
most (of) la plupart (de); **the most (of)** le/la/les plus (de)
mother mère *f.*; **mother-in-law, stepmother** belle-mère *f.* (*pl.* belles-mères)
mountain montagne *f.*; **mountain bike** vélo *m.* tout terrain (VTT); **old rounded mountain range** massif *m.*
mouse souris *f.*; **computer mouse** souris *f.*
mousse: chocolate mousse mousse (*f.*) au chocolat
mouth bouche *f.*
movie theater cinéma *m.*
much beaucoup (de); **how much** combien de; **so much** tellement; **too much** trop (de)
muscle muscle *m.*
museum musée *m.*; **art (natural science) museum** musée d'art (de sciences naturelles); **museum curator** conservateur/trice (*m., f.*) de musée
mushroom champignon *m.*
music musique *f.*
musician musicien(ne) *m., f.*
must: one must (not) il (ne) faut (pas); **must (to have to)** devoir *irreg.*
mutton mouton *m.*

name: to be named s'appeler; **his (her) name is** il (elle) s'appelle; **my name is** je m'appelle
napkin serviette *f.*
narrow étroit(e)
national holiday fête (*f.*) nationale
nauseated: to feel nauseated avoir (*irreg.*) mal au cœur
near près (de)
nearly presque
necessary: it is necessary il est nécessaire, il faut; **it is not necessary** il n'est pas nécessaire
need: to need avoir (*irreg.*) besoin de
neighbor voisin(e) *m., f.*
neighborhood quartier *m.*
nephew neveu *m.*
network (*system*) réseau *m.*; **television network** chaîne *f.*
never ne... jamais
new nouveau (nouvel, nouvelle, nouveaux, nouvelles); **New Year's Day** nouvel an *m.*
news actualités *f. pl.*, informations *f. pl.*; **news program** actualités *f. pl.*, informations *f. pl.*
newspaper journal *m.* (*pl.* journaux); **newspaper section, column** rubrique *f.*
next *adj.* prochain(e); *adv.* ensuite; puis; **the next day** le lendemain *m.*
nice (*person*) gentil(le); sympathique (*fam.* sympa); (*weather*) beau; **it's nice out** il fait beau; **Nice to meet you** Enchanté(e)
niece nièce *f.*
night nuit *f.*; **nightclub** boîte (*f.*) de nuit
nine neuf
nineteen dix-neuf
ninety quatre-vingt-dix
ninth neuvième
no non; **no doubt** sans doute; **no one** ne... personne
nobody ne... personne
noncarbonated *adj.* plat(e)
nonsmoking (train) car wagon (*m.*) non-fumeurs
noon midi *m.*
normally d'habitude
north nord *m.*
North America Amérique (*f.*) du Nord
nose nez *m.*; **runny nose** le nez qui coule
not ne... pas; **not anymore** ne... plus; **not at all, absolutely not** ne... pas du tout; **not ever** ne... jamais; **not one, not any** ne... aucun(e); **not yet** ne... pas encore

notebook cahier *m.*

nothing ne... rien

novel roman *m.*

novelist romancier/ière *m., f.*

November novembre *m.*

now maintenant

numerous nombreux/euse

nurse infirmier/ière *m., f.*; **nurse's aide** garde-malade *m., f.*

obey obéir (à)

obituary nécrologie *f.*; **obituary column** nécrologie *f.*

obtain obtenir (*irreg.*)

ocean océan *m.*

o'clock: it's (five) o'clock il est (cinq) heures; **at (five) o'clock** à (cinq) heures

October octobre *m.*

of de; **of course** bien sûr (que oui); **of course not** bien sûr que non; **of it/them/there** en

offer *v.* offrir (*irreg.*)

office bureau *m.* (*pl.* bureaux)

often souvent

oil (olive, sesame) huile *f.* (d'olive, de sésame)

okay d'accord; **I'm okay** ça va; **okay?** d'accord?; OK?

old vieux (vieil, vieille, vieux, vieilles); **elderly, in old age** au/du troisième âge; **old age** vieillesse *f.*; **old portion of an Arab city** médina *f.*

omelet omelette *f.*

on sur; **on foot** à pied; **on the street** dans la rue; **on the banks (shore, edge) of** au bord de; **on the front page** à la une; **on the Internet** sur Internet; **on the left/right** à gauche/droite; **on time** à l'heure; **on vacation** en vacances

one (*numeral*) un; (*number, amount*) un(e)

onion oignon *m.*

only ne... que; seulement

open *v.* ouvrir (*irreg.*)

opening (*of an art exhibit*) vernissage *m.*

opera opéra *m.*

or ou

orange *adj.* orange *inv.*

orchard verger *m.*

orchestra orchestre *m.*

order: in order that afin que; pour que; **in order to** afin de

other autre

out: to go out sortir

outdoors en plein air

oven four *m.*; **microwave oven** four à micro-ondes

over au-dessus de

overcoat manteau *m.*

overlook (the port) donner sur (le port)

owe devoir (*irreg.*)

owner (*of a bar, restaurant*) patron(ne) *m., f.*

pad of paper bloc-notes *m.*

page page *f.*; **home page** page d'accueil; **on the front page** à la une; **personal home page** page perso

pain douleur *f.*; **to have pain in** avoir (*irreg.*) mal à

painter peintre / femme peintre *m., f.*

painting (*action, art*) peinture *f.*; (*picture*) tableau *m.*

Pakistan Pakistan *m.*

Pakistani *adj.* pakistanais(e)

pants pantalon *m. s.*

paper: pad of paper bloc-notes *m.*; **paper handkerchief** mouchoir (*m.*) en papier; **sheet of paper** feuille (*f.*) de papier

parents parents *m., pl.*

park *n.* parc *m.*; *v.* stationner

parking lot, parking garage parking *m.*

parsley persil *m.*

part partie *f.*

party fête *f.*; **to have a party** faire (*irreg.*) la fête; **political party** parti (*m.*) politique

pass (by) passer (par); **to pass a course (exam)** réussir à un cours (à un examen)

passenger passager/ère *m., f.*

Passover pâque *f.*

passport passeport *m.*

past: in the past autrefois

pasta pâtes *f. pl.*

pastry pâtisserie *f.*; **pastry baker** pâtissier/ière *m., f.*; **pastry shop** pâtisserie *f.*

patience: to lose patience perdre patience

pay payer; **to pay attention** faire (*irreg.*) attention

peanut cacahouète *f.* (*alt. spelling* cacahuète)

peas petits pois *m. pl.*; **chick-peas** pois (*m. pl.*) chiches

pedestrian street rue (*f.*) piétonne

pen stylo *m.*

pencil crayon *m.*

penmanship écriture *f.*

people gens *m. pl.*

pepper poivre *m.*

per par

permit *v.* permettre

perhaps peut-être

person personne *f.*; **person who is afraid of technology** technophobe *m., f.*

philosophy philosophie *f.*

phone: See **telephone.**

photograph: photographie (*fam.* photo) *f.*; **to take photographs** faire (*irreg.*) de la photographie; **to take a photograph** prendre (*irreg.*) une photo

photographer photographe *m., f.*

physics physique *f.*

piano piano *m.*

pick (*flowers*) cueillir (*irreg.*); **to pick up** (*toys, etc.*) ramasser; **to pick up** (*the telephone receiver*) décrocher

picnic: to have a picnic faire (*irreg.*) un pique-nique, piqueniquer

pie tarte *f.*

piece (of) morceau *m.* (de)

pig porc *m.*

pink rose

pita (bread) (pain) pita *m.*

pizza pizza *f.*

place (*location*) endroit *m.*; lieu *m.* (*pl.* lieux); **in your place** à ta (votre) place; **to take place** avoir (*irreg.*) lieu

plain *n.* plaine *f.*

plant *v.* planter

plate assiette *f.*

plateau plateau *m.*

platform quai *m.*

play *v.* jouer; *n.* pièce *f.* (de théâtre); **to play** (*a sport*) jouer à; faire du sport; **to play** (*a musical instrument*) jouer de

pleasure: It's a pleasure (*to meet you*) Enchanté(e)

poem poème *m.*

poet poète / femme poète *m., f.*

poetry poésie *f.*

political party parti (*m.*) politique

pollution pollution *f.*

pool (*swimming*) piscine *f.*

poor pauvre

pork porc *m.*; **pork butcher shop (delicatessen)** charcuterie *f.*; **pork products** charcuterie *f.*

port port *m.*

position (*job*) poste *m.*

possible: it is possible that il est possible que; il se peut que

poster affiche *f.*

pot: large iron cooking pot marmite *f.*

potato pomme (*f.*) de terre

poultry volaille *f.*

pound (*approx. half kilo*) livre *f.*
pour verser
prefer aimer mieux; préférer; **it is
    preferable** il est préférable
prescription ordonnance *f.*
pretty joli(e)
preview (*of an art exhibit*) vernissage *m.*
probable probable
probably sans doute
produce *v.* produire *irreg.*
producer producteur/trice *m., f.*
profession profession *f.*
professor professeur *m.*
program émission *f.*; programme *m.*
promise *v.* promettre *irreg.*
proud fier (fière)
psychology psychologie *f.*
pullover pull-over (*fam.* pull) *m.*
punch (*a ticket*) composter
punk music punk *m.*
pupil élève *m., f.*
purple violet(te)
pursue poursuivre *irreg.*
push *v.* pousser
put mettre *irreg.*; **to put on a piece of
    clothing** mettre (*irreg.*) un vêtement;
    **to put on makeup, to make up (one's
    eyes, one's lips)** se maquiller (les yeux,
    les lèvres)

quarter: quarter past (*the hour*) et quart;
    quarter to (*the hour*) moins le
    quart
Quebec Québec *m.*; **from Quebec**
    québécois(e)
quickly vite

rabbit lapin *m.*
race: running race course (*f.*) à pied
radio radio *f.*; **to put/turn on the
    radio** mettre (*irreg.*) la radio; **radio
    station** station (*f.*) de radio
raï music raï *m.*
railroad tracks voie (*f.*) de chemin de
    fer
rain: it's raining il pleut
raisin raisin (*m.*) sec
Ramadan ramadan *m.*
rapid rapide; **rapidly** rapidement;
    vite
rarely rarement
read lire *irreg.*
reading lecture *f.*
ready prêt(e)
realize se rendre compte
receive recevoir *irreg.*
recipe recette *f.*
recognize reconnaître *irreg.*
recycle recycler; **recycling** re-
    cyclage *m.*

red rouge
reduce réduire *irreg.*
reflect (on) réfléchir (à)
refrigerator réfrigérateur (*fam.* frigo) *m.*
refuge: to take refuge se réfugier
refuse (to do) refuser (de)
reggae music reggae *m.*
register (check in) *v.* enregistrer
regret regretter
reheat réchauffer
relatives parents *m., pl.*
relief (*topography*) relief *m.*
remember se rappeler; se souvenir *irreg.*
    (de)
render (*make*) rendre
renovation rénovation *f.*
rent *v.* louer
repeat répéter
replace remplacer
reporter reporter *m.*
require exiger
research recherche *f.*; **to research**
    rechercher
reserved (*person*) discret/ète
reside habiter
residence résidence *f.*; **university
    dormitory** résidence universitaire
Resistance fighter résistant(e) *m., f.*
resource ressource *f.*
rest *v.* se reposer
restaurant restaurant *m.*
retire prendre (*irreg.*) sa retraite
retiree (*person*) retraité(e) *m., f.*
return (*something*) rendre; **to return**
    retourner
rice riz *m.*
rich riche
ride: ride a horse monter à cheval
ridiculous ridicule
right: to/on the right à droite; **it is
    right (not right)** il est juste (injuste);
    is that right? c'est ça?; **isn't
    that right?** n'est-ce pas?, Non?;
    c'est ca?; **right away** tout de
    suite
river: rivière *f.*; **large river** fleuve *m.*
rock: to go rock climbing faire (*irreg.*) de
    l'escalade
rock music rock *m.*
roll (*bread*) petit pain *m.*
roller skating roller *m.*; **to roller
    skate** faire du roller
room (*in a home*) pièce *f.*; **bathroom**
    salle (*f.*) de bains; **bedroom** chambre
    f.; **classroom** salle (*f.*) de classe;
    dining room salle (*f.*) à manger;
    living room salle (*f.*) de séjour
route chemin *m.*; route *f.*
rug tapis *m.*
run: to run into (*meet*) rencontrer

running (*jogging*) footing *m.* jogging
    m.; **running race** course (*f.*) à
    pied
runny nose le nez qui coule
rush hour heures (*f. pl.*) de pointe
Russia Russie *f.*
Russian *adj.* russe

sad triste; **it is sad** il est triste
sail *v.* faire (*irreg.*) de la voile
sailboat bateau (*m.*) à voile
Saint's day fête *f.*
salad salade *f.*
salary salaire *m.*
salesclerk vendeur/euse *m., f.*
salmon saumon *m.*
salt sel *m.*
same même
sandwich sandwich *f.*
Saturday samedi *m.*
sauce sauce *f.*
saucepan casserole *f.*
sausage saucisson *m.*; **link sausage**
    saucisse *f.*
say dire *irreg.*
scarf écharpe; (*lightweight*) foulard
scene scène *f.*
school: elementary school école *f.*;
    secondary school lycée *m.*
science: natural science sciences (*f. pl.*)
    naturelles
screen écran *m.*
sea mer *f.*
seafood fruits (*m. pl.*) de mer
search for rechercher
season saison *f.*
seat siège *m.*; **aisle (window) seat**
    siège (*m.*) couloir (fenêtre);
    (reserved) seat place *f.*
second deuxième
secretary secrétaire *m., f.*
section (*newspaper*) rubrique *f.*
security guard agent(e) (*m., f.*) de
    sécurité
see voir *irreg.*; **see you soon** à bientôt;
    see you tomorrow à demain; **to
    see again** revoir *irreg.*
seem avoir (*irreg.*) l'air; sembler; paraître
    irreg.
sell vendre
send envoyer
September septembre *m.*
series série *f.*
serve servir *irreg.*
service service *m.*
set (*TV, theater, cinema*) plateau *m.*; **to
    set the table** mettre (*irreg.*) la table
seven sept
seventeen dix-sept
seventh septième

seventy soixante-dix

several plusieurs; quelques

shape: in good (great) shape en bonne (pleine) forme

share *v.* partager

shave *v.* se raser

sheep mouton *m.*

sheet (of paper) feuille *f.* (de papier)

shirt chemise *f.*

shocking étonnant(e)

shoe chaussure *f.*

shoot at tirer sur

shopping: to go shopping faire du shopping

shore: on the shore of au bord de

short court(e); **in short** *interj.* enfin

short story conte *m.*

shorts short *m. s.*

should: one should (you should, etc.) (not) il (ne) faut (pas)

shoulder épaule *f.*

show *v.* montrer; indiquer; *n.* spectacle *m.*; **could you show me the way to** est-ce que vous pourriez m'indiquer le chemin pour aller à

shrimp crevettes *f. pl.*

sick malade; **to become sick** tomber malade

sideboard buffet *m.*

significant fort(e)

signpost poteau (*m.*) indicateur

silently silencieusement

since (*time*) depuis

singer chanteur/euse *m., f.*

single (*unmarried*) célibataire

sir (Mr.) monsieur (M.)

sister sœur *f.*; **sister-in-law, stepsister** belle-sœur *f.* (*pl.* belles-sœurs)

site site *m.*; **touriste site** site touristique; **website** site Web

situation comedy (sitcom) sitcom *f.*

six six

sixteen seize

sixth sixième

sixty soixante; **in one's sixties** (*age*) dans la soixantaine *f.*

ska music ska *m.*

skateboarding skate *m.*

ski *v.* skier, faire (*irreg.*) du ski; **ski run** piste *f.*; **to cross-country ski** faire (*irreg.*) du ski de fond

skip: to skip class sécher un cours

skirt jupe *f.*

sky ciel *m.*; **the sky is cloudy (clear)** le ciel est couvert (clair)

sleep dormir *irreg.*

slow lent(e); **to slow the advance** retarder l'avance

small petit(e)

smell *v.* sentir *irreg.*

smoking (nonsmoking) train car wagon (*m.*) fumeurs (non-fumeurs)

snow: it's snowing il neige

snowboard *v.* faire (*irreg.*) du surf de neige

so *conj.* alors; **so** (*very*) tellement; **so that** afin que; **pour que**

soap opera feuilleton *m.*

soccer football (*fam.* foot) *m.*

society column carnet (*m.*) du jour

sock chaussette *f.*

sofa canapé *m.*

soil terre *f.*

soldier soldat *m.*

sole seul(e)

some des; quelques; *pron.* en

someone quelqu'un

something quelque chose

sometimes parfois; quelquefois

son fils *m.*

song chanson *f.*

soon bientôt; **see you soon** à bientôt

sore: to have a sore . . . avoir mal (*irreg.*) à

sorry: to be sorry (that) être (*irreg.*) désolé(e) (que)

soup soupe *f.*

south sud *m.*

South America Amérique *f.* du Sud

soy sauce sauce (*f.*) de soja

Spain Espagne *f.*

Spanish *adj.* espagnol(e)

speak parler

special event spectacle *m.*

speed limit limite (*f.*) de vitesse

spend: to spend time on mettre du temps à

spice épice *f.*

sponge éponge *f.*

spoon cuillère *f.*

sport: play/do sports faire du sport

sports center centre (*m.*) sportif

sports coat veste *f.*

sports fan fanatique (*m., f.*) du sport

spring printemps *m.*

squash courge *f.*

stage (*in a process*) étape *f.*; (*theater*) scène *f.*

stamp timbre *m.*

stand: to stand up se lever (*irreg.*); **to stand in line** faire (*irreg.*) la queue

star (*of a show, movie*) vedette *f.*

station: (*bus, métro*) **station stop** arrêt *m.*; **radio station** station (*f.*) de radio; **television station** chaîne *f.*; **train station** gare *f.*

stay *v.* rester

steam *v.* faire (*irreg.*) cuire à la vapeur

step: stepbrother beau-frère *m.*; **stepfather** beau-père *m.*; **stepmother** belle-mère *f.*; **stepsister** belle-sœur *f.*

stereo chaîne (*f.*) stéréo

still encore; toujours

stomach estomac *m.*; **to have a stomachache** avoir mal au ventre

stop *v.* cesser (de); **stop** (*bus, subway*) arrêt *m.*; **last stop** terminus *m.*

store magasin *m.*; **bread store** boulangerie *f.*; **butcher shop** boucherie *f.*; **dairy products store** crémerie *f.*; **department store** grand magasin *m.*; **fish store** poissonnerie *f.*; **grocery store** épicerie *f.*, supermarché *m.*; **pastry shop** pâtisserie *f.*; **pork butcher shop** charcuterie *f.*

storm (*thunder and lightning*) orage *m.*

story histoire *f.*; **short story** conte *m.*

stove cuisinière *f.*

straight (ahead) tout droit

street: on (Mouffetard) street dans la rue (Mouffetard) **on the street** dans la rue **pedestrian street** rue (*f.*) piétonne

strength: with strength fort

strike *v.* frapper

strong fort(e)

student (*university*) etudiant(e) *m., f.*

studies études *f. pl.*

studio studio *m.*

study *v.* étudier; **to study** (*a subject*) faire (*irreg.*) des études en; **to study for (a lesson, an exam)** préparer (une leçon, un examen)

subject (*school*) matière *f.*

suburb banlieue *f.*

subway métro *m.*; **subway system** réseau (*m.*) du métro

succeed réussir (à); **to succeed in (doing)** arriver à

such tel(le); **such a** un(e) tel(le)

sudden soudain(e)

suddenly soudain

suffer souffrir *irreg.*

sugar sucre *m.*

suit (*man's*) costume *m.*, complet *m.*; (*woman's*) tailleur *m.*

suitcase valise *f.*

summer été *m.*

Sunday dimanche *m.*

sunglasses lunettes (*f. pl.*) de soleil

sunny: it's sunny out il fait du soleil

superintendent: building superintendent gardien(ne) (*m., f.*) d'immeuble

supermarket supermarché *m.*

suppose: I suppose je suppose

sure sûr(e); certain(e)

surf: to surf the Web naviguer (surfer) le Web

surprised surpris(e)

surprising étonnant(e)

survive survivre *irreg.*

sweatshirt sweatshirt (*fam.* sweat) *m.*

sweet sucré(e)

swim *v.* nager

swimming pool piscine *f.*

system (*network*) réseau *m.*; **subway system** reseau du métro

table table *f.*; **to set the table** mettre (*irreg.*) la table

tablecloth nappe *f.*

tablet (*medicinal*) comprimé *m.*

take prendre *irreg.*; **all it takes is** il suffit de; **I take it** je suppose; **to take a course** suivre un cours; **to take (a long) time** prendre du temps; **to take a trip** faire (*irreg.*) un voyage, voyager; **to take a walk** faire (*irreg.*) une promenade, se promener; **to take an exam** passer un examen; **to take a photograph** prendre (irreg.) une photo; **to take photographs** faire (*irreg.*) de la photographie; **to take place** avoir (*irreg.*) lieu; **to take refuge** se réfugier

talk *v.* parler

talkative bavard(e)

tall grand(e)

tea thé *m.*

teach enseigner

teacher (*elementary school*) instituteur/trice *m.*, *f.*, maître (maîtresse) *m.*, *f.*

teaching enseignement *m.*; **foreign language teaching** enseignement des langues étrangères; **secondary school teaching** enseignement secondaire

team équipe *f.*

telephone téléphone *m.*; **cell phone** portable *m.*; **telephone booth** cabine (*f.*) téléphonique; **to telephone** téléphoner (à)

television télévision (*fam.* télé) *f.*; **television station** chaîne *f.*; **to put/ turn on the television** mettre (*irreg.*) la télévision

tell dire; **to tell about** raconter

temperature température *f.*

ten dix

tennis tennis *m.*

tenth dixième

terminus terminus *m.*

terrific formidable

thank you merci

that *adj.* ce, cet, cette; *rel. pron.* que; *rel. pron.* qui; **that is** c'est; **that is not** ce n'est pas; **that (one)** celle, celui

theater théâtre *m.*

then ensuite; puis; alors

there *adv.* là; *pron.* y; **there is/are** (*pointing out*) voilà; (*counting*) il y a; **there is/are not** il n'y a pas de

therefore alors

these *adj.* ces; *pron.* celles, ceux; **these are (not)** ce (ne) sont (pas)

thesis thèse *m.*

they are (not) ce (ne) sont (pas)

thing chose *f.*

think penser; **to think (about)** réfléchir (à)

third troisième

thirsty: to be thirsty avoir (*irreg.*) soif

thirteen treize

thirty trente; **in one's thirties** (*age*) dans la trentaine

this *adj.* ce, cet, cette; **this is** c'est; **this is not** ce n'est pas; **this (one)** celle, celui

those *adj.* ces; *pron.* celles, ceux; **those are (not)** ce (ne) sont pas

thousand mille

three trois

thrilled ravi(e)

throat gorge *f.*

throughout (*time*) au cours de

thunder and lightening storm orage *m.*

Thursday jeudi *m.*

ticket billet *m.*; **one-way (round trip) ticket** billet aller simple (aller-retour) **ticket window** guichet *m.*

tie cravate *f.*

time fois *f.*; temps *m.*; heure *f.*; **at what time . . . ?** à quelle heure... ?; **from time to time** de temps en temps; **for a long time** longtemps; **full-time** à plein temps; **half-time** à mi-temps; **on time** à l'heure; **time off** congé *m.*; **to have a good time** s'amuser; **to spend time on** mettre (*irreg.*) du temps à; **to take (a long) time** prendre du temps; **what time is it?** quelle heure est-il?

tired fatigué(e)

tissue (*facial*) mouchoir (*m.*) en papier

to à; en

today aujourd'hui

together ensemble

tomato tomate *f.*

tomorrow demain; **see you tomorrow** à demain

too: too much, too many trop (de); **that's too bad** c'est dommage; **it is too bad that** il est dommage que

tooth dent *f.*

topography relief *m.*

tourist site site (*m.*) touristique

toward vers

track piste *f.*; **railroad tracks** voie (*f.*) de chemin de fer

trade (*craft*) métier *m.*

traffic circulation *f.*; **traffic jam** embouteillage *m.*; **traffic light** feu *m.*

trail piste *f.*

train train *m.*; **high-speed train** train à grande vitesse (*fam.* TGV); **train car** wagon *m.*; **train station** gare *f.*; **to train** (*teach*) former

traitor traître/tresse *m.*, *f.*

transfer *v.* faire/prendre (*irreg.*) une correspondance

translate traduire *irreg.*

translation traduction *f.*

trap piège *m.*

treason trahison *m.*

tree arbre *f.*

trip voyage *m.*; **to take a trip** faire (*irreg.*) un voyage, voyager

troops troupes *f. pl.*

trousers pantalon *m. s.*

truck camion *m.*

true vrai(e); **is it true that . . . ?** est-ce vrai que... ?; **that is (it's) true** c'est vrai

try essayer

T-shirt tee-shirt *m.*

Tuesday mardi *m.*

tuna thon *m.*

turn *v.* tourner; **turn around** retourner; **turn on the radio (TV, light)** mettre (*irreg.*) la radio (télé, lumière)

turnip navet *m.*

twelve douze

twentieth vingtième

twenty vingt

twenty-first vingt et unième

two deux

ugly laid(e)

uncertain incertain(e)

uncle oncle *m.*

under sous

understand comprendre *irreg.*

unemployed au chômage

unhappy malheureux/euse

United States États-Unis *m. pl.*

university université *f.*; **university residence** (*dormitory*) résidence (*f.*) universitaire; **university student** étudiant(e) *m.*, *f.*

unless sans que

unlikely: it is unlikely (that) il est peu probable (que)

until jusqu'à; jusqu'à ce que
up: to get up, stand up se lever; **to go up** monter
use *v.* employer
useful utile
useless (*no use*) inutile
usually d'habitude

vacation vacances *f. pl.*; **on vacation** en vacances
valley vallée *f.*
veal veau *m.*
vegetable légume *m.*
very très; **very well** très bien
videocassette recorder (VCR) magnétoscope *m.*
Vietnam Viêtnam *m.*
Vietnamese *adj.* vietnamien(ne)
view: to have a view of (the port) donner sur (le port)
village village *m.*
vine vigne *f.*
vineyard vignoble *m.*
visa visa *m.*
visit: to visit (*a person*) rendre visite à; **to visit** (*a place*) visiter
visual arts arts (*m. pl.*) plastiques
volleyball volley-ball *m.*

wait (for) attendre
wake up se réveiller
walk: to take a walk faire (*irreg.*) une promenade, se promener
wall mur *m.*
want avoir (*irreg.*) envie de; vouloir *irreg.*
war guerre *f.*
wardrobe (*furniture*) armoire *f.*
warmth chaleur *f.*
wash: to get washed, wash up se laver
watch *v.* regarder
water eau (*f.*); **(carbonated, noncarbonated) mineral water** eau minérale (gazeuse, plate)
waterski *v.* faire (*irreg.*) du ski nautique
way route *f.*; chemin *m.*; **could you show me the way to** est-ce que

vous pourriez m'indiquer le chemin pour aller à
weak faible
weapon arme (*f.*)
wear porter
weather temps *m.*; **weather report** météo *f.*; **what's the weather?** quel temps fait-il?
website site (*m.*) Web
Wedding anniversary anniversaire (*m.*) de mariage
Wednesday mercredi *m.*
week semaine *f.*
weekend week-end *m.*
weight training musculation *f.*
weird bizarre
welcome accueil *m.*; **to welcome** accueillir *irreg.*
well *adv.* bien; **I'm well.** Ça va bien.; **very well** très bien; **well** *interj.* enfin; **well behaved** gentil(le); **well known** réputé(e)
west ouest *m.*
what *interr. pron.* que; qu'est-ce que; qu'est-ce qui; quoi; **at what time?** à quelle heure?; **what courses are you taking?** quels cours est-ce que tu suis (vous suivez)?; **what is it/this/that?** qu'est-ce que c'est?; **what is/are . . . like?** comment est/sont… ?; **what's the weather?** quel temps fait-il?; **what time is it?** quelle heure est-il?
wheat blé *m.*
when quand; *rel. pron.* où
where *adv.* où; *rel. pron.* où; **where is . . . ?** où se trouve… ?
whether si
which *interr. adj.* quel (quelle, quels, quelles); *rel. pron.* que; qui
while pendant
white blanc(he)
who *interr. pron.* qui; qui est-ce qui; *rel. pron.* qui **who is it/this/that?** qui est-ce?
whole: the whole . . . tout le / toute la…
whom *interr. pron.* qui; *rel. pron.* que

why pourquoi
wide large
widowed veuf (veuve)
wife femme *f.*
willing: to be willing vouloir (*irreg.*) bien
window fenêtre *f.*; **ticket window** guichet *m.*; **window seat** siège (*m.*) fenêtre
windsurf faire (*irreg.*) de la planche à voile
windy: it's windy out il fait du vent
wine vin *m.*; **red (white, rosé) wine** vin rouge (blanc, rosé); **wine growing** viticulture *f.*
winter hiver *m.*
wish *v.* souhaiter
with avec; **with dignity** dignement; **with strength, with effort** fort
without sans; sans que
woman femme *f.*
wonderful formidable
work travail *m.*; **to work** travailler; **work (of art, literature, music); body of work** œuvre *f.*
workbook cahier *m.*
world monde *m.*
world music world music *f.*
worried inquiet/inquiète
worry *v.* (**about**) s'inquiéter (de, pour)
write écrire *irreg.*; **to write a check** faire (*irreg.*) un chèque
writer écrivain/femme écrivain) *m., f.*
wrong faux/fausse

year an *m.*; année *f.*; **to be (twenty) years old** avoir (vingt) ans
yellow jaune
yes oui; **yes, of course!** bien sûr que oui!
yesterday hier
yogurt yaourt *m.*
you: and you? et vous (toi)?
youth jeunesse *f.*

zero zéro
zucchini courgette *f.*

McGraw-Hill is proud to present an innovative new film-based program designed to motivate and inspire beginning French students:

LE CHEMIN DU RETOUR

Imagine... a French film created for your beginning French course. *Le Chemin du retour* was developed to provide learners with a cinematic view of French language and culture.

Centered around Camille Leclair, a young French journalist who is investigating her grandfather's hidden past, *Le Chemin du retour* is a two-hour feature-length film that takes students on an incredible journey throughout parts of the French-speaking world, introducing them to the richness of the French language and Francophone cultures. *Le Chemin du retour* is filled with drama, culturally authentic language and locations, as wells as historical footage.

With *Le Chemin du retour*, students will learn the basics of French in the functional context provided by the film. The unique approach of the film offers instructors a systematic and easy way to implement the program, with on-screen pre- and post-viewing activities that help students verify comprehension of the story. The *Student Viewer's Handbook* is designed to assess students' comprehension of the film and to provide additional readings in French. When used in conjunction with a regular French course syllabus, Le *Chemin du retour* and the *Student Viewer's Handbook* play an important part in students' ability to gain proficiency in French language and cultures.

For more information on *Le Chemin du retour* and its accompanying print materials, contact your local McGraw-Hill sales representative. Visit the McGraw-Hill website at **www.worldlanguages.com**, or call (800) 338-3987.

McGraw-Hill Higher Education

A Division of The **McGraw-Hill** Companies

ISBN 0-07-289760-0

90000

9 780072 897609

www.mhhe.com